C000145714

The Eleven Comedies
Vol. 1

by Aristophanes

Wilder Publications, LLC.
PO Box 3005
Radford VA 24143-3005

ISBN 10: 1-61720-564-8
ISBN 13: 978-1-61720-564-4

Table of Contents:

Translator's Foreword

Perhaps the first thing to strike us—paradoxical as it may sound to say so—about the Athenian 'Old Comedy' is its *modernness*. Of its very nature, satiric drama comes later than Epic and Lyric poetry, Tragedy or History; Aristophanes follows Homer and Simonides, Sophocles and Thucydides. Of its essence, it is free from many of the conventions and restraining influences of earlier forms of literature, and enjoys much of the liberty of choice of subject and licence of method that marks present-day conditions of literary production both on and off the stage. Its very existence presupposes a fuller and bolder intellectual life, a more advanced and complex city civilization, a keener taste and livelier faculty of comprehension in the people who appreciate it, than could anywhere be found at an earlier epoch. Speaking broadly and generally, the Aristophanic drama has more in common with modern ways of looking at things, more in common with the conditions of the modern stage, especially in certain directions—burlesque, extravaganza, musical farce, and even 'pantomime,' than with the earlier and graver products of the Greek mind.

The eleven plays, all that have come down to us out of a total of over forty staged by our author in the course of his long career, deal with the events of the day, the incidents and personages of contemporary Athenian city life, playing freely over the surface of things familiar to the audience and naturally provoking their interest and rousing their prejudices, dealing with contemporary local gossip, contemporary art and literature, and above all contemporary politics, domestic and foreign. All this *farrago* of miscellaneous subjects is treated in a frank, uncompromising spirit of criticism and satire, a spirit of broad fun, side-splitting laughter and reckless high spirits. Whatever lends itself to ridicule is instantly seized upon; odd, eccentric and degraded personalities are caricatured, social foibles and vices pilloried, pomposity and sententiousness in the verses of the poets, particularly the tragedians, and most particularly in Euripides—the pet aversion and constant butt of Aristophanes' satire—are parodied. All is fish that comes to the Comic dramatists net, anything that will raise a laugh is fair game.

"It is difficult to compare the Aristophanic Comedy to any one form of modern literature, dramatic or other. It perhaps most resembles what we now call burlesque; but it had also very much in it of broad farce and comic opera, and something also (in the hits at the fashions and follies of the day with which it abounded) of the modern pantomime. But it was something more, and more important to the Athenian public than any or all of these could have been. Almost always more or less political, and sometimes intensely personal, and always with some purpose more or less important underlying its wildest vagaries and coarsest buffooneries, it supplied the place of the political journal, the literary review, the popular caricature and the party pamphlet, of our own times. It combined the attractions and influence of all these; for its grotesque masks and elaborate 'spectacle' addressed the eye as strongly as the author's keenest witticisms did the ear of his audience."

Rollicking, reckless, uproarious fun is the key-note; though a more serious intention is always latent underneath. Aristophanes was a strong—sometimes an unscrupulous—partisan; he was an uncompromising Conservative of the old school, an ardent admirer of the vanishing aristocratic régime, an anti-Imperialist—'Imperialism' was a *democratic* craze at Athens—and never lost an opportunity of throwing scorn on Cleon the demagogue, his political *bête noire* and personal enemy, Cleon's henchmen of the popular faction, and the War party generally. Gravity, solemnity, seriousness, are conspicuous by their absence; even that 'restraint' which is the salient characteristic of Greek expression in literature no less than in Art, is largely relaxed in the rough-and-tumble, informal, miscellaneous *modern* phantasmagoria of these diverting extravaganzas.

At the same time we must not be misled by the word 'Comedy' to bring Aristophanes' work into comparison with what we call Comedy now. This is quite another thing—confined to a representation of incidents of private, generally polite life, and made up of the intrigues and entanglements of social and domestic situations. Such a Comedy the Greeks did produce, but at a date fifty or sixty years subsequent to Aristophanes' day, and recognized by themselves as belonging to an entirely different genre. Hence the distinction drawn between 'The Old Comedy,' of which Cratinus and his younger contemporaries, Eupolis and Aristophanes, were the leading representatives, and which was at high-water mark just before and during the course of the great struggle of the Peloponnesian War, and 'The New Comedy,' a comedy of manners, the two chief exponents of which were Philemon and Menander, writing after Athens had fallen under the Macedonian yoke, and politics were excluded altogether from the stage. Menander's plays in turn were the originals of those produced by Plautus and Terence at Rome, whose existing Comedies afford some faint idea of what the lost masterpieces of their Greek predecessor must have been. Unlike the 'Old,' the 'New Comedy' had no Chorus and no 'Parabasis.'

This remarkable and distinctive feature, by-the-bye, of the Old Comedy, the 'Parabasis' to wit, calls for a word of explanation. It was a direct address on the Author's part to the audience, delivered in verse of a special metre, generally towards the close of the representation, by the leader of the Chorus, but expressing the personal opinions and predilections of the poet, and embodying any remarks upon current topics and any urgent piece of advice which he was particularly anxious to insist on. Often it was made the vehicle for special appeal to the sympathetic consideration of the spectators for the play and its merits. These 'parabases,' so characteristic of the Aristophanic comedy, are conceived in the brightest and wittiest vein, and abound in topical allusions and personal hits that must have constituted them perhaps the most telling part of the whole performance.

Aristophanes deals with all questions; for him the domain of the Comic Poet has no limits, his mission is as wide as human nature. It is to Athens he addresses himself, to the city as a whole; his criticism embraces morals no less than politics, poetry no less than philosophy; he does not hesitate to assail the rites and dogmas of Paganism; whatever affords subject for laughter or vituperation lies within his province; there he is in his element, scourge in hand, his heart ablaze with indignation, pitiless, and utterly careless of all social distinctions.

In Politics Aristophanes belongs to the party of the Aristocracy. He could not do otherwise, seeing that the democratic principle was then triumphant; Comedy is never laudatory, it lives upon criticism, it must bite to the quick to win a hearing; its strength, its vital force is contradiction. Thus the abuses of democracy and demagogy were the most favourable element possible for the development of Aristophanes' genius, just because his merciless satire finds more abundant subject-matter there than under any other form of civil constitution. Then are we actually to believe that the necessity of his profession as a comic poet alone drove him into the faction of the malcontents? This would surely be to wilfully mistake the dignity of character and consistency of conviction which are to be found underlying all his productions. Throughout his long career as a dramatist his predilections always remain the same, as likewise his antipathies, and in many respects the party he champions so ardently had claims to be regarded as representing the best interests of the state. It is but just therefore to proclaim Aristophanes as having deserved well of his country, and to admit the genuine courage he displayed in attacking before the people the people's own favourites, assailing in word those who held the sword. To mock at the folly of a nation that lets itself be cajoled by vain and empty flatteries, to preach peace to fellow-citizens enamoured of war, was to fulfil a dangerous rôle, that would never have appealed, we may feel sure, to a mere vulgar ambition.

Moreover his genius, pre-eminently Greek as it is, has an instinctive horror of all excesses, and hits out at them wherever he marks their existence, whether amongst the great or the humble of the earth. Supposing the Aristocracy, having won the victory the Poet desired, had fallen in turn into oppression and misgovernment, doubtless Aristophanes would have lashed its members with his most biting sarcasms. It is just because Liberty is dear to his heart that he hates government by Demagogues; he would fain free the city from the despotism of a clique of wretched intriguers that oppressed her. But at the same time the Aristocracy favoured by our Author was not such as comes by birth and privilege, but such as is won and maintained by merit and high service to the state.

In matters of morality his satires have the same high aims. How should a corrupted population recover purity, if not by returning to the old unsullied sources from which earlier generations had drawn their inspiration? Accordingly we find Aristophanes constantly bringing on the stage the "men of Marathon," the vigorous generation to which Athens owed her freedom and her greatness. It is no mere childish commonplace with our poet, this laudation of a past age; the facts of History prove he was in the right, all the novelties he condemns were as a matter of fact so many causes that brought about Athenian decadence. Directly the citizen receives payment for attending the Assembly, he is no longer a perfectly free agent in the disposal of his vote; besides, the practice is equivalent to setting a premium on idleness, and so ruining all proper activity; a populace maintained by the state loses all energy, falls into a lethargy and dies. The life of the forum is a formidable solvent of virtue and vigour; by dint of speechifying, men forget how to act. Another thing was the introduction of 'the new education,' imported by 'the Sophists,' which substituted for serious studies, definitely limited and systematically pursued, a crowd of vague and subtle speculations; it was a mental gymnastic that gave suppleness to the wits, it is true, but only by corrupting and deteriorating the moral sense, a system that in the long run was merely destructive. Such, then, was the threefold poison that was destroying Athenian morality—the triobolus, the noisy assemblies in the Agora, the doctrines of the Sophists; the antidote was the recollection of former virtue and past prosperity, which the Poet systematically revives in contrast with the turpitudes and trivialities of the present day. There is no turning back the course of history; but if Aristophanes' efforts have remained abortive, they are not therefore inglorious. Is the moralist to despair and throw away his pen, because in so many cases his voice finds no echo?

Again we find Aristophanes' literary views embodying the same good sense which led him to see the truth in politics and morals. Here likewise it is not the individual he attacks; his criticism is general. His adversary is not the individual Euripides, but under his name depraved taste and the abandonment of that noble simplicity which had produced the masterpieces of the age of Pericles. Euripides was no ordinary writer, that is beyond question; but the very excellence of his qualities made his influence only the more dangerous.

Literary reform is closely connected with moral regeneration, the decadence of the one being both cause and effect of the deterioration of the other. The author who should succeed in purifying the public taste would come near restoring to repute healthy and honest views of life. Aristophanes essayed the task both by criticism and example—by criticism, directing the shafts of his ridicule at over-emphasis and over-subtlety, by example, writing himself in inimitable perfection the beautiful Attic dialect, which was being enervated and effeminated and spoiled in the hands of his opponents.

Even the Gods were not spared by the Aristophanic wit and badinage; in 'Plutus,' in 'The Birds,' in 'The Frogs,' we see them very roughly handled. To wonder at these profane drolleries, however, is to fail altogether to grasp the privileges of ancient comedy and the very nature of Athenian society. The Comic Poets exercised unlimited rights of making fun; we do not read in history of a single one of the class having ever been called to the bar of justice to answer for the audacity of his dramatic efforts. The same liberty extended to religious matters; the Athenian people, keen, delicately organized, quick to see a joke and loving laughter for its own sake, even when the point told against themselves, this people of mockers felt convinced the Gods appreciated raillery just as well as men did. Moreover, the Greeks do not appear to have had any very strong attachment to Paganism as a matter of dogmatic belief. To say nothing of the enlightened classes, who saw in this vast hierarchy of divinities only an ingenious allegory, the populace even was mainly concerned with the processions and songs and dances, the banquets and spectacular shows and all the external pomp and splendour of a cult the magnificence and varied rites of which amused its curiosity. But serious faith, ardent devotion, dogmatic discussion, is there a trace of these things? A sensual and poetic type of religion, Paganism was accepted at Athens only by the imagination, not by the reason; its ceremonies were duly performed, without any real piety touching the heart. Thus the audience felt no call to champion the cause of their deities when held up to ribaldry on the open stage; they left them to defend themselves—if they could.

Thus Aristophanes, we see, covered the whole field of thought; he scourged whatever was vicious or ridiculous, whether before the altars of the Gods, in the schools of the Sophists, or on the Orators' platform. But the wider the duty he undertook, the harder it became to fulfil this duty adequately. How satisfy a public made up of so many and such diverse elements, so sharply contrasted by birth, fortune, education, opinion, interest? How hold sway over a body of spectators, who were at the same time judges? To succeed in the task he was bound to be master of all styles of diction—at one and the same time a dainty poet and a diverting buffoon. It is just this universality of genius, this combination of the most eminent and various qualities, that has won Aristophanes a place apart among satirists; and if it be true to say that well-written works never die, the style alone of his Comedies would have assured their immortality.

No writer, indeed, has been more pre-eminent in that simple, clear, precise, elegant diction that is the peculiar glory of Attic literature, the brilliant yet concise quality of which the authors of no other Greek city were quite able to attain. He shows, each in its due turn, vigour and suppleness of language, he exercises a sure and spontaneous choice of correct terms, the proper combination of harmonious phrases, he goes straight to his object, he aims well and hits hard, even when he seems to be merely grazing the surface. Under his apparent negligence lies concealed the high perfection of accomplished art. This applies to the dialogues. In the choruses, Aristophanes speaks the tongue of Pindar and Sophocles; he follows the footsteps of those two mighty masters of the choric hymn into the highest regions of poetry; his lyric style is bold, impetuous, abounding in verve and brilliance, yet without the high-flown inspiration ever involving a lapse from good taste.

One of the forms in which he is fondest of clothing his conceptions is allegory; it may truly lie said that the stage of Aristophanes is a series of caricatures where every idea has taken on a corporeal presentment and is reproduced under human lineaments. To personify the abstract notion, to dress it up in the shape of an animated being for its better comprehension by the public, is in fact a proceeding altogether in harmony with the customs and conventions of Ancient Comedy. The Comic Poet never spares us a single detail of everyday life, no matter how commonplace or degrading; he pushes the materialistic delineation of the passions and vices to the extreme limit of obscene gesture and the most cynical shamelessness of word and act.

This scorn of propriety, this unchecked licence of speech, has often been made a subject of reproach against Aristophanes, and it appears to the best modern critics that the poet would have been not a whit less diverting or effective had he respected the dictates of common decency. But it is only fair, surely, before finally condemning our Author, to consider whether the times in which he lived, the origin itself of the Greek Comedy, and the constitution of the audience, do not entitle him at any rate to claim the benefit of extenuating circumstances. We must not forget that Comedy owes its birth to those festivals at which Priapus was adored side by side with Bacchus, and that 'Phallophoria' (carrying the symbols of generation in procession) still existed as a religious rite at the date when Aristophanes was composing his plays. Nor must we forget that theatrical performances were at Athens forbidden pleasures to women and children. Above all we should take full account of the code of social custom and morality then prevailing. The Ancients never understood modesty quite in the same way as our refined modern civilization does; they spoke of everything without the smallest reticence, and expressions which would revolt the least squeamish amongst ourselves did not surprise or shock the most fastidious. We ought not, therefore, to blame too severely the Comic Poet, who after all was only following in this respect the habits of his age; and if his pictures are often repulsively bestial, let us lay most blame to the account of a state of society which deserved to be painted in such odiously black colours. Doubtless Aristophanes might have given less Prominence to these cynical representations, instead of revelling in them, as he really seems to have done; men of taste and refinement, and there must have been such even among his audience, would have thought all the better of him! But it was the populace filled the bulk of the benches, and the populace loved coarse laughter and filthy words. The Poet supplied what the majority demanded; he was not the man to sacrifice one of the easiest and surest means of winning applause and popularity.

Aristophanes enjoyed an ample share of glory in his lifetime, and posterity has ratified the verdict given by his contemporaries. The epitaph is well-known which Plato composed for him, after his death: "The Graces, seeking an imperishable sanctuary, found the soul of Aristophanes." Such eulogy may appear excessive to one who re-peruses after the lapse of twenty centuries these pictures of a vanished world. But if, despite the profound differences of custom, taste and opinion which separate our own age from that of the Greeks, despite the obscurity of a host of passages whose especial point lay in their reference to some topic of the moment, and which inevitably leave us cold at the present day—if, despite all this, we still feel ourselves carried away, charmed, diverted, dominated by this dazzling *verve*, these copious outpourings of imagination, wit and poesy, let us try to realize in thought what must have been the unbounded pleasure of an Athenian audience listening to one of our Author's satires. Then every detail was realized, every nuance of criticism appreciated; every allusion told, and the model was often actually sitting in the semicircle of the auditorium facing the copy at that time being presented on the stage. "What a passion of excitement! What transports of enthusiasm and angry protest! What bursts of uncontrollable merriment! What thunders of applause! How the Comic Poet must have felt himself a King, indeed, in presence of these popular storms which, like the god of the sea, he could arouse and allay at his good will and pleasure!"

To return for a moment to the coarseness of language so often pointed to as a blot in Aristophanes. "The great comedian has been censured and apologized for on this ground, over and over again. His personal exculpation must always rest upon the fact, that the wildest licence in which he indulged was not only recognized as permissible, but actually enjoined as part of the ceremonial at these festivals of Bacchus; that it was not only in accordance with public taste, but was consecrated as a part of the national religion.... But the coarseness of Aristophanes is not corrupting. There is nothing immoral in his plots, nothing really dangerous in his broadest humour. Compared with some of our old English dramatists, he is morality itself. And when we remember the plots of some French and English plays which now attract fashionable audiences, and the character of some modern French and English novels not unfrequently found (at any rate in England) upon drawing-room tables, the least that can be said is, that we had better not cast stones at Aristophanes." Moreover, it should be borne in mind that Athenian custom did not sanction the presence of women—at least women of reputable character—at these performances.

The particular plays, though none are free from it, which most abound in this ribald fun—for fun it always is, never mere pruriency for its own sake, Aristophanes has a deal of the old 'esprit gaulois' about him—are the 'Peace' and, as might be expected from its theme, lending itself so readily to suggestive allusions and situations, above all the 'Lysistrata.' The 'Thesmophoriazusae' and 'Ecclesiazusae' also take ample toll in this sort of the 'risqué' situations incidental to their plots, the dressing up of men as women in the former, and of women as men in the latter. Needless to say, no faithful translator will emasculate his author by expurgation, and the reader will here find Aristophanes' Comedies as Aristophanes wrote them, not as Mrs. Grundy might wish him to have written them.

These performances took place at the Festivals of Dionysus (Bacchus), either the Great Dionysia or the minor celebration of the Lenaea, and were in a sense religious ceremonials—at any rate under distinct religious sanction. The representations were held in the Great Theatre of Dionysus, under the slope of the Acropolis, extensive remains of which still exist; several plays were brought out at each festival in competition, and prizes, first and second, were awarded to the most successful productions—rewards which were the object of the most intense ambition.

Next to nothing is known of the private life of Aristophanes, and that little, beyond the two or three main facts given below, is highly dubious, not to say apocryphal. He was born about 444 B.C., probably at Athens. His father held property in Aegina, and the family may very likely have come originally from that island. At any rate, this much is certain, that the author's arch-enemy Cleon made more than one judicial attempt to prove him of alien birth and therefore not properly entitled to the rights of Athenian citizenship; but in this he entirely failed. The great Comedian had three sons, but of these and their career history says nothing whatever. Such incidents and anecdotes of our author's literary life as have come down to us are all connected with one or other of the several plays, and will be found alluded to in the special Introductions prefixed to these. He died about 380 B.C.—the best and central years of his life and work thus coinciding with the great national period of stress and struggle, the Peloponnesian War, 431-404 B.C. He continued to produce plays for the Athenian stage for the long period of thirty-seven years; though only eleven Comedies, out of a reputed total of forty, have survived.

A word or two as to existing translations of Aristophanes. These, the English ones at any rate, leave much to be desired; indeed it is not too much to say that there is no version of our Author in the language which gives the general reader anything like an adequate notion of these Plays. We speak of prose renderings. Aristophanes has been far more fortunate in his verse translators—Mitchell, who published four Comedies in this form in 1822, old-fashioned, but still helpful, Hookham Frere, five plays (1871), both scholarly and spirited, and last but not least, Mr. Bickley Rogers, whose excellent versions have appeared at intervals since 1867. But from their very nature these cannot afford anything like an exact idea of the 'ipsissima verba' of the Comedies, while all slur over or omit altogether passages in any way 'risqué.' There remains only our old friend 'Bohn' ("The Comedies of Aristophanes; a literal Translation by W. J. Hickie"), and what stuff 'Bohn' is! By very dint of downright literalness—though not, by-the-bye, always downright accuracy—any true notion of the Author's meaning is quite obscured. The letter kills the spirit.

The French prose versions are very good. That by C. Poyard (in the series of "Chefs-d'oeuvre des Littératures Anciennes") combines scholarly precision with an easy, racy, vernacular style in a way that seems impossible to any but a French scholar.

The order here adopted for the successive plays differs slightly from that observed in most editions; but as these latter do not agree amongst themselves, this small assumption of licence appears not unwarrantable. Chronologically 'The Acharnians' (426 B.C.) should come first; but it seems more convenient to group it with the two other "Comedies of the War," the whole trilogy dealing with the hardships involved by the struggle with the Lacedaemonians and the longings of the Athenian people for the blessings of peace. This leaves 'The Knights' to open the whole series—the most important politically of all Aristophanes' productions, embodying as it does his trenchant attack on the great demagogue Cleon and striking the keynote of the author's general attitude as advocate of old-fashioned conservatism against the new democracy, its reckless 'Imperialism' and the unscrupulous and self-seeking policy, so the aristocratic party deemed it, of its accredited leaders.

Order, as thus rearranged, approximate date, and *motif* (in brief) of each of the eleven Comedies are given below:

'The Knights': 424 B.C.—eighth year of the War. Attacks Cleon, the Progressives, and the War policy generally.

Comedies of the War:—

'The Acharnians': 426 B.C.—sixth year of the War. Insists on the miseries consequent on the War, especially affecting the rural population, as represented by the Acharnian Dicaeopolis and his fellow demesmen. Incidentally makes fun of the tragedian Euripides.

'Peace': 422 B.C.—tenth year of the War. Further insists on the same theme, and enlarges on the blessings of Peace. The hero Trygaeus flies to Olympus, mounted on a beetle, to bring back the goddess

Peace to earth.

'Lysistrata': 411 B.C.—twenty-first year of the War. A burlesque conspiracy entered into by the confederated women of Hellas, led by Lysistrata the Athenian, to compel the men to conclude peace.

'The Clouds': 423 B.C.—satirizes Socrates, the 'Sophists,' and the 'New Education.'

'The Wasps': 422 B.C. Makes fun of the Athenian passion for litigation, and the unsatisfactory organization of the Courts. Contains the incident of the mock trial of the thievish house-dog.

'The Birds': 414 B.C. Euelpides and Pisthetaerus, disgusted with the state of things at Athens, build a new and improved city, Cloud-cuckoo-town, in the kingdom of the birds. Some see an allusion to the Sicilian expedition, and Alcibiades' Utopian schemes.

'The Frogs': 405 B.C. A satire on Euripides and the 'New Tragedy.' Dionysus, patron of the Drama, dissatisfied with the contemporary condition of the Art, goes down to Hades to bring back to earth a poet of the older and worthier school.

'The Thesmophoriazusae': 412 B.C. Another literary satire; Euripides, summoned as a notorious defamer of women to defend himself before the dames of Athens assembled in solemn conclave at the Thesmophoria, or festival of Demeter and Persephone, induces his father-in-law, Mnesilochus, to dress up in women's clothes, penetrate thus disguised into the assemblage, and plead the poet's cause, but with scant success.

'The Ecclesiazusae': 392 B.C. Pokes fun at the ideal Utopias, such as Plato's 'Republic,' based on sweeping social and economic changes, greatly in vogue with the Sophists of the day. The women of the city disguise themselves as men, slip into the Public Assembly and secure a majority of votes. They then pass a series of decrees providing for community of goods and community of women, which produce, particularly the latter, a number of embarrassing and diverting consequences.

'Plutus': 408 and 388 B.C. A whimsical allegory more than a regular comedy. Plutus, the god of wealth, has been blinded by Zeus; discovered in the guise of a ragged beggarman and succoured by Chremylus, an old man who has ruined himself by generosity to his friends, he is restored to sight by Aesculapius. He duly rewards Chremylus, and henceforth apportions this world's goods among mankind on juster principles—enriching the just, but condemning the unjust to poverty.

The Knights

Introduction

This was the fourth play in order of time produced by Aristophanes on the Athenian stage; it was brought out at the Lenaean Festival, in January, 424 B.C. Of the author's previous efforts, two, 'The Revellers' and 'The Babylonians,' were apparently youthful essays, and are both lost. The other, 'The Acharnians,' forms the first of the three Comedies dealing directly with the War and its disastrous effects and urging the conclusion of Peace; for this reason it is better ranged along with its sequels, the 'Peace' and the 'Lysistrata,' and considered in conjunction with them.

In many respects 'The Knights' may be reckoned the great Comedian's masterpiece, the direct personal attack on the then all-powerful Cleon, with its scathing satire and tremendous invective, being one of the most vigorous and startling things in literature. Already in 'The Acharnians' he had threatened to "cut up Cleon the Tanner into shoe-leather for the Knights," and he now proceeds to carry his menace into execution, "concentrating the whole force of his wit in the most unscrupulous and merciless fashion against his personal enemy." In the first-mentioned play Aristophanes had attacked and satirized the whole general policy of the democratic party—and incidentally Cleon, its leading spirit and mouthpiece since the death of Pericles; he had painted the miseries of war and invasion arising from this mistaken and mischievous line of action, as he regarded it, and had dwelt on the urgent necessity of peace in the interests of an exhausted country and ruined agriculture. Now he turns upon Cleon personally, and pays him back a hundredfold for the attacks the demagogue had made in the Public Assembly on the daring critic, and the abortive charge which the same unscrupulous enemy had brought against him in the Courts of having "slandered the city in the presence of foreigners." "In this bitterness of spirit the play stands in strong contrast with the good-humoured burlesque of 'The Acharnians' and the 'Peace,' or, indeed, with any other of the author's productions which has reached us."

The characters are five only. First and foremost comes Demos, 'The People,' typifying the Athenian democracy, a rich householder—a self-indulgent, superstitious, weak creature. He has had several overseers or factors in succession, to look after his estate and manage his slaves. The present one is known as 'the Paphlagonian,' or sometimes as 'the Tanner,' an unprincipled, lying, cheating, pilfering scoundrel, fawning and obsequious to his master, insolent towards his subordinates. Two of these are Nicias and Demosthenes. Here we have real names. Nicias was High Admiral of the Athenian navy at the time, and Demosthenes one of his Vice-Admirals; both held still more important commands later in connection with the Sicilian Expedition of 415-413 B.C. Fear of consequences apparently prevented the poet from doing the same in the case of Cleon, who is, of course, intended under the names of 'the Paphlagonian' and 'the Tanner.' Indeed, so great was the terror inspired by the great man that no artist was found bold enough to risk his powerful vengeance by caricaturing his features, and no actor dared to represent him on the stage. Aristophanes is said to have played the part himself, with his face, in the absence of a mask, smeared with wine-lees, roughly mimicking the purple and bloated visage of the demagogue. The remaining character is 'the Sausage-seller,' who is egged on by Nicias and Demosthenes to oust 'the Paphlagonian' from Demos' favour by outvying him in his own arts of impudent flattery, noisy boasting and unscrupulous allurement. After a fierce and stubbornly contested trial of wits and interchange of 'Billingsgate,' 'the Sausage-seller' beats his rival at his own weapons and gains his object; he supplants the disgraced favourite, who is driven out of the house with ignominy.

The Comedy takes its title, as was often the case, from the Chorus, which is composed of Knights—the order of citizens next to the highest at Athens, and embodying many of the old aristocratic preferences and prejudices.

The drama was adjudged the first prize—the 'Satyrs' of Cratinus being placed second—by acclamation, as such a masterpiece of wit and intrepidity certainly deserved to be; but, as usual, the political result was nil. The piece was applauded in the most enthusiastic manner, the satire on the sovereign multitude was forgiven, and—Cleon remained in as much favour as ever.

The Knights

DRAMATIS PERSONAE

DEMOSTHENES.
NICIAS.
AGORACRITUS, a Sausage-seller.
CLEON. DEMOS, an old man, typifying the Athenian people.
CHORUS OF KNIGHTS.

SCENE: In front of Demos' house at Athens.

DEMOSTHENES. Oh! alas! alas! Oh! woe! oh! woe! Miserable Paphlagonian! may the gods destroy both him and his cursed advice! Since that evil day when this new slave entered the house he has never ceased belabouring us with blows.

NICIAS. May the plague seize him, the arch-fiend—him and his lying tales!

DEMOSTHENES. Hah! my poor fellow, what is your condition?

NICIAS. Very wretched, just like your own.

DEMOSTHENES. Then come, let us sing a duet of groans in the style of Olympus.

DEMOSTHENES AND NICIAS. Boo, hoo! boo, hoo! boo, hoo! boo, hoo! boo, hoo! boo, hoo!!

DEMOSTHENES. Bah! 'tis lost labour to weep! Enough of groaning! Let us consider how to save our pelts.

NICIAS. But how to do it! Can you suggest anything?

DEMOSTHENES. Nay! you begin. I cede you the honour.

NICIAS. By Apollo! no, not I. Come, have courage! Speak, and then I will say what I think.

DEMOSTHENES. "Ah! would you but tell me what I should tell you!"

NICIAS. I dare not. How could I express my thoughts with the pomp of Euripides?

DEMOSTHENES. Oh! prithee, spare me! Do not pelt me with those vegetables, but find some way of leaving our master.

NICIAS. Well, then! Say "Let-us-bolt," like this, in one breath.

DEMOSTHENES. I follow you—"Let-us-bolt."

NICIAS. Now after "Let-us-bolt" say "at-top-speed!"

DEMOSTHENES. "At-top-speed!"

NICIAS. Splendid! Just as if you were masturbating yourself; first slowly, "Let-us-bolt"; then quick and firmly, "at-top-speed!"

DEMOSTHENES. Let-us-bolt, let-us-bolt-at-top-speed!

NICIAS. Hah! does that not please you?

DEMOSTHENES. I' faith, yes! yet I fear me your omen bodes no good to my hide.

NICIAS. How so?

DEMOSTHENES. Because hard rubbing abrades the skin when folk masturbate themselves.

NICIAS. The best thing we can do for the moment is to throw ourselves at the feet of the statue of some god.

DEMOSTHENES. Of which statue? Any statue? Do you then believe there are gods?

NICIAS. Certainly.

DEMOSTHENES. What proof have you?

NICIAS. The proof that they have taken a grudge against me. Is that not enough?

DEMOSTHENES. I'm convinced it is. But to pass on. Do you consent to my telling the spectators of our troubles?

NICIAS. 'Twould not be amiss, and we might ask them to show us by their manner, whether our facts and actions are to their liking.

DEMOSTHENES. I will begin then. We have a very brutal master, a perfect glutton for beans, and most bad-tempered; 'tis Demos of the Pnyx, an intolerable old man and half deaf. The beginning of last month he bought a slave, a Paphlagonian tanner, an arrant rogue, the incarnation of calumny. This man of leather knows his old master thoroughly; he plays the fawning cur, flatters, cajoles; wheedles, and dupes him at will with little scraps of leavings, which he allows him to get. "Dear Demos," he will say, "try a single case and you will have done enough; then take your bath, eat, swallow and devour; here are three obols." Then the Paphlagonian filches from one of us what we have prepared and makes a present of it to our old man. T'other day I had just kneaded a Spartan cake at Pylos; the cunning rogue came behind my back, sneaked it and offered the cake, which was my invention, in his own name. He keeps us at a distance and suffers none but himself to wait upon the master; when Demos is dining, he keeps close to his side with a thong in his hand and puts the orators to flight. He keeps singing oracles to him, so that the old man now thinks of nothing but the Sibyl. Then, when he sees him thoroughly obfuscated, he uses all his cunning and piles up lies and calumnies against the household; then we are scourged and the Paphlagonian runs about among the slaves to demand contributions with threats and gathers 'em in with both hands. He will say, "You see how I have had Hylas beaten! Either content me or die at once!" We are forced to give, for else the old man tramples on us and makes us spew forth all our body contains. There must be an end to it, friend. Let us see! what can be done? Who will get us out of this mess?

NICIAS. The best thing, chum, is our famous "Let-us-bolt!"

DEMOSTHENES. But none can escape the Paphlagonian, his eye is everywhere. And what a stride! He has one leg on Pylos and the other in the Assembly; his rump is exactly over the land of the Chaonians, his hands are with the Aetolians and his mind with the Clopidians.

NICIAS. 'Tis best then to die; but let us seek the most heroic death.

DEMOSTHENES. Let me bethink me, what is the most heroic?

NICIAS. Let us drink the blood of a bull; 'tis the death which Themistocles chose.

DEMOSTHENES. No, not that, but a bumper of good unmixed wine in honour of the Good Genius; perchance we may stumble on a happy thought.

NICIAS. Look at him! "Unmixed wine!" Your mind is on drink intent? Can a man strike out a brilliant thought when drunk?

DEMOSTHENES. Without question. Go, ninny, blow yourself out with water; do you dare to accuse wine of clouding the reason? Quote me more marvellous effects than those of wine. Look! when a man drinks, he is rich, everything he touches succeeds, he gains lawsuits, is happy and helps his friends. Come, bring hither quick a flagon of wine, that I may soak my brain and get an ingenious idea.

NICIAS. Eh, my god! What can your drinking do to help us?

DEMOSTHENES. Much. But bring it to me, while I take my seat. Once drunk, I shall strew little ideas, little phrases, little reasonings everywhere.

NICIAS (returning with a flagon). It is lucky I was not caught in the house stealing the wine.

DEMOSTHENES. Tell me, what is the Paphlagonian doing now?

NICIAS. The wretch has just gobbled up some confiscated cakes; he is drunk and lies at full-length a-snoring on his hides.

DEMOSTHENES. Very well, come along, pour me out wine and plenty of it.

NICIAS. Take it and offer a libation to your Good Genius; taste, taste the liquor of the genial soil of Pramnium.

DEMOSTHENES. Oh, Good Genius! 'Tis thy will, not mine.

NICIAS. Prithee, tell me, what is it?

DEMOSTHENES. Run indoors quick and steal the oracles of the Paphlagonian, while he is asleep.

NICIAS. Bless me! I fear this Good Genius will be but a very Bad Genius for me.

DEMOSTHENES. And set the flagon near me, that I may moisten my wit to invent some brilliant notion.

NICIAS (*enters the house and returns at once*). How the Paphlagonian grunts and snores! I was able to seize the sacred oracle, which he was guarding with the greatest care, without his seeing me.

DEMOSTHENES. Oh! clever fellow! Hand it here, that I may read. Come, pour me out some drink, bestir yourself! Let me see what there is in it. Oh! prophecy! Some drink! some drink! Quick!

NICIAS. Well! what says the oracle?

DEMOSTHENES. Pour again.

NICIAS. Is "pour again" in the oracle?

DEMOSTHENES. Oh, Bacis!

NICIAS. But what is in it?

DEMOSTHENES. Quick! some drink!

NICIAS. Bacis is very dry!

DEMOSTHENES. Oh! miserable Paphlagonian! This then is why you have so long taken such precautions; your horoscope gave you qualms of terror.

NICIAS. What does it say?

DEMOSTHENES. It says here how he must end.

NICIAS. And how?

DEMOSTHENES. How? the oracle announces clearly that a dealer in oakum must first govern the city.

NICIAS. First dealer. And after him, who?

DEMOSTHENES. After him, a sheep-dealer.

NICIAS. Two dealers, eh? And what is this one's fate?

DEMOSTHENES. To reign until a greater scoundrel than he arises; then he perishes and in his place the leather-seller appears, the Paphlagonian robber, the bawler, who roars like a torrent.

NICIAS. And the leather-seller must destroy the sheep-seller?

DEMOSTHENES. Yes.

NICIAS. Oh! woe is me! Where can another seller be found, is there ever a one left?

DEMOSTHENES. There is yet one, who plies a firstrate trade.

NICIAS. Tell me, pray, what is that?

DEMOSTHENES. You really want to know?

NICIAS. Yes.

DEMOSTHENES. Well then! 'tis a sausage-seller who must overthrow him.

NICIAS. A sausage-seller! Ah! by Posidon! what a fine trade! But where can this man be found?

DEMOSTHENES. Let us seek him.

NICIAS. Lo! there he is, going towards the market-place; 'tis the gods, the gods who send him!

DEMOSTHENES. This way, this way, oh, lucky sausage-seller, come forward, dear friend, our saviour, the saviour of our city.

SAUSAGE-SELLER. What is it? Why do you call me?

DEMOSTHENES. Come here, come and learn about your good luck, you who are Fortune's favourite!

NICIAS. Come! Relieve him of his basket-tray and tell him the oracle of the god; I will go and look after the Paphlagonian.

DEMOSTHENES. First put down all your gear, then worship the earth and the gods.

SAUSAGE-SELLER. 'Tis done. What is the matter?

DEMOSTHENES. Happiness, riches, power; to-day you have nothing, to-morrow you will have all, oh! chief of happy Athens.

SAUSAGE-SELLER. Why not leave me to wash my tripe and to sell my sausages instead of making game of me?

DEMOSTHENES. Oh! the fool! Your tripe! Do you see these tiers of people?

SAUSAGE-SELLER. Yes.

DEMOSTHENES. You shall be master to them all, governor of the market, of the harbours, of the Pnyx; you shall trample the Senate under foot, be able to cashier the generals, load them with fetters, throw them into gaol, and you will play the debauchee in the Prytaneum.

SAUSAGE-SELLER. What! I?

DEMOSTHENES. You, without a doubt. But you do not yet see all the glory awaiting you. Stand on your basket and look at all the islands that surround Athens.

SAUSAGE-SELLER. I see them. What then?

DEMOSTHENES. Look at the storehouses and the shipping.

SAUSAGE-SELLER. Yes, I am looking.

DEMOSTHENES. Exists there a mortal more blest than you? Furthermore, turn your right eye towards Caria and your left towards Chalcedon.

SAUSAGE-SELLER. 'Tis then a blessing to squint!

DEMOSTHENES. No, but 'tis you who are going to trade away all this. According to the oracle you must become the greatest of men.

SAUSAGE-SELLER. Just tell me how a sausage-seller can become a great man.

DEMOSTHENES. That is precisely why you will be great, because you are a sad rascal without shame, no better than a common market rogue.

SAUSAGE-SELLER. I do not hold myself worthy of wielding power.

DEMOSTHENES. Oh! by the gods! Why do you not hold yourself worthy? Have you then such a good opinion of yourself? Come, are you of honest parentage?

SAUSAGE-SELLER. By the gods! No! of very bad indeed.

DEMOSTHENES. Spoilt child of fortune, everything fits together to ensure your greatness.

SAUSAGE-SELLER. But I have not had the least education. I can only read, and that very badly.

DEMOSTHENES. That is what may stand in your way, almost knowing how to read. The demagogues will neither have an educated nor an honest man; they require an ignoramus and a rogue. But do not, do not let go this gift, which the oracle promises.

SAUSAGE-SELLER. But what does the oracle say?

DEMOSTHENES. Faith! it is put together in very fine enigmatical style, as elegant as it is clear: "When the eagle-tanner with the hooked claws shall seize a stupid dragon, a blood-sucker, it will be an end to the hot Paphlagonian pickled garlic. The god grants great glory to the sausage-sellers unless they prefer to sell their wares."

SAUSAGE-SELLER. In what way does this concern me? Pray instruct my ignorance.

DEMOSTHENES. The eagle-tanner is the Paphlagonian.

SAUSAGE-SELLER. What do the hooked claws mean?

DEMOSTHENES. It means to say, that he robs and pillages us with his claw-like hands.

SAUSAGE-SELLER. And the dragon?

DEMOSTHENES. That is quite clear. The dragon is long and so also is the sausage; the sausage like the dragon is a drinker of blood. Therefore the oracle says, that the dragon will triumph over the eagle-tanner, if he does not let himself be cajoled with words.

SAUSAGE-SELLER. The oracles of the gods summon me! Faith! I do not at all understand how I can be capable of governing the people.

DEMOSTHENES. Nothing simpler. Continue your trade. Mix and knead together all the state business as you do for your sausages. To win the people, always cook them some savoury that pleases them. Besides, you possess all the attributes of a demagogue; a screeching, horrible voice, a perverse, cross-grained nature and the language of the market-place. In you all is united which is needful for governing. The oracles are in your favour, even including that of Delphi. Come, take a chaplet, offer a libation to the god of Stupidity and take care to fight vigorously.

SAUSAGE-SELLER. Who will be my ally? for the rich fear the Paphlagonian and the poor shudder at the sight of him.

DEMOSTHENES. You will have a thousand brave Knights, who detest him, on your side; also the honest citizens amongst the spectators, those who are men of brave hearts, and finally myself and the god. Fear not, you will not see his features, for none have dared to make a mask resembling him. But the public have wit enough to recognize him.

NICIAS. Oh! mercy! here is the Paphlagonian!

CLEON. By the twelve gods! Woe betide you, who have too long been conspiring against Demos. What means this Chalcidian cup? No doubt you are provoking the Chalcidians to revolt. You shall be killed, butchered, you brace of rogues.

DEMOSTHENES. What! are you for running away? Come, come, stand firm, bold Sausage-seller, do not betray us. To the rescue, oh! Knights. Now is the time. Simon, Panaetius, get you to the right wing; they are coming on; hold tight and return to the charge. I can see the dust of their horses' hoofs; they are galloping to our aid. Courage! Repel, attack them, put them to flight.

CHORUS. Strike, strike the villain, who has spread confusion amongst the ranks of the Knights, this public robber, this yawning gulf of plunder, this devouring Charybdis, this villain, this villain, this villain! I cannot say the word too often, for he is a villain a thousand times a day. Come, strike, drive, hurl him over and crush him to pieces; hate him as we hate him; stun him with your blows and your shouts. And beware lest he escape you; he knows the way Eucrates took straight to a bran sack for concealment.

CLEON. Oh! veteran Heliasts, brotherhood of the three obols, whom I fostered by bawling at random, help me; I am being beaten to death by rebels.

CHORUS. And 'tis justice; you devour the public funds that all should share in; you treat the officers answerable for the revenue like the fruit of the fig tree, squeezing them to find which are still green or more or less ripe; and, when you find one simple and timid, you force him to come from the Chersonese, then you seize him by the middle, throttle him by the neck, while you twist his shoulder back; he falls and you devour him. Besides, you know very well how to select from among the citizens those who are as meek as lambs, rich, without guile and loathers of lawsuits.

CLEON. Eh! what! Knights, are you helping them? But, if I am beaten, 'tis in your cause, for I was going to propose to erect you a statue in the city in memory of your bravery.

CHORUS. Oh! the impostor! the dull varlet! See! he treats us like old dotards and crawls at our feet to deceive us; but the cunning wherein lies his power shall this time recoil on himself; he trips up himself by resorting to such artifices.

CLEON. Oh Citizens! oh people! see how these brutes are bursting my belly.

CHORUS. What shouts! but 'tis this very bawling that incessantly upsets the city!

SAUSAGE-SELLER. I can shout too—and so loud that you will flee with fear.

CHORUS. If you shout louder than he does, I will strike up the triumphal hymn; if you surpass him in impudence, the cake is ours.

CLEON. I denounce this fellow; he has had tasty stews exported from Athens for the Spartan fleet.

SAUSAGE-SELLER. And I denounce him, who runs into the Prytaneum with empty belly and comes out with it full.

DEMOSTHENES. And by Zeus! he carries off bread, meat, and fish, which is forbidden. Pericles himself never had this right.

CLEON. You are travelling the right road to get killed.

SAUSAGE-SELLER. I'll bawl three times as loud as you.

CLEON. I will deafen you with my yells.

SAUSAGE-SELLER. And I you with my bellowing.

CLEON. I shall calumniate you, if you become a Strategus.

SAUSAGE-SELLER. Dog, I will lay your back open with the lash.

CLEON. I will make you drop your arrogance.

SAUSAGE-SELLER. I will baffle your machinations.

CLEON. Dare to look me in the face!

SAUSAGE-SELLER. I too was brought up in the market-place.

CLEON. I will cut you to shreds if you whisper a word.

SAUSAGE-SELLER. I will daub you with dung if you open your mouth.

CLEON. I own I am a thief; do you admit yourself another.

SAUSAGE-SELLER. By our Hermes of the market-place, if caught in the act, why, I perjure myself before those who saw me.

CLEON. These are my own special tricks. I will denounce you to the Prytanes as the owner of sacred tripe, that has not paid tithe.

CHORUS. Oh! you scoundrel! you impudent bawler! everything is filled with your daring, all Attica, the Assembly, the Treasury, the decrees, the tribunals. As a furious torrent you have overthrown our city; your outcries have deafened Athens and, posted upon a high rock, you have lain in wait for the tribute moneys as the fisherman does for the tunny-fish.

CLEON. I know your tricks; 'tis an old plot resoled.

SAUSAGE-SELLER. If you know naught of soling, I understand nothing of sausages; you, who cut bad leather on the slant to make it look stout and deceive the country yokels. They had not worn it a day before it had stretched some two spans.

DEMOSTHENES 'Tis the very trick he served me; both my neighbours and my friends laughed heartily at me, and before I reached Pergasae I was swimming in my shoes.

CHORUS. Have you not always shown that blatant impudence, which is the sole strength of our orators? You push it so far, that you, the head of the State, dare to milk the purses of the opulent aliens and, at sight of you, the son of Hippodamus melts into tears. But here is another man, who gives me pleasure, for he is a much greater rascal than you; he will overthrow you; 'tis easy to see, that he will beat you in roguery, in brazenness and in clever turns. Come, you, who have been brought up among the class which to-day gives us all our great men, show us that a liberal education is mere tomfoolery.

SAUSAGE-SELLER. Just hear what sort of fellow that fine citizen is.

CLEON. Will you not let me speak?

SAUSAGE-SELLER. Assuredly not, for I also am a sad rascal.

CHORUS. If he does not give in at that, tell him your parents were sad rascals too.

CLEON. Once more, will you not let me speak?

SAUSAGE-SELLER. No, by Zeus!

CLEON. Yes, by Zeus, but you shall!

SAUSAGE-SELLER. No, by Posidon! We will fight first to see who shall speak first.

CLEON. I will die sooner.

SAUSAGE-SELLER. I will not let you....

CHORUS. Let him, in the name of the gods, let him die.

CLEON. What makes you so bold as to dare to speak to my face?

SAUSAGE-SELLER. 'Tis that I know both how to speak and how to cook.

CLEON. Hah! the fine speaker! Truly, if some business matter fell your way, you would know thoroughly well how to attack it, to carve it up alive! Shall I tell you what has happened to you? Like so many others, you have gained some petty lawsuit against some alien. Did you drink enough water to inspire you? Did you mutter over the thing sufficiently through the night, spout it along the street, recite it to all you met? Have you bored your friends enough with it? 'Tis then for this you deem yourself an orator. Ah! poor fool!

SAUSAGE-SELLER. And what do you drink yourself then, to be able all alone by yourself to dumbfound and stupefy the city so with your clamour?

CLEON. Can you match me with a rival? Me! When I have devoured a good hot tunny-fish and drunk on top of it a great jar of unmixed wine, I hold up the Generals of Pylos to public scorn.

SAUSAGE-SELLER. And I, when I have bolted the tripe of an ox together with a sow's belly and swallowed the broth as well, I am fit, though slobbering with grease, to bellow louder than all orators and to terrify Nicias.

CHORUS. I admire your language so much; the only thing I do not approve is that you swallow all the broth yourself.

CLEON. E'en though you gorged yourself on sea-dogs, you would not beat the Milesians.

SAUSAGE-SELLER. Give me a bullock's breast to devour, and I am a man to traffic in mines.

CLEON. I will rush into the Senate and set them all by the ears.

SAUSAGE-SELLER. And I will lug out your gut to stuff like a sausage.

CLEON. As for me, I will seize you by the rump and hurl you head foremost through the door.

CHORUS. In any case, by Posidon, 'twill only be when you have thrown *me* there first.

CLEON. Beware of the carcan!

SAUSAGE-SELLER. I denounce you for cowardice.

CLEON. I will tan your hide.

SAUSAGE-SELLER. I will flay you and make a thief's pouch with the skin.

CLEON. I will peg you out on the ground.

SAUSAGE-SELLER. I will slice you into mince-meat.

CLEON. I will tear out your eyelashes.

SAUSAGE-SELLER. I will slit your gullet.

DEMOSTHENES. We will set his mouth open with a wooden stick as the cooks do with pigs; we will tear out his tongue, and, looking down his gaping throat, will see whether his inside has any pimples.

CHORUS. Thus then at Athens we have something more fiery than fire, more impudent than impudence itself! 'Tis a grave matter; come, we will push and jostle him without mercy. There, you grip him tightly under the arms; if he gives way at the onset, you will find him nothing but a craven; I know my man.

SAUSAGE-SELLER. That he has been all his life and he has only made himself a name by reaping another's harvest; and now he has tied up the ears he gathered over there, he lets them dry and seeks to sell them.

CLEON. I do not fear you as long as there is a Senate and a people which stands like a fool, gaping in the air.

CHORUS. What unparalleled impudence! 'Tis ever the same brazen front. If I don't hate you, why, I'm ready to take the place of the one blanket Cratinus wets; I'll offer to play a tragedy by Morsimus. Oh! you cheat! who turn all into money, who flutter from one extortion to another; may you disgorge as quickly as you have crammed yourself! Then only would I sing, "Let us drink, let us drink to this happy event!" Then even the son of Iulius, the old niggard, would empty his cup with transports of joy, crying, "Io, Paean! Io, Bacchus!"

CLEON. By Posidon! You! would you beat me in impudence! If you succeed, may I no longer have my share of the victims offered to Zeus on the city altar.

SAUSAGE-SELLER. And I, I swear by the blows that have so oft rained upon my shoulders since infancy, and by the knives that have cut me, that I will show more effrontery than you; as sure as I have rounded this fine stomach by feeding on the pieces of bread that had cleansed other folk's greasy fingers.

CLEON. On pieces of bread, like a dog! Ah! wretch! you have the nature of a dog and you dare to fight a cynecephalus?

SAUSAGE-SELLER. I have many another trick in my sack, memories of my childhood's days. I used to linger around the cooks and say to them, "Look, friends, don't you see a swallow? 'tis the herald of springtime." And while they stood, their noses in the air, I made off with a piece of meat.

CHORUS. Oh! most clever man! How well thought out! You did as the eaters of artichokes, you gathered them before the return of the swallows.

SAUSAGE-SELLER. They could make nothing of it; or, if they suspected a trick, I hid the meat in my breeches and denied the thing by all the gods; so that an orator, seeing me at the game, cried, "This child will get on; he has the mettle that makes a statesman."

CHORUS. He argued rightly; to steal, perjure yourself and make a receiver of your rump are three essentials for climbing high.

CLEON. I will stop your insolence, or rather the insolence of both of you. I will throw myself upon you like a terrible hurricane ravaging both land and sea at the will of its fury.

SAUSAGE-SELLER. Then I will gather up my sausages and entrust myself to the kindly waves of fortune so as to make you all the more enraged.

DEMOSTHENES. And I will watch in the bilges in case the boat should make water.

CLEON. No, by Demeter! I swear, 'twill not be with impunity that you have thieved so many talents from the Athenians.

CHORUS (to the Sausage-seller). Oh! oh! reef your sail a bit! Here is Boreas blowing calumniously.

CLEON. I know that you got ten talents out of Potidaea.

SAUSAGE-SELLER. Hold! I will give you one; but keep it dark!

CHORUS. Hah! that will please him mightily; now you can travel under full sail.

SAUSAGE-SELLER. Yes, the wind has lost its violence.

CLEON. I will bring four suits against you, each of one hundred talents.

SAUSAGE-SELLER. And I twenty against you for shirking duty and more than a thousand for robbery.

CLEON. I maintain that your parents were guilty of sacrilege against the goddess.

SAUSAGE-SELLER. And I, that one of your grandfathers was a satellite....

CLEON. To whom? Explain!

SAUSAGE-SELLER. To Byrsina, the mother of Hippias.

CLEON. You are an impostor.

SAUSAGE-SELLER. And you are a rogue.

CHORUS. Hit him hard.

CLEON. Oh, oh, dear! The conspirators are murdering me!

CHORUS. Strike, strike with all your might; bruise his belly, lashing him with your guts and your tripe; punish him with both arms! Oh! vigorous assailant and intrepid heart! Have you not routed him totally in this duel of abuse? how shall I give tongue to my joy and sufficiently praise you?

CLEON. Ah! by Demeter! I was not ignorant of this plot against me; I knew it was forming, that the chariot of war was being put together.

CHORUS (to Sausage-seller). Look out, look out! Come, outfence him with some wheelwright slang?

SAUSAGE-SELLER. His tricks at Argos do not escape me. Under pretence of forming an alliance with the Argives, he is hatching a plot with the Lacedaemonians there; and I know why the bellows are blowing and the metal that is on the anvil; 'tis the question of the prisoners.

CHORUS. Well done! Forge on, if he be a wheelwright.

SAUSAGE-SELLER. And there are men at Sparta who are hammering the iron with you; but neither gold nor silver nor prayers nor anything else shall impede my denouncing your trickery to the Athenians.

CLEON. As for me, I hasten to the Senate to reveal your plotting, your nightly gatherings in the city, your trafficking with the Medes and with the Great King, and all you are foraging for in Boeotia.

SAUSAGE-SELLER. What price then is paid for forage by Boeotians?

CLEON. Oh! by Heracles! I will tan your hide.

CHORUS. Come, if you have both wit and heart, now is the time to show it, as on the day when you hid the meat in your breeches, as you say. Hasten to the Senate, for he will rush there like a tornado to calumniate us all and give vent to his fearful bellowings.

SAUSAGE-SELLER. I am going, but first I must rid myself of my tripe and my knives; I will leave them here.

CHORUS. Stay! rub your neck with lard; in this way you will slip between the fingers of calumny.

SAUSAGE-SELLER. Spoken like a finished master of fence.

CHORUS. Now, bolt down these cloves of garlic.

SAUSAGE-SELLER. Pray, what for?

CHORUS. Well primed with garlic, you will have greater mettle for the fight. But hurry, hurry, bestir yourself!

SAUSAGE-SELLER. That's just what I am doing.

CHORUS. And, above all, bite your foe, rend him to atoms, tear off his comb and do not return until you have devoured his wattles. Go! make your attack with a light heart, avenge me and may Zeus guard you! I burn to see you return the victor and laden with chaplets of glory. And you, spectators, enlightened critics of all kinds of poetry, lend an ear to my anapaests.

CHORUS. Had one of the old authors asked to mount this stage to recite his verses, he would not have found it hard to persuade me. But our poet of to-day is likewise worthy of this favour; he shares our hatred, he dares to tell the truth, he boldly braves both waterspouts and hurricanes. Many among you, he tells us, have expressed wonder, that he has not long since had a piece presented in his own name, and have asked the reason why. This is what he bids us say in reply to your questions; 'tis not without grounds that he has courted the shade, for, in his opinion, nothing is more difficult than to cultivate the comic Muse; many court her, but very few secure her favours. Moreover, he knows that you are fickle by nature and betray your poets when they grow old. What fate befell Magnes, when his hair went white? Often enough has he triumphed over his rivals; he has sung in all keys, played the lyre and fluttered wings; he turned into a Lydian and even into a gnat, daubed himself with green to become a frog. All in vain! When young, you applauded him; in his old age you hooted and mocked him, because his genius for raillery had gone. Cratinus again was like a torrent of glory rushing across the plain, uprooting oak, plane tree and rivals and bearing them pell-mell in its wake. The only songs at the banquet were, 'Doro, shod with lying tales' and 'Adepts of the Lyric Muse'; so great was his renown. Look at him now! he drivels, his lyre has neither strings nor keys, his voice quivers, but you have no pity for him, and you let him wander about as he can, like Connas, his temples circled with a withered chaplet; the poor old fellow is dying of thirst; he who, in honour of his glorious past, should be in the Prytaneum drinking at his ease, and instead of trudging the country should be sitting amongst the first row of the spectators, close to the statue of Dionysus and loaded with perfumes. Crates, again, have you done hounding him with your rage and your hisses? True, 'twas but meagre fare that his sterile Muse could offer you; a few ingenious fancies formed the sole ingredients, but nevertheless he knew how to stand firm and to recover from his falls. 'Tis such examples that frighten our poet; in addition, he would tell himself, that before being a pilot, he must first know how to row, then to keep watch at the prow, after that how to gauge the winds, and that only then would he be able to command his vessel. If then you approve this wise caution and his resolve that he would not bore you with foolish nonsense, raise loud waves of applause in his favour this day, so that, at this Lenaean feast, the breath of your favour may swell the sails of his trumphant galley and the poet may withdraw proud of his success, with head erect and his face beaming with delight.

Posidon, god of the racing steed, I salute you, you who delight in their neighing and in the resounding clatter of their brass-shod hoofs, god of the swift galleys, which, loaded with mercenaries, cleave the seas with their azure beaks, god of the equestrian contests, in which young rivals, eager for glory, ruin themselves for the sake of distinction with their chariots in the arena, come and direct our chorus; Posidon with the trident of gold, you, who reign over the dolphins, who are worshipped at Sunium and at Geraestus beloved of Phormio, and dear to the whole city above all the immortals, I salute you!

Let us sing the glory of our forefathers; ever victors, both on land and sea, they merit that Athens, rendered famous by these, her worthy sons, should write their deeds upon the sacred peplus. As soon as they saw the enemy, they at once sprang at him without ever counting his strength. Should one of them fall in the conflict, he would shake off the dust, deny his mishap and begin the struggle anew. Not one of these Generals of old time would have asked Cleaenetus to be fed at the cost of the state; but our present men refuse to fight, unless they get the honours of the Prytaneum and precedence in their seats. As for us, we place our valour gratuitously at the service of Athens and of her gods; our only hope is, that, should peace ever put a term to our toils, you will not grudge us our long, scented hair nor our delicate care for our toilet.

Oh! Pallas, guardian of Athens, you, who reign over the most pious city, the most powerful, the richest in warriors and in poets, hasten to my call, bringing in your train our faithful ally in all our expeditions and combats, Victory, who smiles on our choruses and fights with us against our rivals. Oh! goddess! manifest yourself to our sight; this day more than ever we deserve that you should ensure our triumph.

We will sing likewise the exploits of our steeds! they are worthy of our praises; in what invasions, what fights have I not seen them helping us! But especially admirable were they, when they bravely leapt upon the galleys, taking nothing with them but a coarse wine, some cloves of garlic and onions; despite this, they nevertheless seized the sweeps just like men, curved their backs over the thwarts and shouted, "Hippopopoh! Give way! Come, all pull together! Come, come! How! Samphoras! Are you not rowing?" They rushed down upon the coast of Corinth, and the youngest hollowed out beds in the sand with their hoofs or went to fetch coverings; instead of luzern, they had no food but crabs, which they caught on the strand and even in the sea; so that Theorus causes a Corinthian crab to say, "'Tis a cruel fate, oh Posidon! neither my deep hiding-places, whether on land or at sea, can help me to escape the Knights."

Welcome, oh, dearest and bravest of men! How distracted I have been during your absence! But here you are back, safe and sound. Tell us about the fight you have had.

SAUSAGE-SELLER. The important thing is that I have beaten the Senate.

CHORUS. All glory to you! Let us burst into shouts of joy! You speak well, but your deeds are even better. Come, tell me everything in detail; what a long journey would I not be ready to take to hear your tale! Come, dear friend, speak with full confidence to your admirers.

SAUSAGE-SELLER. The story is worth hearing. Listen! From here I rushed straight to the Senate, right in the track of this man; he was already letting loose the storm, unchaining the lightning, crushing the Knights beneath huge mountains of calumnies heaped together and having all the air of truth; he called you conspirators and his lies caught root like weeds in every mind; dark were the looks on every side and brows were knitted. When I saw that the Senate listened to him favourably and was being tricked by his imposture, I said to myself, "Come, gods of rascals and braggarts, gods of all fools, toad-eaters and braggarts and thou, market-place, where I was bred from my earliest days, give me unbridled audacity, an untiring chatter and a shameless voice." No sooner had I ended this prayer than a lewd man broke wind on my right. "Hah! 'tis a good omen," said I, and prostrated myself; then I burst open the door by a vigorous push with my back, and, opening my mouth to the utmost, shouted, "Senators, I wanted you to be the first to hear the good news; since the War broke out, I have never seen anchovies at a lower price!" All faces brightened at once and I was voted a chaplet for my good tidings; and I added, "With a couple of words I will reveal to you, how you can have quantities of anchovies for an obol; 'tis to seize on all the dishes the merchants have." With mouths gaping with admiration, they applauded me. However, the Paphlagonian winded the matter and, well knowing the sort of language which pleases the Senate best, said, "Friends, I am resolved to offer one hundred oxen to the goddess in recognition of this happy event." The Senate at once veered to his side. So when I saw myself defeated by this ox filth, I outbade the fellow, crying, "Two hundred!" And beyond this I moved, that a vow be made to Diana of a thousand goats if the next day anchovies should only be worth an obol a hundred. And the Senate looked towards me again. The other, stunned with the blow, grew delirious in his speech, and at last the Prytanes and the guards dragged him out. The Senators then stood talking noisily about the anchovies. Cleon, however, begged them to listen to the Lacedaemonian envoy, who had come to make proposals of peace; but all with one accord, cried, "'Tis certainly not the moment to think of peace now! If anchovies are so cheap, what need have we of peace? Let the war take its course!" And with loud shouts they demanded that the Prytanes should close the sitting and then leapt over the rails in all directions. As for me, I slipped away to buy all the coriander seed and leeks there were on the market and gave it to them gratis as seasoning for their anchovies. 'Twas marvellous! They loaded me with praises and caresses; thus I conquered the Senate with an obol's worth of leeks, and here I am.

CHORUS. Bravo! you are the spoilt child of Fortune. Ah! our knave has found his match in another, who has far better tricks in his sack, a thousand kinds of knaveries and of wily words. But the fight begins afresh; take care not to weaken; you know that I have long been your most faithful ally.

SAUSAGE-SELLER. Ah! ah! here comes the Paphlagonian! One would say, 'twas a hurricane lashing the sea and rolling the waves before it in its fury. He looks as if he wanted to swallow me up alive! Ye gods! what an impudent knave!

CLEON. To my aid, my beloved lies! I am going to destroy you, or my name is lost.

SAUSAGE-SELLER. Oh! how he diverts me with his threats! His bluster makes me laugh! And I dance the *mothon* for joy, and sing at the top of my voice, cuckoo!

CLEON. Ah! by Demeter! if I do not kill and devour you, may I die!

SAUSAGE-SELLER. If you do not devour me? and I, if I do not drink your blood to the last drop, and then burst with indigestion.

CLEON. I, I will strangle you, I swear it by the precedence which Pylos gained me.

SAUSAGE-SELLER. By the precedence! Ah! might I see you fall from your precedence into the hindmost seat!

CLEON. By heaven! I will put you to the torture.

SAUSAGE-SELLER. What a lively wit! Come, what's the best to give you to eat? What do you prefer? A purse?

CLEON. I will tear out your inside with my nails.

SAUSAGE-SELLER. And I will cut off your victuals at the Prytaneum.

CLEON. I will haul you before Demos, who will mete out justice to you.

SAUSAGE-SELLER. And I too will drag you before him and belch forth more calumnies than you.

CLEON. Why, poor fool, he does not believe you, whereas I play with him at will.

SAUSAGE-SELLER. So that Demos is your property, your contemptible creature.

CLEON. 'Tis because I know the dishes that please him.

SAUSAGE-SELLER. And these are little mouthfuls, which you serve to him like a clever nurse. You chew the pieces and place some in small quantities in his mouth, while you swallow three parts yourself.

CLEON. Thanks to my skill, I know exactly how to enlarge or contract this gullet.

SAUSAGE-SELLER. I can do as much with my rump.

CLEON. Hah! my friend, you tricked me at the Senate, but have a care! Let us go before Demos.

SAUSAGE-SELLER. That's easily done; come, let's along without delay.

CLEON. Oh, Demos! Come, I adjure you to help me, my father!

SAUSAGE-SELLER. Come, oh, my dear little Demos; come and see how I am insulted.

DEMOS. What a hubbub! To the Devil with you, bawlers! alas! my olive branch, which they have torn down! Ah! 'tis you, Paphlagonian. And who, pray, has been maltreating you?

CLEON. You are the cause of this man and these young people having covered me with blows.

DEMOS. And why?

CLEON Because you love me passionately, Demos.

DEMOS. And you, who are you?

SAUSAGE-SELLER. His rival. For many a long year have I loved you, have I wished to do you honour, I and a crowd of other men of means. But this rascal here has prevented us. You resemble those young men who do not know where to choose their lovers; you repulse honest folk; to earn your favours, one has to be a lamp-seller, a cobbler, a tanner or a currier.

CLEON. I am the benefactor of the people.

SAUSAGE-SELLER. In what way, an it please you?

CLEON. In what way? I supplanted the Generals at Pylos, I hurried thither and I brought back the Laconian captives.

SAUSAGE-SELLER. And I, whilst simply loitering, cleared off with a pot from a shop, which another fellow had been boiling.

CLEON. Demos, convene the assembly at once to decide which of us two loves you best and most merits your favour.

SAUSAGE-SELLER. Yes, yes, provided it be not at the Pnyx.

DEMOS. I could not sit elsewhere; 'tis at the Pnyx, that you must appear before me.

SAUSAGE-SELLER. Ah! great gods! I am undone! At home this old fellow is the most sensible of men, but the instant he is seated on those cursed stone seats, he is there with mouth agape as if he were hanging up figs by their stems to dry.

CHORUS. Come, loose all sail. Be bold, skilful in attack and entangle him in arguments which admit of no reply. It is difficult to beat him, for he is full of craft and pulls himself out of the worst corners. Collect all your forces to come forth from this fight covered with glory, but take care! Let him not assume the attack, get ready your grapples and advance with your vessel to board him!

CLEON. Oh! guardian goddess of our city! oh! Athené! if it be true that next to Lysicles, Cynna and Salabaccha none have done so much good for the Athenian people as I, suffer me to continue to be fed at the Prytaneum without working; but if I hate you, if I am not ready to fight in your defence alone and against all, may I perish, be sawn to bits alive and my skin be cut up into thongs.

SAUSAGE-SELLER. And I, Demos, if it be not true, that I love and cherish you, may I be cooked in a stew; and if that is not saying enough, may I be grated on this table with some cheese and then hashed, may a hook be passed through my testicles and let me be dragged thus to the Ceramicus!

CLEON. Is it possible, Demos, to love you more than I do? And firstly, as long as you have governed with my consent, have I not filled your treasury, putting pressure on some, torturing others or begging of them, indifferent to the opinion of private individuals, and solely anxious to please you?

SAUSAGE-SELLER. There is nothing so wonderful in all that, Demos; I will do as much; I will thieve the bread of others to serve up to you. No, he has neither love for you nor kindly feeling; his only care is to warm himself with your wood, and I will prove it. You, who, sword in hand, saved Attica from the Median yoke at Marathon; you, whose glorious triumphs we love to extol unceasingly, look, he cares little whether he sees you seated uncomfortably upon a stone; whereas I, I bring you this cushion, which I have sewn with my own hands. Rise and try this nice soft seat. Did you not put enough strain on your breeches at Salamis?

DEMOS. Who are you then? Can you be of the race of Harmodius? Upon my faith, 'tis nobly done and like a true friend of Demos.

CLEON. Petty flattery to prove him your goodwill!

SAUSAGE-SELLER. But you have caught him with even smaller baits!

CLEON. Never had Demos a defender or a friend more devoted than myself; on my head, on my life, I swear it!

SAUSAGE-SELLER. You pretend to love him and for eight years you have seen him housed in casks, in crevices and dovecots, where he is blinded with the smoke, and you lock him in without pity; Archeptolemus brought peace and you tore it to ribbons; the envoys who come to propose a truce you drive from the city with kicks in their backsides.

CLEON. This is that Demos may rule over all the Greeks; for the oracles predict that, if he is patient, he must one day sit as judge in Arcadia at five obols per day. Meanwhile, I will nourish him, look after him and, above all, I will ensure to him his three obols.

SAUSAGE-SELLER. No, little you care for his reigning in Arcadia, 'tis to pillage and impose on the allies at will that you reckon; you wish the War to conceal your rogueries as in a mist, that Demos may see nothing of them, and harassed by cares, may only depend on yourself for his bread. But if ever peace is restored to him, if ever he returns to his lands to comfort himself once more with good cakes, to greet his cherished olives, he will know the blessings you have kept him out of, even though paying him a salary; and, filled with hatred and rage, he will rise, burning with desire to vote against you. You know this only too well; 'tis for this you rock him to sleep with your lies.

CLEON. Is it not shameful, that you should dare thus to calumniate me before Demos, me, to whom Athens, I swear it by Demeter, already owes more than it ever did to Themistocles?

SAUSAGE-SELLER. Oh! citizens of Argos, do you hear what he says? You dare to compare yourself to Themistocles, who found our city half empty and left it full to overflowing, who one day gave us the Piraeus for dinner, and added fresh fish to all our usual meals. You, on the contrary, you, who compare yourself with Themistocles, have only sought to reduce our city in size, to shut it within its walls, to chant oracles to us. And Themistocles goes into exile, while you gorge yourself on the most excellent fare.

CLEON. Oh! Demos! Am I compelled to hear myself thus abused, and merely because I love you?

DEMOS. Silence! stop your abuse! All too long have I been your tool.

SAUSAGE-SELLER. Ah! my dear little Demos, he is a rogue, who has played you many a scurvy trick; when your back is turned, he taps at the root the lawsuits initiated by the peculators, swallows the proceeds wholesale and helps himself with both hands from the public funds.

CLEON. Tremble, knave; I will convict you of having stolen thirty thousand drachmae.

SAUSAGE-SELLER. For a rascal of your kidney, you shout rarely! Well! I am ready to die if I do not prove that you have accepted more than forty minae from the Mitylenaeans.

CHORUS. This indeed may be termed talking. Oh, benefactor of the human race, proceed and you will be the most illustrious of the Greeks. You alone shall have sway in Athens, the allies will obey you, and, trident in hand, you will go about shaking and overturning everything to enrich yourself. But, stick to your man, let him not go; with lungs like yours you will soon have him finished.

CLEON. No, my brave friends, no, you are running too fast; I have done a sufficiently brilliant deed to shut the mouth of all enemies, so long as one of the bucklers of Pylos remains.

SAUSAGE-SELLER. Of the bucklers! Hold! I stop you there and I hold you fast. For if it be true, that you love the people, you would not allow these to be hung up with their rings; but 'tis with an intent you have done this. Demos, take knowledge of his guilty purpose; in this way you no longer can punish him at your pleasure. Note the swarm of young tanners, who really surround him, and close to them the sellers of honey and cheese; all these are at one with him. Very well! you have but to frown, to speak of ostracism and they will rush at night to these bucklers, take them down and seize our granaries.

DEMOS. Great gods! what! the bucklers retain their rings! Scoundrel! ah! too long have you had me for your tool, cheated and played with me!

CLEON. But, dear sir, never you believe all he tells you. Oh! never will you find a more devoted friend than me; unaided, I have known how to put down the conspiracies; nothing that is a-hatching in the city escapes me, and I hasten to proclaim it loudly.

SAUSAGE-SELLER. You are like the fishers for eels; in still waters they catch nothing, but if they thoroughly stir up the slime, their fishing is good; in the same way 'tis only in troublous times that you line your pockets. But come, tell me, you, who sell so many skins, have you ever made him a present of a pair of soles for his slippers? and you pretend to love him!

DEMOS. No, he has never given me any.

SAUSAGE-SELLER. That alone shows up the man; but I, I have bought you this pair of shoes; accept them.

DEMOS. None ever, to my knowledge, has merited so much from the people; you are the most zealous of all men for your country and for my toes.

CLEON. Can a wretched pair of slippers make you forget all that you owe me? Is it not I who curbed Gryttus, the filthiest of the lewd, by depriving him of his citizen rights?

SAUSAGE-SELLER. Ah! noble inspector of back passages, let me congratulate you. Moreover, if you set yourself against this form of lewdness, this pederasty, 'twas for sheer jealousy, knowing it to be the school for orators. But you see this poor Demos without a cloak and that at his age too! so little do you care for him, that in mid-winter you have not given him a garment with sleeves. Here, Demos, here is one, take it!

DEMOS. This even Themistocles never thought of; the Piraeus was no doubt a happy idea, but meseems this tunic is quite as fine an invention.

CLEON. Must you have recourse to such jackanapes' tricks to supplant me?

SAUSAGE-SELLER. No, 'tis your own tricks that I am borrowing, just as a guest, driven by urgent need, seizes some other man's shoes.

CLEON. Oh! you shall not outdo me in flattery! I am going to hand Demos this garment; all that remains to you, you rogue, is to go and hang yourself.

DEMOS. Faugh! may the plague seize you! You stink of leather horribly.

SAUSAGE-SELLER. Why, 'tis to smother you that he has thrown this cloak around you on top of the other; and it is not the first plot he has planned against you. Do you remember the time when silphium was so cheap?

DEMOS. Aye, to be sure I do!

SAUSAGE-SELLER. Very well! it was Cleon who had caused the price to fall so low so that all could eat it and the jurymen in the Courts were almost poisoned with farting in each others' faces.

DEMOS. Hah! why, indeed, a scavenger told me the same thing.

SAUSAGE-SELLER. Were you not yourself in those days quite red in the gills with farting?

DEMOS. Why, 'twas a trick worthy of Pyrrandrus!

CLEON. With what other idle trash will you seek to ruin me, you wretch!

SAUSAGE-SELLER. Oh! I shall be more brazen than you, for 'tis the goddess who has commanded me.

CLEON. No, on my honour, you will not! Here, Demos, feast on this dish; it is your salary as a dicast, which you gain through me for doing naught.

SAUSAGE-SELLER. Hold! here is a little box of ointment to rub into the sores on your legs.

CLEON. I will pluck out your white hairs and make you young again.

SAUSAGE-SELLER. Take this hare's scut to wipe the rheum from your eyes.

CLEON. When you wipe your nose, clean your fingers on my head.

SAUSAGE-SELLER. No, on mine.

CLEON. On mine. (*To the Sausage-seller.*) I will have you made a trierarch and you will get ruined through it; I will arrange that you are given an old vessel with rotten sails, which you will have to repair constantly and at great cost.

CHORUS. Our man is on the boil; enough, enough, he is boiling over; remove some of the embers from under him and skim off his threats.

CLEON. I will punish your self-importance; I will crush you with imposts; I will have you inscribed on the list of the rich.

SAUSAGE-SELLER. For me no threats—only one simple wish. That you may be having some cuttle-fish fried on the stove just as you are going to set forth to plead the cause of the Milesians, which, if you gain, means a talent in your pocket; that you hurry over devouring the fish to rush off to the Assembly; suddenly you are called and run off with your mouth full so as not to lose the talent and choke yourself. There! that is my wish.

CHORUS. Splendid! by Zeus, Apollo and Demeter!

DEMOS. Faith! here is an excellent citizen indeed, such as has not been seen for a long time. 'Tis truly a man of the lowest scum! As for you, Paphlagonian, who pretend to love me, you only feed me on garlic. Return me my ring, for you cease to be my steward.

CLEON. Here it is, but be assured, that if you bereave me of my power, my successor will be worse than I am.

DEMOS. This cannot be my ring; I see another device, unless I am going purblind.

SAUSAGE-SELLER. What was your device?

DEMOS. A fig-leaf, stuffed with bullock's fat.

SAUSAGE-SELLER. No, that is not it.

DEMOS. What is it then?

SAUSAGE-SELLER. 'Tis a gull with beak wide open, haranguing from the top of a stone.

DEMOS. Ah! great gods!

SAUSAGE-SELLER. What is the matter?

DEMOS. Away! away out of my sight! 'Tis not my ring he had, 'twas that of Cleonymus. (*To the Sausage-seller.*) Hold, I give you this one; you shall be my steward.

CLEON. Master, I adjure you, decide nothing till you have heard my oracles.

SAUSAGE-SELLER. And mine.

CLEON. If you believe him, you will have to suck his tool for him.

SAUSAGE-SELLER. If you listen to him, you'll have to let him skin your penis to the very stump.

CLEON. My oracles say that you are to reign over the whole earth, crowned with chaplets.

SAUSAGE-SELLER. And mine say that, clothed in an embroidered purple robe, you shall pursue Smicythes and her spouse, standing in a chariot of gold and with a crown on your head.

DEMOS. Go, fetch me your oracles, that the Paphlagonian may hear them.

SAUSAGE-SELLER. Willingly.

DEMOS. And you yours.

CLEON. I run.

SAUSAGE-SELLER. And I run too; nothing could suit me better!

CHORUS. Oh! happy day for us and for our children, if Cleon perish. Yet just now I heard some old cross-grained pleaders on the market-place who hold not this opinion discoursing together. Said they, "If Cleon had not had the power we should have lacked two most useful tools, the pestle and the soup-ladle." You also know what a pig's education he has had; his school-fellows can recall that he only liked the Dorian style and would study no other; his music-master in displeasure sent him away, saying: "This youth in matters of harmony, will only learn the Dorian style because 'tis akin to bribery."

CLEON. There, behold and look at this heap; and yet I do not bring all.

SAUSAGE-SELLER. Ugh! I pant and puff under the weight and yet I do not bring all.

DEMOS. What are these?

CLEON. Oracles.

DEMOS. All these?

CLEON. Does that astonish you? Why, I have another whole boxful of them.

SAUSAGE-SELLER. And I the whole of my attics and two rooms besides.

DEMOS. Come, let us see, whose are these oracles?

CLEON. Mine are those of Bacis.

DEMOS (to the Sausage-seller). And whose are yours?

SAUSAGE-SELLER. Glanis's, the elder brother of Bacis.

DEMOS. And of what do they speak?

CLEON. Of Athens, of Pylos, of you, of me, of all.

DEMOS. And yours?

SAUSAGE-SELLER. Of Athens, of lentils, of Lacedaemonians, of fresh mackerel, of scoundrelly flour-sellers, of you, of me. Ah! ha! now let him gnaw his own penis with chagrin!

DEMOS. Come, read them out to me and especially that one I like so much, which says that I shall become an eagle and soar among the clouds.

CLEON. Then listen and be attentive! "Son of Erectheus, understand the meaning of the words, which the sacred tripods set resounding in the sanctuary of Apollo. Preserve the sacred dog with the jagged teeth, that barks and howls in your defence; he will ensure you a salary and, if he fails, will perish as the victim of the swarms of jays that hunt him down with their screams."

DEMOS. By Demeter! I do not understand a word of it. What connection is there between Erectheus, the jays and the dog?

CLEON. 'Tis I who am the dog, since I bark in your defence. Well! Phoebus commands you to keep and cherish your dog.

SAUSAGE-SELLER. 'Tis not so spoken by the god; this dog seems to me to gnaw at the oracles as others gnaw at doorposts. Here is exactly what Apollo says of the dog.

DEMOS. Let us hear, but I must first pick up a stone; an oracle which speaks of a dog might bite me.

SAUSAGE-SELLER. "Son of Erectheus, beware of this Cerberus that enslaves freemen; he fawns upon you with his tail, when you are dining, but he is lying in wait to devour your dishes, should you turn your head an instant; at night he sneaks into the kitchen and, true dog that he is, licks up with one lap of his tongue both your dishes and ... the islands."

DEMOS. Faith, Glanis, you speak better than your brother.

CLEON. Condescend again to hear me and then judge: "A woman in sacred Athens will be delivered of a lion, who shall fight for the people against clouds of gnats with the same ferocity as if he were defending his whelps; care ye for him, erect wooden walls around him and towers of brass." Do you understand that?

DEMOS. Not the least bit in the world.

CLEON. The god tells you here to look after me, for, 'tis I who am your lion.

DEMOS. How! You have become a lion and I never knew a thing about it?

SAUSAGE-SELLER. There is only one thing which he purposely keeps from you; he does not say what this wall of wood and brass is in which Apollo warns you to keep and guard him.

DEMOS. What does the god mean, then?

SAUSAGE-SELLER. He advises you to fit him into a five-holed wooden collar.

DEMOS. Hah! I think that oracle is about to be fulfilled.

CLEON. Do not believe it; these are but jealous crows, that caw against me; but never cease to cherish your good hawk; never forget that he brought you those Lacedaemonian fish, loaded with chains.

SAUSAGE-SELLER. Ah! if the Paphlagonian ran any risk that day, 'twas because he was drunk. Oh, too credulous son of Cecrops, do you accept that as a glorious exploit? A woman would carry a heavy burden if only a man had put it on her shoulders. But to fight! Go to! he would shit himself, if ever it came to a tussle.

CLEON. Note this Pylos in front of Pylos, of which the oracle speaks, "Pylos is before Pylos."

DEMOS. How "in front of Pylos"? What does he mean by that?

SAUSAGE-SELLER. He says he will seize upon your bath-tubs.

DEMOS. Then I shall not bathe to-day.

SAUSAGE-SELLER. No, as he has stolen our baths. But here is an oracle about the fleet, to which I beg your best attention.

DEMOS. Read on! I am listening; let us first see how we are to pay our sailors.

SAUSAGE-SELLER. "Son of Aegeus, beware of the tricks of the dog-fox, he bites from the rear and rushes off at full speed; he is nothing but cunning and perfidy." Do you know what the oracle intends to say?

DEMOS. The dog-fox is Philostratus.

SAUSAGE-SELLER. No, no, 'tis Cleon; he is incessantly asking you for light vessels to go and collect the tributes, and Apollo advises you not to grant them.

DEMOS. What connection is there between a galley and a dog-fox?

SAUSAGE-SELLER. What connection? Why, 'tis quite plain—a galley travels as fast as a dog.

DEMOS. Why, then, does the oracle not say dog instead of dog-fox?

SAUSAGE-SELLER. Because he compares the soldiers to young foxes, who, like them, eat the grapes in the fields.

DEMOS. Good! Well then! how am I to pay the wages of my young foxes?

SAUSAGE-SELLER. I will undertake that, and in three days too! But listen to this further oracle, by which Apollo puts you on your guard against the snares of the greedy fist.

DEMOS. Of what greedy fist?

SAUSAGE-SELLER. The god in this oracle very clearly points to the hand of Cleon, who incessantly holds his out, saying, "Fill it."

CLEON. 'Tis false! Phoebus means the hand of Diopithes. But here I have a winged oracle, which promises you shall become an eagle and rule over all the earth.

SAUSAGE-SELLER. I have one, which says that you shall be King of the Earth and of the Sea, and that you shall administer justice in Ecbatana, eating fine rich stews the while.

CLEON. I have seen Athené in a dream, pouring out full vials of riches and health over the people.

SAUSAGE-SELLER. I too have seen the goddess, descending from the Acropolis with an owl perched upon her helmet; on your head she was pouring out ambrosia, on that of Cleon garlic pickle.

DEMOS. Truly Glanis is the wisest of men. I shall yield myself to you; guide me in my old age and educate me anew.

CLEON. Ah! I adjure you! not yet; wait a little; I will promise to distribute barley every day.

DEMOS. Ah! I will not hear another word about barley; you have cheated me too often already, both you and Theophanes.

CLEON. Well then! you shall have flour-cakes all piping hot.

SAUSAGE-SELLER. I will give you cakes too, and nice cooked fish; you will only have to eat.

DEMOS. Very well, mind you keep your promises. To whichever of you twain shall treat me best I hand over the reins of state.

CLEON. I will be first.

SAUSAGE-SELLER. No, no, I will.

CHORUS. Demos, you are our all-powerful sovereign lord; all tremble before you, yet you are led by the nose. You love to be flattered and fooled; you listen to the orators with gaping mouth and your mind is led astray.

DEMOS. 'Tis rather you who have no brains, if you think me so foolish as all that; it is with a purpose that I play this idiot's role, for I love to drink the lifelong day, and so it pleases me to keep a thief for my minister. When he has thoroughly gorged himself, then I overthrow and crush him.

CHORUS. What profound wisdom! If it be really so, why! all is for the best. Your ministers, then, are your victims, whom you nourish and feed up expressly in the Pnyx, so that, the day your dinner is ready, you may immolate the fattest and eat him.

DEMOS. Look, see how I play with them, while all the time they think themselves such adepts at cheating me. I have my eye on them when they thieve, but I do not appear to be seeing them; then I thrust a judgment down their throat as it were a feather, and force them to vomit up all they have robbed from me.

CLEON. Oh! the rascal!

SAUSAGE-SELLER. Oh! the scoundrel!

CLEON. Demos, all is ready these three hours; I await your orders and I burn with desire to load you with benefits.

SAUSAGE-SELLER. And I ten, twelve, a thousand hours, a long, long while, an infinitely long while.

DEMOS. As for me, 'tis thirty thousand hours that I have been impatient; very long, infinitely long that I have cursed you.

SAUSAGE-SELLER. Do you know what you had best do?

DEMOS. If I do not, tell me.

SAUSAGE-SELLER. Declare the lists open and we will contend abreast to determine who shall treat you the best.

DEMOS. Splendid! Draw back in line!

CLEON. I am ready.

DEMOS. Off you go!

SAUSAGE-SELLER (to Cleon). I shall not let you get to the tape.

DEMOS. What fervent lovers! If I am not to-day the happiest of men, 'tis because I shall be the most disgusted.

CLEON. Look! 'tis I who am the first to bring you a seat.

SAUSAGE-SELLER. And I a table.

CLEON. Hold, here is a cake kneaded of Pylos barley.

SAUSAGE–SELLER. Here are crusts, which the ivory hand of the goddess has hallowed.

DEMOS. Oh! Mighty Athené! How large are your fingers!

CLEON. This is pea-soup, as exquisite as it is fine; 'tis Pallas the victorious goddess at Pylos who crushed the peas herself.

SAUSAGE-SELLER. Oh, Demos! the goddess watches over you; she is stretching forth over your head ... a stew-pan full of broth.

DEMOS. And should we still be dwelling in this city without this protecting stew-pan?

CLEON. Here are some fish, given to you by her who is the terror of our foes.

SAUSAGE-SELLER. The daughter of the mightiest of the gods sends you this meat cooked in its own gravy, along with this dish of tripe and some paunch.

DEMOS. 'Tis to thank me for the Peplos I offered to her; 'tis well.

CLEON. The goddess with the terrible plume invites you to eat this long cake; you will row the harder on it.

SAUSAGE-SELLER. Take this also.

DEMOS. And what shall I do with this tripe?

SAUSAGE-SELLER. She sends it you to belly out your galleys, for she is always showing her kindly anxiety for our fleet. Now drink this beverage composed of three parts of water to two of wine.

DEMOS. Ah! what delicious wine, and how well it stands the water.

SAUSAGE-SELLER. 'Twas the goddess who came from the head of Zeus that mixed this liquor with her own hands.

CLEON. Hold, here is a piece of good rich cake.

SAUSAGE-SELLER. But I offer you an entire cake.

CLEON. But you cannot offer him stewed hare as I do.

SAUSAGE-SELLER. Ah! great gods! stewed hare! where shall I find it? Oh! brain of mine, devise some trick!

CLEON. Do you see this, poor fellow?

SAUSAGE-SELLER. A fig for that! Here are folk coming to seek me.

CLEON. Who are they?

SAUSAGE-SELLER. Envoys, bearing sacks bulging with money.

CLEON. (*Hearing money mentioned Clean turns his head, and Agoracritus seizes the opportunity to snatch away the stewed hare.*) Where, where, I say?

SAUSAGE-SELLER. Bah! What's that to you? Will you not even now let the strangers alone? Demos, do you see this stewed hare which I bring you?

CLEON. Ah! rascal! you have shamelessly robbed me.

SAUSAGE-SELLER. You have robbed too, you robbed the Laconians at Pylos.

DEMOS. An you pity me, tell me, how did you get the idea to filch it from him?

SAUSAGE-SELLER. The idea comes from the goddess; the theft is all my own.

CLEON. And I had taken such trouble to catch this hare.

SAUSAGE-SELLER. But 'twas I who had it cooked.

DEMOS (to Cleon). Get you gone! My thanks are only for him who served it.

CLEON. Ah! wretch! have you beaten me in impudence!

SAUSAGE-SELLER. Well then, Demos, say now, who has treated you best, you and your stomach? Decide!

DEMOS. How shall I act here so that the spectators shall approve my judgment?

SAUSAGE-SELLER. I will tell you. Without saying anything, go and rummage through my basket, and then through the Paphlagonian's, and see what is in them; that's the best way to judge.

DEMOS. Let us see then, what is there in yours?

SAUSAGE-SELLER. Why, 'tis empty, dear little father; I have brought everything to you.

DEMOS. This is a basket devoted to the people.

SAUSAGE-SELLER. Now hunt through the Paphlagonian's. Well?

DEMOS. Oh! what a lot of good things! Why! 'tis quite full! Oh! what a huge great part of this cake he kept for himself! He had only cut off the least little tiny piece for me.

SAUSAGE-SELLER. But this is what he has always done. Of everything he took, he only gave you the crumbs, and kept the bulk.

DEMOS. Oh! rascal! was this the way you robbed me? And I was loading you with chaplets and gifts!

CLEON. 'Twas for the public weal I robbed.

DEMOS (to Cleon). Give me back that crown; I will give it to him.

SAUSAGE-SELLER. Return it quick, quick, you gallows-bird.

CLEON. No, for the Pythian oracle has revealed to me the name of him who shall overthrow me.

SAUSAGE-SELLER. And that name was mine, nothing can be clearer.

CLEON. Reply and I shall soon see whether you are indeed the man whom the god intended. Firstly, what school did you attend when a child?

SAUSAGE-SELLER. 'Twas in the kitchens I was taught with cuffs and blows.

CLEON. What's that you say? Ah! this is truly what the oracle said. And what did you learn from the master of exercises?

SAUSAGE-SELLER. I learnt to take a false oath without a smile, when I had stolen something.

CLEON. Oh! Phoebus Apollo, god of Lycia! I am undone! And when you had become a man, what trade did you follow?

SAUSAGE-SELLER. I sold sausages and did a bit of fornication.

CLEON. Oh! my god! I am a lost man! Ah! still one slender hope remains. Tell me, was it on the market-place or near the gates that you sold your sausages?

SAUSAGE-SELLER. Near the gates, in the market for salted goods.

CLEON Alas! I see the prophecy of the god is verily come true. Alas! roll me home. I am a miserable, ruined man. Farewell, my chaplet! 'Tis death to me to part with you. So you are to belong to another; 'tis certain he cannot be a greater thief, but perhaps he may be a luckier one.

SAUSAGE-SELLER. Oh! Zeus, the protector of Greece! 'tis to you I owe this victory!

DEMOSTHENES. Hail! illustrious conqueror, but forget not, that if you have become a great man, 'tis thanks to me; I ask but a little thing; appoint me secretary of the law-court in the room of Phanus.

DEMOS (to the Sausage-seller). But what is your name then? Tell me.

SAUSAGE-SELLER. My name is Agoracritus, because I have always lived on the market-place in the midst of lawsuits.

DEMOS. Well then, Agoracritus, I stand by you; as for the Paphlagonian, I hand him over to your mercy.

AGORACRITUS. Demos, I will care for you to the best of my power, and all shall admit that no citizen is more devoted than I to this city of simpletons.

CHORUS. What fitter theme for our Muse, at the close as at the beginning of his work, than this, to sing the hero who drives his swift steeds down the arena? Why afflict Lysistratus with our satires on his poverty, and Thumantis, who has not so much as a lodging? He is dying of hunger and can be seen at Delphi, his face bathed in tears, clinging to your quiver, oh, Apollo! and supplicating you to take him out of his misery.

An insult directed at the wicked is not to be censured; on the contrary, the honest man, if he has sense, can only applaud. Him, whom I wish to brand with infamy, is little known himself; 'tis the brother of Arignotus. I regret to quote this name which is so dear to me, but whoever can distinguish black from white, or the Orthian mode of music from others, knows the virtues of Arignotus, whom his brother, Ariphrades, in no way resembles. He gloats in vice, is not merely a dissolute man and utterly debauched—but he has actually invented a new form of vice; for he pollutes his tongue with abominable pleasures in brothels licking up that nauseous moisture and befouling his beard as he tickles the lips of lewd women's private parts. Whoever is not horrified at such a monster shall never drink from the same cup with me.

At times a thought weighs on me at night; I wonder whence comes this fearful voracity of Cleonymus. 'Tis said, that when dining with a rich host, he springs at the dishes with the gluttony of a wild beast and never leaves the bread-bin until his host seizes him round the knees, exclaiming, "Go, go, good gentleman, in mercy go, and spare my poor table!"

'Tis said that the triremes assembled in council and that the oldest spoke in these terms, "Are you ignorant, my sisters, of what is plotting in Athens? They say, that a certain Hyperbolus, a bad citizen and an infamous scoundrel, asks for a hundred of us to take them to sea against Chalcedon." All were indignant, and one of them, as yet a virgin, cried, "May god forbid that I should ever obey him! I would prefer to grow old in the harbour and be gnawed by worms. No! by the gods I swear it, Nauphanté, daughter of Nauson, shall never bend to his law; 'tis as true as I am made of wood and pitch. If the Athenians vote for the proposal of Hyperbolus, let them! we will hoist full sail and seek refuge by the temple of Theseus or the shrine of the Euminides. No! he shall not command us! No! he shall not play with the city to this extent! Let him sail by himself for Tartarus, if such please him, launching the boats in which he used to sell his lamps."

AGORACRITUS. Maintain a holy silence! Keep your mouths from utterance! call no more witnesses; close these tribunals, which are the delight of this city, and gather at the theatre to chant the Paean of thanksgiving to the gods for a fresh favour.

CHORUS. Oh! torch of sacred Athens, saviour of the Islands, what good tidings are we to celebrate by letting the blood of the victims flow in our market-places?

AGORACRITUS. I have freshened Demos up somewhat on the stove and have turned his ugliness into beauty.

CHORUS. I admire your inventive genius; but, where is he?

AGORACRITUS. He is living in ancient Athens, the city of the garlands of violets.

CHORUS. How I should like to see him! What is his dress like, what his manner?

AGORACRITUS. He has once more become as he was in the days when he lived with Aristides and Miltiades. But you will judge for yourselves, for I hear the vestibule doors opening. Hail with your shouts of gladness the Athens of old, which now doth reappear to your gaze, admirable, worthy of the songs of the poets and the home of the illustrious Demos.

CHORUS. Oh! noble, brilliant Athens, whose brow is wreathed with violets, show us the sovereign master of this land and of all Greece.

AGORACRITUS. Lo! here he is coming with his hair held in place with a golden band and in all the glory of his old-world dress; perfumed with myrrh, he spreads around him not the odour of lawsuits, but of peace.

CHORUS. Hail! King of Greece, we congratulate you upon the happiness you enjoy; it is worthy of this city, worthy of the glory of Marathon.

DEMOS. Come, Agoracritus, come, my best friend; see the service you have done me by freshening me up on your stove.

AGORACRITUS. Ah! if you but remembered what you were formerly and what you did, you would for a certainty believe me to be a god.

DEMOS. But what did I? and how was I then?

AGORACRITUS. Firstly, so soon as ever an orator declared in the assembly "Demos, I love you ardently; 'tis I alone, who dream of you and watch over your interests"; at such an exordium you would look like a cock flapping his wings or a bull tossing his horns.

DEMOS. What, I?

AGORACRITUS. Then, after he had fooled you to the hilt, he would go.

DEMOS. What! they would treat me so, and I never saw it!

AGORACRITUS. You knew only how to open and close your ears like a sunshade.

DEMOS. Was I then so stupid and such a dotard?

AGORACRITUS. Worse than that; if one of two orators proposed to equip a fleet for war and the other suggested the use of the same sum for paying out to the citizens, 'twas the latter who always carried the day. Well! you droop your head! you turn away your face?

DEMOS. I redden at my past errors.

AGORACRITUS. Think no more of them; 'tis not you who are to blame, but those who cheated you in this sorry fashion. But, come, if some impudent lawyer dared to say, "Dicasts, you shall have no wheat unless you convict this accused man!" what would you do? Tell me.

DEMOS. I would have him removed from the bar, I would bind Hyperbolus about his neck like a stone and would fling him into the Barathrum.

AGORACRITUS. Well spoken! but what other measures do you wish to take?

DEMOS. First, as soon as ever a fleet returns to the harbour, I shall pay up the rowers in full.

AGORACRITUS. That will soothe many a worn and chafed bottom.

DEMOS. Further, the hoplite enrolled for military service shall not get transferred to another service through favour, but shall stick to that given him at the outset.

AGORACRITUS. This will strike the buckler of Cleonymus full in the centre.

DEMOS. None shall ascend the rostrum, unless their chins are bearded.

AGORACRITUS. What then will become of Clisthenes and of Strato?

DEMOS. I wish only to refer to those youths, who loll about the perfume shops, babbling at random, "What a clever fellow is Pheax! How cleverly he escaped death! how concise and convincing is his style! what phrases! how clear and to the point! how well he knows how to quell an interruption!"

AGORACRITUS. I thought you were the lover of those pathic minions.

DEMOS. The gods forefend it! and I will force all such fellows to go a-hunting instead of proposing decrees.

AGORACRITUS. In that case, accept this folding-stool, and to carry it this well-grown, big-testicled slave lad. Besides, you may put him to any other purpose you please.

DEMOS. Oh! I am happy indeed to find myself as I was of old!

AGORACRITUS. Aye, you deem yourself happy, when I shall have handed you the truces of thirty years. Truces! step forward!

DEMOS. Great gods! how charming they are! Can I do with them as I wish? where did you discover them, pray?

AGORACRITUS. 'Twas that Paphlagonian who kept them locked up in his house, so that you might not enjoy them. As for myself, I give them to you; take them with you into the country.

DEMOS. And what punishment will you inflict upon this Paphlagonian, the cause of all my troubles?

AGORACRITUS. 'Twill not be over-terrible. I condemn him to follow my old trade; posted near the gates, he must sell sausages of asses' and dogs'-meat; perpetually drunk, he will exchange foul language with prostitutes and will drink nothing but the dirty water from the baths.

DEMOS. Well conceived! he is indeed fit to wrangle with harlots and bathmen; as for you, in return for so many blessings, I invite you to take the place at the Prytaneum which this rogue once occupied. Put on this frog-green mantle and follow me. As for the other, let 'em take him away; let him go sell his sausages in full view of the foreigners, whom he used formerly so wantonly to insult.

FINIS OF "THE KNIGHTS"

The Acharnians

Introduction

This is the first of the series of three Comedies—'The Acharnians,' 'Peace' and 'Lysistrata'—produced at intervals of years, the sixth, tenth and twenty-first of the Peloponnesian War, and impressing on the Athenian people the miseries and disasters due to it and to the scoundrels who by their selfish and reckless policy had provoked it, the consequent ruin of industry and, above all, agriculture, and the urgency of asking Peace. In date it is the earliest play brought out by the author in his own name and his first work of serious importance. It was acted at the Lenaean Festival, in January, 426 B.C., and gained the first prize, Cratinus being second.

Its diatribes against the War and fierce criticism of the general policy of the War party so enraged Cleon that, as already mentioned, he endeavoured to ruin the author, who in 'The Knights' retorted by a direct and savage personal attack on the leader of the democracy. The plot is of the simplest. Dicaeopolis, an Athenian citizen, but a native of Acharnae, one of the agricultural *demes* and one which had especially suffered in the Lacedaemonian invasions, sick and tired of the ill-success and miseries of the War, makes up his mind, if he fails to induce the people to adopt his policy of "peace at any price," to conclude a private and particular peace of his own to cover himself, his family, and his estate. The Athenians, momentarily elated by victory and over-persuaded by the demagogues of the day—Cleon and his henchmen, refuse to hear of such a thing as coming to terms. Accordingly Dicaeopolis dispatches an envoy to Sparta on his own account, who comes back presently with a selection of specimen treaties in his pocket. The old man tastes and tries, special terms are arranged, and the play concludes with a riotous and uproarious rustic feast in honour of the blessings of Peace and Plenty. Incidentally excellent fun is poked at Euripides and his dramatic methods, which supply matter for so much witty badinage in several others of our author's pieces.

Other specially comic incidents are: the scene where the two young daughters of the famished Megarian are sold in the market at Athens as sucking-pigs—a scene in which the convenient similarity of the Greek words signifying a pig and the 'pudendum muliebre' respectively is utilized in a whole string of ingenious and suggestive 'double entendres' and ludicrous jokes; another where the Informer, or Market-Spy, is packed up in a crate as crockery and carried off home by the Boeotian buyer.

The drama takes its title from the Chorus, composed of old men of Acharnae.

The Acharnians

DICAEOPOLIS (*alone*). What cares have not gnawed at my heart and
how few have been the pleasures in my life! Four, to be exact, while my
troubles have been as countless as the grains of sand on the shore! Let me see
of what value to me have been these few pleasures? Ah! I remember that I
was delighted in soul when Cleon had to disgorge those five talents; I was in
ecstasy and I love the Knights for this deed; 'it is an honour to Greece.' But
the day when I was impatiently awaiting a piece by Aeschylus, what tragic

despair it caused me when the herald called, "Theognis, introduce your Chorus!" Just imagine how this blow struck straight at my heart! On the other hand, what joy Dexitheus caused me at the musical competition, when he played a Boeotian melody on the lyre! But this year by contrast! Oh! what deadly torture to hear Chaeris perform the prelude in the Orthian mode!—Never, however, since I began to bathe, has the dust hurt my eyes as it does to-day. Still it is the day of assembly; all should be here at daybreak, and yet the Pnyx is still deserted. They are gossiping in the market-place, slipping hither and thither to avoid the vermilioned rope. The Prytanes even do not come; they will be late, but when they come they will push and fight each other for a seat in the front row. They will never trouble themselves with the question of peace. Oh! Athens! Athens! As for myself, I do not fail to come here before all the rest, and now, finding myself alone, I groan, yawn, stretch, break wind, and know not what to do; I make sketches in the dust, pull out my loose hairs, muse, think of my fields, long for peace, curse town life and regret my dear country home, which never told me to 'buy fuel, vinegar or oil'; there the word 'buy,' which cuts me in two, was unknown; I harvested everything at will. Therefore I have come to the assembly fully prepared to bawl, interrupt and abuse the speakers, if they talk of aught but peace. But here come the Prytanes, and high time too, for it is midday! As I foretold, hah! is it not so? They are pushing and fighting for the front seats.

HERALD. Move on up, move on, move on, to get within the consecrated area.

AMPHITHEUS. Has anyone spoken yet?

HERALD. Who asks to speak?

AMPHITHEUS. I do.

HERALD. Your name?

AMPHITHEUS. Amphitheus.

HERALD. You are no man.

AMPHITHEUS. No! I am an immortal! Amphitheus was the son of Ceres and Triptolemus; of him was born Celeus. Celeus wedded Phaencreté, my grandmother, whose son was Lucinus, and, being born of him, I am an immortal; it is to me alone that the gods have entrusted the duty of treating with the Lacedaemonians. But, citizens, though I am immortal, I am dying of hunger; the Prytanes give me naught.

A PRYTANIS. Guards!

AMPHITHEUS. Oh, Triptolemus and Ceres, do ye thus forsake your own blood?

DICAEOPOLIS. Prytanes, in expelling this citizen, you are offering an outrage to the Assembly. He only desired to secure peace for us and to sheathe the sword.

PRYTANIS. Sit down and keep silence!

DICAEOPOLIS. No, by Apollo, will I not, unless you are going to discuss the question of peace.

HERALD. The ambassadors, who are returned from the Court of the King!

DICAEOPOLIS. Of what King? I am sick of all those fine birds, the peacock ambassadors and their swagger.

HERALD. Silence!

DICAEOPOLIS. Oh! oh! by Ecbatana, what assumption!

AN AMBASSADOR. During the archonship of Euthymenes, you sent us to the Great King on a salary of two drachmae per diem.

DICAEOPOLIS. Ah! those poor drachmae!

AMBASSADOR. We suffered horribly on the plains of the Caÿster, sleeping under a tent, stretched deliciously on fine chariots, half dead with weariness.

DICAEOPOLIS. And I was very much at ease, lying on the straw along the battlements!

AMBASSADOR. Everywhere we were well received and forced to drink delicious wine out of golden or crystal flagons....

DICAEOPOLIS. Oh, city of Cranaus, thy ambassadors are laughing at thee!

AMBASSADOR. For great feeders and heavy drinkers are alone esteemed as men by the barbarians.

DICAEOPOLIS. Just as here in Athens, we only esteem the most drunken debauchees.

AMBASSADOR. At the end of the fourth year we reached the King's Court, but he had left with his whole army to ease himself, and for the space of eight months he was thus easing himself in midst of the golden mountains.

DICAEOPOLIS. And how long was he replacing his dress?

AMBASSADOR. The whole period of a full moon; after which he returned to his palace; then he entertained us and had us served with oxen roasted whole in an oven.

DICAEOPOLIS. Who ever saw an oxen baked in an oven? What a lie!

AMBASSADOR. On my honour, he also had us served with a bird three times as large as Cleonymus, and called the Boaster.

DICAEOPOLIS. And do we give you two drachmae, that you should treat us to all this humbug?

AMBASSADOR. We are bringing to you, Pseudartabas, the King's Eye.

DICAEOPOLIS. I would a crow might pluck out thine with his beak, thou cursed ambassador!

HERALD. The King's Eye!

DICAEOPOLIS. Eh! Great gods! Friend, with thy great eye, round like the hole through which the oarsman passes his sweep, you have the air of a galley doubling a cape to gain the port.

AMBASSADOR. Come, Pseudartabas, give forth the message for the Athenians with which you were charged by the Great King.

PSEUDARTABAS. Jartaman exarx 'anapissonnai satra.

AMBASSADOR. Do you understand what he says?

DICAEOPOLIS. By Apollo, not I!

AMBASSADOR. He says, that the Great King will send you gold. Come, utter the word 'gold' louder and more distinctly.

DICAEOPOLIS. Thou shalt not have gold, thou gaping-arsed Ionian.

DICAEOPOLIS. Ah! may the gods forgive me, but that is clear enough.

AMBASSADOR. What does he say?

DICAEOPOLIS. That the Ionians are debauchees and idiots, if they expect to receive gold from the barbarians.

AMBASSADOR. Not so, he speaks of medimni of gold.

DICAEOPOLIS. What medimni? Thou art but a great braggart; but get your way, I will find out the truth by myself. Come now, answer me clearly, if you do not wish me to dye your skin red. Will the Great King send us gold? (*Pseudartabas makes a negative sign.*) Then our ambassadors are seeking to deceive us? (*Pseudartabas signs affirmatively.*) These fellows make signs like any Greek; I am sure that they are nothing but Athenians. Oh, ho! I recognize one of these eunuchs; it is Clisthenes, the son of Sibyrtius. Behold the effrontery of this shaven rump! How! great baboon, with such a beard do you seek to play the eunuch to us? And this other one? Is it not Straton?

HERALD. Silence! Let all be seated. The Senate invites the King's Eye to the Prytaneum.

DICAEOPOLIS. Is this not sufficient to drive one to hang oneself? Here I stand chilled to the bone, whilst the doors of the Prytaneum fly wide open to lodge such rascals. But I will do something great and bold. Where is Amphitheus? Come and speak with me.

AMPHITHEUS. Here I am.

DICAEOPOLIS. Take these eight drachmae and go and conclude a truce with the Lacedaemonians for me, my wife and my children; I leave you free, my dear citizens, to send out embassies and to stand gaping in the air.

HERALD. Bring in Theorus, who has returned from the Court of Sitalces.

THEORUS. I am here.

DICAEOPOLIS. Another humbug!

THEORUS. We should not have remained long in Thrace....

DICAEOPOLIS. Forsooth, no, if you had not been well paid.

THEORUS. ... If the country had not been covered with snow; the rivers were ice-bound at the time that Theognis brought out his tragedy here; during the whole of that time I was holding my own with Sitalces, cup in hand; and, in truth, he adored you to such a degree, that he wrote on the walls, "How beautiful are the Athenians!" His son, to whom we gave the freedom of the city, burned with desire to come here and eat chitterlings at the feast of the Apaturia; he prayed his father to come to the aid of his new country and Sitalces swore on his goblet that he would succour us with such a host that the Athenians would exclaim, "What a cloud of grasshoppers!"

DICAEOPOLIS. May I die if I believe a word of what you tell us! Excepting the grasshoppers, there is not a grain of truth in it all!

THEORUS. And he has sent you the most warlike soldiers of all Thrace.

DICAEOPOLIS. Now we shall begin to see clearly.

HERALD. Come hither, Thracians, whom Theorus brought.

DICAEOPOLIS. What plague have we here?

THEORUS. 'Tis the host of the Odomanti.

DICAEOPOLIS. Of the Odomanti? Tell me what it means. Who has mutilated their tools like this?

THEORUS. If they are given a wage of two drachmae, they will put all Boeotia to fire and sword.

DICAEOPOLIS. Two drachmae to those circumcised hounds! Groan aloud, ye people of rowers, bulwark of Athens! Ah! great gods! I am undone; these Odomanti are robbing me of my garlic! Will you give me back my garlic?

THEORUS. Oh! wretched man! do not go near them; they have eaten garlic.

DICAEOPOLIS. Prytanes, will you let me be treated in this manner, in my own country and by barbarians? But I oppose the discussion of paying a wage to the Thracians; I announce an omen; I have just felt a drop of rain.

HERALD. Let the Thracians withdraw and return the day after to-morrow; the Prytanes declare the sitting at an end.

DICAEOPOLIS. Ye gods, what garlic I have lost! But here comes Amphitheus returned from Lacedaemon. Welcome, Amphitheus.

AMPHITHEUS. No, there is no welcome for me and I fly as fast as I can, for I am pursued by the Acharnians.

DICAEOPOLIS. Why, what has happened?

AMPHITHEUS. I was hurrying to bring your treaty of truce, but some old dotards from Acharnae got scent of the thing; they are veterans of Marathon, tough as oak or maple, of which they are made for sure—rough and ruthless. They all set to a-crying, "Wretch! you are the bearer of a treaty, and the enemy has only just cut our vines!" Meanwhile they were gathering stones in their cloaks, so I fled and they ran after me shouting.

DICAEOPOLIS. Let 'em shout as much as they please! But have you brought me a treaty?

AMPHITHEUS. Most certainly, here are three samples to select from, this one is five years old; take it and taste.

DICAEOPOLIS. Faugh!

AMPHITHEUS. Well?

DICAEOPOLIS. It does not please me; it smells of pitch and of the ships they are fitting out.

AMPHITHEUS. Here is another, ten years old; taste it.

DICAEOPOLIS. It smells strongly of the delegates, who go round the towns to chide the allies for their slowness.

AMPHITHEUS. This last is a truce of thirty years, both on sea and land.

DICAEOPOLIS. Oh! by Bacchus! what a bouquet! It has the aroma of nectar and ambrosia; this does not say to us, "Provision yourselves for three days." But it lisps the gentle numbers, "Go whither you will." I accept it, ratify it, drink it at one draught and consign the Acharnians to limbo. Freed from the war and its ills, I shall keep the Dionysia in the country.

AMPHITHEUS. And I shall run away, for I'm mortally afraid of the Acharnians.

CHORUS. This way all! Let us follow our man; we will demand him of everyone we meet; the public weal makes his seizure imperative. Ho, there! tell me which way the bearer of the truce has gone; he has escaped us, he has disappeared. Curse old age! When I was young, in the days when I followed Phayllus, running with a sack of coals on my back, this wretch would not have eluded my pursuit, let him be as swift as he will; but now my limbs are stiff; old Lacratides feels his legs are weighty and the traitor escapes me. No, no, let us follow him; old Acharnians like ourselves shall not be set at naught by a scoundrel, who has dared, great gods! to conclude a truce, when I wanted the war continued with double fury in order to avenge my ruined lands. No mercy for our foes until I have pierced their hearts like a sharp reed, so that they dare never again ravage my vineyards. Come, let us seek the rascal; let us look everywhere, carrying our stones in our hands; let us hunt him from place to place until we trap him; I could never, never tire of the delight of stoning him.

DICAEOPOLIS. Peace! profane men!

CHORUS. Silence all! Friends, do you hear the sacred formula? Here is he, whom we seek! This way, all! Get out of his way, surely he comes to offer an oblation.

DICAEOPOLIS. Peace, profane men! Let the basket-bearer come forward, and thou, Xanthias, hold the phallus well upright.

WIFE OF DICAEOPOLIS. Daughter, set down the basket and let us begin the sacrifice.

DAUGHTER OF DICAEOPOLIS. Mother, hand me the ladle, that I may spread the sauce on the cake.

DICAEOPOLIS. It is well! Oh, mighty Bacchus, it is with joy that, freed from military duty, I and all mine perform this solemn rite and offer thee this sacrifice; grant, that I may keep the rural Dionysia without hindrance and that this truce of thirty years may be propitious for me.

WIFE OF DICAEOPOLIS. Come, my child, carry the basket gracefully and with a grave, demure face. Happy he, who shall be your possessor and embrace you so firmly at dawn, that you belch wind like a weasel. Go forward, and have a care they don't snatch your jewels in the crowd.

DICAEOPOLIS. Xanthias, walk behind the basket-bearer and hold the phallus well erect; I will follow, singing the Phallic hymn; thou, wife, look on from the top of the terrace. Forward! Oh, Phales, companion of the orgies of Bacchus, night reveller, god of adultery, friend of young men, these past six years I have not been able to invoke thee. With what joy I return to my farmstead, thanks to the truce I have concluded, freed from cares, from fighting and from Lamachuses! How much sweeter, Phales, oh, Phales, is it to surprise Thratta, the pretty wood-maid, Strymodorus' slave, stealing wood from Mount Phelleus, to catch her under the arms, to throw her on the ground and possess her! Oh, Phales, Phales! If thou wilt drink and bemuse thyself with me, we will to-morrow consume some good dish in honour of the peace, and I will hang up my buckler over the smoking hearth.

CHORUS. It is he, he himself. Stone him, stone him, stone him, strike the wretch. All, all of you, pelt him, pelt him!

DICAEOPOLIS. What is this? By Heracles, you will smash my pot.

CHORUS. It is you that we are stoning, you miserable scoundrel.

DICAEOPOLIS. And for what sin, Acharnian Elders, tell me that!

CHORUS. You ask that, you impudent rascal, traitor to your country; you alone amongst us all have concluded a truce, and you dare to look us in the face!

DICAEOPOLIS. But you do not know *why* I have treated for peace. Listen!

CHORUS. Listen to you? No, no, you are about to die, we will annihilate you with our stones.

DICAEOPOLIS. But first of all, listen. Stop, my friends.

CHORUS. I will hear nothing; do not address me; I hate you more than I do Cleon, whom one day I shall flay to make sandals for the Knights. Listen to your long speeches, after you have treated with the Laconians! No, I will punish you.

DICAEOPOLIS. Friends, leave the Laconians out of debate and consider only whether I have not done well to conclude my truce.

CHORUS. Done well! when you have treated with a people who know neither gods, nor truth, nor faith.

DICAEOPOLIS. We attribute too much to the Laconians; as for myself, I know that they are not the cause of all our troubles.

CHORUS. Oh, indeed, rascal! You dare to use such language to me and then expect me to spare you!

DICAEOPOLIS. No, no, they are not the cause of all our troubles, and I who address you claim to be able to prove that they have much to complain of in us.

CHORUS. This passes endurance; my heart bounds with fury. Thus you dare to defend our enemies.

DICAEOPOLIS. Were my head on the block I would uphold what I say and rely on the approval of the people.

CHORUS. Comrades, let us hurl our stones and dye this fellow purple.

DICAEOPOLIS. What black fire-brand has inflamed your heart! You will not hear me? You really will not, Acharnians?

CHORUS. No, a thousand times, no.

DICAEOPOLIS. This is a hateful injustice.

CHORUS. May I die, if I listen.

DICAEOPOLIS. Nay, nay! have mercy, have mercy, Acharnians.

CHORUS. You shall die.

DICAEOPOLIS. Well, blood for blood! I will kill your dearest friend. I have here the hostages of Acharnae; I shall disembowel them.

CHORUS. Acharnians, what means this threat? Has he got one of our children in his house? What gives him such audacity?

DICAEOPOLIS. Stone me, if it please you; I shall avenge myself on this. (*Shows a basket.*) Let us see whether you have any love for your coals.

CHORUS. Great gods! this basket is our fellow-citizen. Stop, stop, in heaven's name!

DICAEOPOLIS. I shall dismember it despite your cries; I will listen to nothing.

CHORUS. How! will you kill this coal-basket, my beloved comrade?

DICAEOPOLIS. Just now, you did not listen to me.

CHORUS. Well, speak now, if you will; tell us, tell us you have a weakness for the Lacedaemonians. I consent to anything; never will I forsake this dear little basket.

DICAEOPOLIS. First, throw down your stones.

CHORUS. There! 'tis done. And you, do you put away your sword.

DICAEOPOLIS. Let me see that no stones remain concealed in your cloaks.

CHORUS. They are all on the ground; see how we shake our garments. Come, no haggling, lay down your sword; we threw away everything while crossing from one side of the stage to the other.

DICAEOPOLIS. What cries of anguish you would have uttered had these coals of Parnes been dismembered, and yet it came very near it; had they perished, their death would have been due to the folly of their fellow-citizens. The poor basket was so frightened, look, it has shed a thick black dust over me, the same as a cuttle-fish does. What an irritable temper! You shout and throw stones, you will not hear my arguments—not even when I propose to speak in favour of the Lacedaemonians with my head on the block; and yet I cling to my life.

CHORUS. Well then, bring out a block before your door, scoundrel, and let us hear the good grounds you can give us; I am curious to know them. Now mind, as you proposed yourself, place your head on the block and speak.

DICAEOPOLIS. Here is the block; and, though I am but a very sorry speaker, I wish nevertheless to talk freely of the Lacedaemonians and without the protection of my buckler. Yet I have many reasons for fear. I know our rustics; they are delighted if some braggart comes, and rightly or wrongly loads both them and their city with praise and flattery; they do not see that such toad-eaters are traitors, who sell them for gain. As for the old men, I know their weakness; they only seek to overwhelm the accused with their votes. Nor have I forgotten how Cleon treated me because of my comedy last year; he dragged me before the Senate and there he uttered endless slanders against me; 'twas a tempest of abuse, a deluge of lies. Through what a slough of mud he dragged me! I nigh perished. Permit me, therefore, before I speak, to dress in the manner most likely to draw pity.

CHORUS. What evasions, subterfuges and delays! Hold! here is the sombre helmet of Pluto with its thick bristling plume; Hieronymus lends it to you; then open Sisyphus' bag of wiles; but hurry, hurry, pray, for our discussion does not admit of delay.

DICAEOPOLIS. The time has come for me to manifest my courage, so I will go and seek Euripides. Ho! slave, slave!

SLAVE. Who's there?

DICAEOPOLIS. Is Euripides at home?

SLAVE. He is and he isn't; understand that, if you have wit for't.

DICAEOPOLIS. How? He is and he isn't!

SLAVE. Certainly, old man; busy gathering subtle fancies here and there, his mind is not in the house, but he himself is; perched aloft, he is composing a tragedy.

DICAEOPOLIS. Oh, Euripides, you are indeed happy to have a slave so quick at repartee! Now, fellow, call your master.

SLAVE. Impossible!

DICAEOPOLIS. So much the worse. But I will not go. Come, let us knock at the door. Euripides, my little Euripides, my darling Euripides, listen; never had man greater right to your pity. It is Dicaeopolis of the Chollidan Deme who calls you. Do you hear?

EURIPIDES. I have no time to waste.

DICAEOPOLIS. Very well, have yourself wheeled out here.

EURIPIDES. Impossible.

DICAEOPOLIS. Nevertheless....

EURIPIDES. Well, let them roll me out; as to coming down, I have not the time.

DICAEOPOLIS. Euripides....

EURIPIDES. What words strike my ear?

DICAEOPOLIS. You perch aloft to compose tragedies, when you might just as well do them on the ground. I am not astonished at your introducing cripples on the stage. And why dress in these miserable tragic rags? I do not wonder that your heroes are beggars. But, Euripides, on my knees I beseech you, give me the tatters of some old piece: for I have to treat the Chorus to a long speech, and if I do it ill it is all over with me.

EURIPIDES. What rags do you prefer? Those in which I rigged out Aeneus on the stage, that unhappy, miserable old man?

DICAEOPOLIS. No, I want those of some hero still more unfortunate.

EURIPIDES. Of Phoenix, the blind man?

DICAEOPOLIS. No, not of Phoenix, you have another hero more unfortunate than him.

EURIPIDES. Now, what tatters *does* he want? Do you mean those of the beggar Philoctetes?

DICAEOPOLIS. No, of another far more the mendicant.

EURIPIDES. Is it the filthy dress of the lame fellow, Bellerophon?

DICAEOPOLIS. No, 'tis not Bellerophon; he, whom I mean, was not only lame and a beggar, but boastful and a fine speaker.

EURIPIDES. Ah! I know, it is Telephus, the Mysian.

DICAEOPOLIS. Yes, Telephus. Give me his rags, I beg of you.

EURIPIDES. Slave! give him Telephus' tatters; they are on top of the rags of Thyestes and mixed with those of Ino.

SLAVE. Catch hold! here they are.

DICAEOPOLIS. Oh! Zeus, whose eye pierces everywhere and embraces all, permit me to assume the most wretched dress on earth. Euripides, cap your kindness by giving me the little Mysian hat, that goes so well with these tatters. I must to-day have the look of a beggar; "be what I am, but not appear to be"; the audience will know well who I am, but the Chorus will be fools enough not to, and I shall dupe 'em with my subtle phrases.

EURIPIDES. I will give you the hat; I love the clever tricks of an ingenious brain like yours.

DICAEOPOLIS. Rest happy, and may it befall Telephus as I wish. Ah! I already feel myself filled with quibbles. But I must have a beggar's staff.

EURIPIDES. Here you are, and now get you gone from this porch.

DICAEOPOLIS. Oh, my soul! You see how you are driven from this house, when I still need so many accessories. But let us be pressing, obstinate, importunate. Euripides, give me a little basket with a lamp alight inside.

EURIPIDES. Whatever do you want such a thing as that for?

DICAEOPOLIS. I do not need it, but I want it all the same.

EURIPIDES. You importune me; get you gone!

DICAEOPOLIS. Alas! may the gods grant you a destiny as brilliant as your mother's.

EURIPIDES. Leave me in peace.

DICAEOPOLIS. Oh! just a little broken cup.

EURIPIDES. Take it and go and hang yourself. What a tiresome fellow!

DICAEOPOLIS. Ah! you do not know all the pain you cause me. Dear, good Euripides, nothing beyond a small pipkin stoppered with a sponge.

EURIPIDES. Miserable man! You are robbing me of an entire tragedy. Here, take it and be off.

DICAEOPOLIS. I am going, but, great gods! I need one thing more; unless I have it, I am a dead man. Hearken, my little Euripides, only give me this and I go, never to return. For pity's sake, do give me a few small herbs for my basket.

EURIPIDES. You wish to ruin me then. Here, take what you want; but it is all over with my pieces!

DICAEOPOLIS. I won't ask another thing; I'm going. I am too importunate and forget that I rouse against me the hate of kings.—Ah! wretch that I am! I am lost! I have forgotten one thing, without which all the rest is as nothing. Euripides, my excellent Euripides, my dear little Euripides, may I die if I ask you again for the smallest present; only one, the last, absolutely the last; give me some of the chervil your mother left you in her will.

EURIPIDES. Insolent hound! Slave, lock the door.

DICAEOPOLIS. Oh, my soul! I must go away without the chervil. Art thou sensible of the dangerous battle we are about to engage upon in defending the Lacedaemonians? Courage, my soul, we must plunge into the midst of it. Dost thou hesitate and art thou fully steeped in Euripides? That's right! do not falter, my poor heart, and let us risk our head to say what we hold for truth. Courage and boldly to the front. I wonder I am so brave!

CHORUS. What do you purport doing? what are you going to say? What an impudent fellow! what a brazen heart! To dare to stake his head and uphold an opinion contrary to that of us all! And he does not tremble to face this peril! Come, it is you who desired it, speak!

DICAEOPOLIS. Spectators, be not angered if, although I am a beggar, I dare in a Comedy to speak before the people of Athens of the public weal; Comedy too can sometimes discern what is right. I shall not please, but I shall say what is true. Besides, Cleon shall not be able to accuse me of attacking Athens before strangers; we are by ourselves at the festival of the Lenaea; the period when our allies send us their tribute and their soldiers is not yet. Here is only the pure wheat without chaff; as to the resident strangers settled among us, they and the citizens are one, like the straw and the ear.

I detest the Lacedaemonians with all my heart, and may Posidon, the god of Taenarus, cause an earthquake and overturn their dwellings! My vines also have been cut. But come (there are only friends who hear me), why accuse the Laconians of all our woes? Some men (I do not say the city, note particularly, that I do not say the city), some wretches, lost in vices, bereft of honour, who were not even citizens of good stamp, but strangers, have accused the Megarians of introducing their produce fraudulently, and not a cucumber, a leveret, a sucking-pig, a clove of garlic, a lump of salt was seen without its being said, "Halloa! these come from Megara," and their being instantly confiscated. Thus far the evil was not serious, and we were the only sufferers. But now some young drunkards go to Megara and carry off the courtesan Simaetha; the Megarians, hurt to the quick, run off in turn with two harlots of the house of Aspasia; and so for three gay women Greece is set ablaze. Then Pericles, aflame with ire on his Olympian height, let loose the lightning, caused the thunder to roll, upset Greece and passed an edict, which ran like the song, "That the Megarians be banished both from our land and from our markets and from the sea and from the continent." Meanwhile the Megarians, who were beginning to die of hunger, begged the Lacedaemonians to bring about the abolition of the decree, of which those harlots were the cause; several times we refused their demand; and from that time there was a horrible clatter of arms everywhere. You will say that Sparta was wrong, but what should she have done? Answer that. Suppose that a Lacedaemonian had seized a little Seriphian dog on any pretext and had sold it, would you have endured it quietly? Far from it, you would at once have sent three hundred vessels to sea, and what an uproar there would have been through all the city! there 'tis a band of noisy soldiery, here a brawl about the election of a Trierarch; elsewhere pay is being distributed, the Pallas figure-heads are being regilded, crowds are surging under the market porticos, encumbered with wheat that is being measured, wine-skins, oar-leathers, garlic, olives, onions in nets; everywhere are chaplets, sprats, flute-girls, black eyes; in the arsenal bolts are being noisily driven home, sweeps are being made and fitted with leathers; we hear nothing but the sound of whistles, of flutes and fifes to encourage the work-folk. That is what you assuredly would have done, and would not Telephus have done the same? So I come to my general conclusion; we have no common sense.

FIRST SEMI-CHORUS. Oh! wretch! oh! infamous man! You are naught but a beggar and yet you dare to talk to us like this! you insult their worships the informers!

SECOND SEMI-CHORUS. By Posidon! he speaks the truth; he has not lied in a single detail.

FIRST SEMI-CHORUS. But though it be true, need he say it? But you'll have no great cause to be proud of your insolence!

SECOND SEMI-CHORUS. Where are you running to? Don't you move; if you strike this man I shall be at you.

FIRST SEMI-CHORUS. Lamachus, whose glance flashes lightning, whose plume petrifies thy foes, help! Oh! Lamachus, my friend, the hero of my tribe and all of you, both officers and soldiers, defenders of our walls, come to my aid; else is it all over with me!

LAMACHUS. Whence comes this cry of battle? where must I bring my aid? where must I sow dread? who wants me to uncase my dreadful Gorgon's head?

DICAEOPOLIS. Oh, Lamachus, great hero! Your plumes and your cohorts terrify me.

CHORUS. This man, Lamachus, incessantly abuses Athens.

LAMACHUS. You are but a mendicant and you dare to use language of this sort?

DICAEOPOLIS. Oh, brave Lamachus, forgive a beggar who speaks at hazard.

LAMACHUS. But what have you said? Let us hear.

DICAEOPOLIS. I know nothing about it; the sight of weapons makes me dizzy. Oh! I adjure you, take that fearful Gorgon somewhat farther away.

LAMACHUS. There.

DICAEOPOLIS. Now place it face downwards on the ground.

LAMACHUS. It is done.

DICAEOPOLIS. Give me a plume out of your helmet.

LAMACHUS. Here is a feather.

DICAEOPOLIS. And hold my head while I vomit; the plumes have turned my stomach.

LAMACHUS. Hah! what are you proposing to do? do you want to make yourself vomit with this feather?

DICAEOPOLIS. Is it a feather? what bird's? a braggart's?

LAMACHUS. Ah! ah! I will rip you open.

DICAEOPOLIS. No, no, Lamachus! Violence is out of place here! But as you are so strong, why did you not circumcise me? You have all you want for the operation there.

LAMACHUS. A beggar dares thus address a general!

DICAEOPOLIS. How? Am I a beggar?

LAMACHUS. What are you then?

DICAEOPOLIS. Who am I? A good citizen, not ambitious; a soldier, who has fought well since the outbreak of the war, whereas you are but a vile mercenary.

LAMACHUS. They elected me....

DICAEOPOLIS. Yes, three cuckoos did! If I have concluded peace, 'twas disgust that drove me; for I see men with hoary heads in the ranks and young fellows of your age shirking service. Some are in Thrace getting an allowance of three drachmae, such fellows as Tisameophoenippus and Panurgipparchides. The others are with Chares or in Chaonia, men like Geretotheodorus and Diomialazon; there are some of the same kidney, too, at Camarina and at Gela, the laughing-stock of all and sundry.

LAMACHUS. They were elected.

DICAEOPOLIS. And why do you always receive your pay, when none of these others ever get any? Speak, Marilades, you have grey hair; well then, have you ever been entrusted with a mission? See! he shakes his head. Yet he is an active as well as a prudent man. And you, Dracyllus, Euphorides or Prinides, have you knowledge of Ecbatana or Chaonia? You say no, do you not? Such offices are good for the son of Caesyra and Lamachus, who, but yesterday ruined with debt, never pay their shot, and whom all their friends avoid as foot passengers dodge the folks who empty their slops out of window.

LAMACHUS. Oh! in freedom's name! are such exaggerations to be borne?

DICAEOPOLIS. Lamachus is well content; no doubt he is well paid, you know.

LAMACHUS. But I propose always to war with the Peloponnesians, both at sea, on land and everywhere to make them tremble, and trounce them soundly.

DICAEOPOLIS. For my own part, I make proclamation to all Peloponnesians, Megarians and Boeotians, that to them my markets are open; but I debar Lamachus from entering them.

CHORUS. Convinced by this man's speech, the folk have changed their view and approve him for having concluded peace. But let us prepare for the recital of the parabasis.

Never since our poet presented Comedies, has he praised himself upon the stage; but, having been slandered by his enemies amongst the volatile Athenians, accused of scoffing at his country and of insulting the people, to-day he wishes to reply and regain for himself the inconstant Athenians. He maintains that he has done much that is good for you; if you no longer allow yourselves to be too much hoodwinked by strangers or seduced by flattery, if in politics you are no longer the ninnies you once were, it is thanks to him. Formerly, when delegates from other cities wanted to deceive you, they had but to style you, "the people crowned with violets," and, at the word "violets" you at once sat erect on the tips of your bums. Or, if to tickle your vanity, someone spoke of "rich and sleek Athens," in return for that 'sleekness' he would get all, because he spoke of you as he would have of anchovies in oil. In cautioning you against such wiles, the poet has done you great service as well as in forcing you to understand what is really the democratic principle. Thus, the strangers, who came to pay their tributes, wanted to see this great poet, who had dared to speak the truth to Athens. And so far has the fame of his boldness reached that one day the Great King, when questioning the Lacedaemonian delegates, first asked them which of the two rival cities was the superior at sea, and then immediately demanded at which it was that the comic poet directed his biting satire. "Happy that city," he added, "if it listens to his counsel; it will grow in power, and its victory is assured." This is why the Lacedaemonians offer you peace, if you will cede them Aegina; not that they care for the isle, but they wish to rob you of your poet. As for you, never lose him, who will always fight for the cause of justice in his Comedies; he promises you that his precepts will lead you to happiness, though he uses neither flattery, nor bribery, nor intrigue, nor deceit; instead of loading you with praise, he will point you to the better way. I scoff at Cleon's tricks and plotting; honesty and justice shall fight my cause; never will you find me a political poltroon, a prostitute to the highest bidder.

I invoke thee, Acharnian Muse, fierce and fell as the devouring fire; sudden as the spark that bursts from the crackling oaken coal when roused by the quickening fan to fry little fishes, while others knead the dough or whip the sharp Thasian pickle with rapid hand, so break forth, my Muse, and inspire thy tribesmen with rough, vigorous, stirring strains.

We others, now old men and heavy with years, we reproach the city; so many are the victories we have gained for the Athenian fleets that we well deserve to be cared for in our declining life; yet far from this, we are ill-used, harassed with law-suits, delivered over to the scorn of stripling orators. Our minds and bodies being ravaged with age, Posidon should protect us, yet we have no other support than a staff. When standing before the judge, we can scarcely stammer forth the fewest words, and of justice we see but its barest shadow, whereas the accuser, desirous of conciliating the younger men, overwhelms us with his ready rhetoric; he drags us before the judge, presses us with questions, lays traps for us; the onslaught troubles, upsets and rends poor old Tithonus, who, crushed with age, stands tongue-tied; sentenced to a fine, he weeps, he sobs and says to his friend, "This fine robs me of the last trifle that was to have bought my coffin."

Is this not a scandal? What! the clepsydra is to kill the white-haired veteran, who, in fierce fighting, has so oft covered himself with glorious sweat, whose valour at Marathon saved the country! 'Twas we who pursued on the field of Marathon, whereas now 'tis wretches who pursue us to the death and crush us! What would Marpsias reply to this? What an injustice, that a man, bent with age like Thucydides, should be brow-beaten by this braggart advocate, Cephisodemus, who is as savage as the Scythian desert he was born in! Is it not to convict him from the outset? I wept tears of pity when I saw an Archer maltreat this old man, who, by Ceres, when he was young and the true Thucydides, would not have permitted an insult from Ceres herself! At that date he would have floored ten miserable orators, he would have terrified three thousand Archers with his shouts; he would have pierced the whole line of the enemy with his shafts. Ah! but if you will not leave the aged in peace, decree that the advocates be matched; thus the old man will only be confronted with a toothless greybeard, the young will fight with the braggart, the ignoble with the son of Clinias; make a law that in future, the old man can only be summoned and convicted at the courts by the aged and the young man by the youth.

DICAEOPOLIS. These are the confines of my market-place. All Peloponnesians, Megarians, Boeotians, have the right to come and trade here, provided they sell their wares to me and not to Lamachus. As market-inspectors I appoint these three whips of Leprean leather, chosen by lot. Warned away are all informers and all men of Phasis. They are bringing me the pillar on which the treaty is inscribed and I shall erect it in the centre of the market, well in sight of all.

A MEGARIAN. Hail! market of Athens, beloved of Megarians. Let Zeus, the patron of friendship, witness, I regretted you as a mother mourns her son. Come, poor little daughters of an unfortunate father, try to find something to eat; listen to me with the full heed of an empty belly. Which would you prefer? To be sold or to cry with hunger.

DAUGHTERS. To be sold, to be sold!

MEGARIAN. That is my opinion too. But who would make so sorry a deal as to buy you? Ah! I recall me a Megarian trick; I am going to disguise you as little porkers, that I am offering for sale. Fit your hands with these hoofs and take care to appear the issue of a sow of good breed, for, if I am forced to take you back to the house, by Hermes! you will suffer cruelly of hunger! Then fix on these snouts and cram yourselves into this sack. Forget not to grunt and to say wee-wee like the little pigs that are sacrificed in the Mysteries. I must summon Dicaeopolis. Where is he? Dicaeopolis, will you buy some nice little porkers?

DICAEOPOLIS. Who are you? a Megarian?

MEGARIAN. I have come to your market.

DICAEOPOLIS. Well, how are things at Megara?

MEGARIAN. We are crying with hunger at our firesides.

DICAEOPOLIS. The fireside is jolly enough with a piper. But what else is doing at Megara, eh?

MEGARIAN. What else? When I left for the market, the authorities were taking steps to let us die in the quickest manner.

DICAEOPOLIS. That is the best way to get you out of all your troubles.

MEGARIAN. True.

DICAEOPOLIS. What other news of Megara? What is wheat selling at?

MEGARIAN. With us it is valued as highly as the very gods in heaven!

DICAEOPOLIS. Is it salt that you are bringing?

MEGARIAN. Are you not holding back the salt?

DICAEOPOLIS. 'Tis garlic then?

MEGARIAN. What! garlic! do you not at every raid grub up the ground with your pikes to pull out every single head?

DICAEOPOLIS. What *do* you bring then?

MEGARIAN. Little sows, like those they immolate at the Mysteries.

DICAEOPOLIS. Ah! very well, show me them.

MEGARIAN. They are very fine; feel their weight. See! how fat and fine.

DICAEOPOLIS. But what is this?

MEGARIAN. A *sow*, for a certainty.

DICAEOPOLIS. You say a sow! of what country, then?

MEGARIAN. From Megara. What! is that not a sow then?

DICAEOPOLIS. No, I don't believe it is.

MEGARIAN. This is too much! what an incredulous man! He says 'tis not a sow; but we will stake, an you will, a measure of salt ground up with thyme, that in good Greek this is called a sow and nothing else.

DICAEOPOLIS. But a sow of the human kind.

MEGARIAN. Without question, by Diocles! of my own breed! Well! What think you? will you hear them squeal?

DICAEOPOLIS. Well, yes, i' faith, I will.

MEGARIAN. Cry quickly, wee sowlet; squeak up, hussy, or by Hermes! I take you back to the house.

GIRL. Wee-wee, wee-wee!

MEGARIAN. Is that a little sow, or not?

DICAEOPOLIS. Yes, it seems so; but let it grow up, and it will be a fine fat cunt.

MEGARIAN. In five years it will be just like its mother.

DICAEOPOLIS. But it cannot be sacrificed.

MEGARIAN. And why not?

DICAEOPOLIS. It has no tail.

MEGARIAN. Because it is quite young, but in good time it will have a big one, thick and red.

DICAEOPOLIS. The two are as like as two peas.

MEGARIAN. They are born of the same father and mother; let them be fattened, let them grow their bristles, and they will be the finest sows you can offer to Aphrodité.

DICAEOPOLIS. But sows are not immolated to Aphrodité.

MEGARIAN. Not sows to Aphrodité! Why, 'tis the only goddess to whom they are offered! the flesh of my sows will be excellent on the spit.

DICAEOPOLIS. Can they eat alone? They no longer need their mother!

MEGARIAN. Certainly not, nor their father.

DICAEOPOLIS. What do they like most?

MEGARIAN. Whatever is given them; but ask for yourself.

DICAEOPOLIS. Speak! little sow.

DAUGHTER. Wee-wee, wee-wee!

DICAEOPOLIS. Can you eat chick-pease?

DAUGHTER. Wee-wee, wee-wee, wee-wee!

DICAEOPOLIS. And Attic figs?

DAUGHTER. Wee-wee, wee-wee!

DICAEOPOLIS. What sharp squeaks at the name of figs. Come, let some figs be brought for these little pigs. Will they eat them? Goodness! how they munch them, what a grinding of teeth, mighty Heracles! I believe those pigs hail from the land of the Voracians. But surely, 'tis impossible they have bolted all the figs!

MEGARIAN. Yes, certainly, bar this one that I took from them.

DICAEOPOLIS. Ah! what funny creatures! For what sum will you sell them?

MEGARIAN. I will give you one for a bunch of garlic, and the other, if you like, for a quart measure of salt.

DICAEOPOLIS. I buy them of you. Wait for me here.

MEGARIAN. The deal is done. Hermes, god of good traders, grant I may sell both my wife and my mother in the same way!

AN INFORMER. Hi! fellow, what countryman are you?

MEGARIAN. I am a pig-merchant from Megara.

INFORMER. I shall denounce both your pigs and yourself as public enemies.

MEGARIAN. Ah! here our troubles begin afresh!

INFORMER. Let go that sack. I will punish your Megarian lingo.

MEGARIAN. Dicaeopolis, Dicaeopolis, they want to denounce me.

DICAEOPOLIS. Who dares do this thing? Inspectors, drive out the Informers. Ah! you offer to enlighten us without a lamp!

INFORMER. What! I may not denounce our enemies?

DICAEOPOLIS. Have a care for yourself, if you don't go off pretty quick to denounce elsewhere.

MEGARIAN. What a plague to Athens!

DICAEOPOLIS. Be reassured, Megarian. Here is the value of your two swine, the garlic and the salt. Farewell and much happiness!

MEGARIAN. Ah! we never have that amongst us.

DICAEOPOLIS. Well! may the inopportune wish apply to myself.

MEGARIAN. Farewell, dear little sows, and seek, far from your father, to munch your bread with salt, if they give you any.

CHORUS. Here is a man truly happy. See how everything succeeds to his wish. Peacefully seated in his market, he will earn his living; woe to Ctesias, and all other informers, who dare to enter there! You will not be cheated as to the value of wares, you will not again see Prepis wiping his foul rump, nor will Cleonymus jostle you; you will take your walks, clothed in a fine tunic, without meeting Hyperbolus and his unceasing quibblings, without being accosted on the public place by any importunate fellow, neither by Cratinus, shaven in the fashion of the debauchees, nor by this musician, who plagues us with his silly improvisations, Artemo, with his arm-pits stinking as foul as a goat, like his father before him. You will not be the butt of the villainous Pauson's jeers, nor of Lysistratus, the disgrace of the Cholargian deme, who is the incarnation of all the vices, and endures cold and hunger more than thirty days in the month.

A BOEOTIAN. By Heracles! my shoulder is quite black and blue. Ismenias, put the penny-royal down there very gently, and all of you, musicians from Thebes, pipe with your bone flutes into a dog's rump.

DICAEOPOLIS. Enough, enough, get you gone. Rascally hornets, away with you! Whence has sprung this accursed swarm of Cheris fellows which comes assailing my door?

BOEOTIAN. Ah! by Iolas! Drive them off, my dear host, you will please me immensely; all the way from Thebes, they were there piping behind me and have completely stripped my penny-royal of its blossom. But will you buy anything of me, some chickens or some locusts?

DICAEOPOLIS. Ah! good day, Boeotian, eater of good round loaves. What do you bring?

BOEOTIAN. All that is good in Boeotia, marjoram, penny-royal, rush-mats, lamp-wicks, ducks, jays, woodcocks, waterfowl, wrens, divers.

DICAEOPOLIS. 'Tis a very hail of birds that beats down on my market.

BOEOTIAN. I also bring geese, hares, foxes, moles, hedgehogs, cats, lyres, martins, otters and eels from the Copaic lake.

DICAEOPOLIS. Ah! my friend, you, who bring me the most delicious of fish, let me salute your eels.

BOEOTIAN. Come, thou, the eldest of my fifty Copaic virgins, come and complete the joy of our host.

DICAEOPOLIS. Oh! my well-beloved, thou object of my long regrets, thou art here at last then, thou, after whom the comic poets sigh, thou, who art dear to Morychus. Slaves, hither with the stove and the bellows. Look at this charming eel, that returns to us after six long years of absence. Salute it, my children; as for myself, I will supply coal to do honour to the stranger. Take it into my house; death itself could not separate me from her, if cooked with beet leaves.

BOEOTIAN. And what will you give me in return?

DICAEOPOLIS. It will pay for your market dues. And as to the rest, what do you wish to sell me?

BOEOTIAN. Why, everything.

DICAEOPOLIS. On what terms? For ready-money or in wares from these parts?

BOEOTIAN. I would take some Athenian produce, that we have not got in Boeotia.

DICAEOPOLIS. Phaleric anchovies, pottery?

BOEOTIAN. Anchovies, pottery? But these we have. I want produce that is wanting with us and that is plentiful here.

DICAEOPOLIS. Ah! I have the very thing; take away an Informer, packed up carefully as crockery-ware.

BOEOTIAN. By the twin gods! I should earn big money, if I took one; I would exhibit him as an ape full of spite.

DICAEOPOLIS. Hah! here we have Nicarchus, who comes to denounce you.

BOEOTIAN. How small he is!

DICAEOPOLIS. But in his case the whole is one mass of ill-nature.

NICARCHUS. Whose are these goods?

DICAEOPOLIS. Mine; they come from Boeotia, I call Zeus to witness.

NICARCHUS. I denounce them as coming from an enemy's country.

BOEOTIAN. What! you declare war against birds?

NICARCHUS. And I am going to denounce you too.

BOEOTIAN. What harm have I done you?

NICARCHUS. I will say it for the benefit of those that listen; you introduce lamp-wicks from an enemy's country.

DICAEOPOLIS. Then you go as far as denouncing a wick.

NICARCHUS. It needs but one to set an arsenal afire.

DICAEOPOLIS. A wick set an arsenal ablaze! But how, great gods?

NICARCHUS. Should a Boeotian attach it to an insect's wing, and, taking advantage of a violent north wind, throw it by means of a tube into the arsenal and the fire once get hold of the vessels, everything would soon be devoured by the flames.

DICAEOPOLIS. Ah! wretch! an insect and a wick would devour everything. (*He strikes him.*)

NICARCHUS (*to the Chorus*). You will bear witness, that he mishandles me.

DICAEOPOLIS. Shut his mouth. Give him some hay; I am going to pack him up as a vase, that he may not get broken on the road.

CHORUS. Pack up your goods carefully, friend; that the stranger may not break it when taking it away.

DICAEOPOLIS. I shall take great care with it, for one would say he is cracked already; he rings with a false note, which the gods abhor.

CHORUS. But what will be done with him?

DICAEOPOLIS. This is a vase good for all purposes; it will be used as a vessel for holding all foul things, a mortar for pounding together law-suits, a lamp for spying upon accounts, and as a cup for the mixing up and poisoning of everything.

CHORUS. None could ever trust a vessel for domestic use that has such a ring about it.

DICAEOPOLIS. Oh! it is strong, my friend, and will never get broken, if care is taken to hang it head downwards.

CHORUS. There! it is well packed now!

BOEOTIAN. Marry, I will proceed to carry off my bundle.

CHORUS. Farewell, worthiest of strangers, take this Informer, good for anything, and fling him where you like.

DICAEOPOLIS. Bah! this rogue has given me enough trouble to pack! Here! Boeotian, pick up your pottery.

BOEOTIAN. Stoop, Ismenias, that I may put it on your shoulder, and be very careful with it.

DICAEOPOLIS. You carry nothing worth having; however, take it, for you will profit by your bargain; the Informers will bring you luck.

A SERVANT OF LAMACHUS. Dicaeopolis!

DICAEOPOLIS. What do want crying this gait?

SERVANT. Lamachus wants to keep the Feast of Cups, and I come by his order to bid you one drachma for some thrushes and three more for a Copaic eel.

DICAEOPOLIS. And who is this Lamachus, who demands an eel?

SERVANT. 'Tis the terrible, indefatigable Lamachus, he, who is always brandishing his fearful Gorgon's head and the three plumes which o'ershadow his helmet.

DICAEOPOLIS. No, no, he will get nothing, even though he gave me his buckler. Let him eat salt fish, while he shakes his plumes, and, if he comes here making any din, I shall call the inspectors. As for myself, I shall take away all these goods; I go home on thrushes' wings and blackbirds' pinions.

CHORUS. You see, citizens, you see the good fortune which this man owes to his prudence, to his profound wisdom. You see how, since he has concluded peace, he buys what is useful in the household and good to eat hot. All good things flow towards him unsought. Never will I welcome the god of war in my house; never shall he chant the 'Harmodius' at my table; he is a sot, who comes feasting with those who are overflowing with good things and brings all sorts of mischief at his heels. He overthrows, ruins, rips open; 'tis vain to make him a thousand offers, "be seated, pray, drink this cup, proffered in all friendship," he burns our vine-stocks and brutally pours out the wine from our vineyards on the ground. This man, on the other hand, covers his table with a thousand dishes; proud of his good fortunes, he has had these feathers cast before his door to show us how he lives.

DICAEOPOLIS. Oh! Peace! companion of fair Aphrodité and of the sweet Graces, how charming are your features and yet I never knew it! Would that Eros might join me to thee, Eros, crowned with roses as Zeuxis shows him to us! Perhaps I seem somewhat old to you, but I am yet able to make you a threefold offering; despite my age, I could plant a long row of vines for you; then beside these some tender cuttings from the fig; finally a young vine-stock, loaded with fruit and all round the field olive trees, which would furnish us with oil, wherewith to anoint us both at the New Moons.

HERALD. List, ye people! As was the custom of your forebears, empty a full pitcher of wine at the call of the trumpet; he, who first sees the bottom, shall get a wine-skin as round and plump as Ctesiphon's belly.

DICAEOPOLIS. Women, children, have you not heard? Faith! do you not heed the herald? Quick! let the hares boil and roast merrily; keep them a-turning; withdraw them from the flame; prepare the chaplets; reach me the skewers that I may spit the thrushes.

CHORUS. I envy you your wisdom and even more your good cheer.

DICAEOPOLIS. What then will you say when you see the thrushes roasting?

CHORUS. Ah! true indeed!

DICAEOPOLIS. Slave! stir up the fire.

CHORUS. See, how he knows his business, what a perfect cook! How well he understands the way to prepare a good dinner!

A HUSBANDMAN. Ah! woe is me!

DICAEOPOLIS. Heracles! What have we here?

HUSBANDMAN. A most miserable man.

DICAEOPOLIS. Keep your misery for yourself.

HUSBANDMAN. Ah! friend! since you alone are enjoying peace, grant me a part of your truce, were it but five years.

DICAEOPOLIS. What has happened to you?

HUSBANDMAN. I am ruined; I have lost a pair of steers.

DICAEOPOLIS. How?

HUSBANDMAN. The Boeotians seized them at Phylé.

DICAEOPOLIS. Ah! poor wretch! and yet you have not left off white?

HUSBANDMAN. Their dung made my wealth.

DICAEOPOLIS. What can I do in the matter?

HUSBANDMAN. Crying for my beasts has lost me my eyesight. Ah! if you care for poor Dercetes of Phylé, anoint mine eyes quickly with your balm of peace.

DICAEOPOLIS. But, my poor fellow, I do not practise medicine.

HUSBANDMAN. Come, I adjure you; perchance I shall recover my steers.

DICAEOPOLIS. 'Tis impossible; away, go and whine to the disciples of Pittalus.

HUSBANDMAN. Grant me but one drop of peace; pour it into this reedlet.

DICAEOPOLIS. No, not a particle; go a-weeping elsewhere.

HUSBANDMAN. Oh! oh! oh! my poor beasts!

CHORUS. This man has discovered the sweetest enjoyment in peace; he will share it with none.

DICAEOPOLIS. Pour honey over this tripe; set it before the fire to dry.

CHORUS. What lofty tones he uses! Did you hear him?

DICAEOPOLIS. Get the eels on the gridiron!

CHORUS. You are killing me with hunger; your smoke is choking your neighbours, and you split our ears with your bawling.

DICAEOPOLIS. Have this fried and let it be nicely browned.

A BRIDESMAID. Dicaeopolis! Dicaeopolis!

DICAEOPOLIS. Who are you?

BRIDESMAID. A young bridegroom sends you these viands from the marriage feast.

DICAEOPOLIS. Whoever he be, I thank him.

BRIDESMAID. And in return, he prays you to pour a glass of peace into this vase, that he may not have to go to the front and may stay at home to do his duty to his young wife.

DICAEOPOLIS. Take back, take back your viands; for a thousand drachmae I would not give a drop of peace; but who are you, pray?

BRIDESMAID. I am the bridesmaid; she wants to say something to you from the bride privately.

DICAEOPOLIS. Come, what do you wish to say? (*The bridesmaid whispers in his ear.*) Ah! what a ridiculous demand! The bride burns with longing to keep by her her husband's weapon. Come! bring hither my truce; to her alone will I give some of it, for she is a woman, and, as such, should not suffer under the war. Here, friend, reach hither your vial. And as to the manner of applying this balm, tell the bride, when a levy of soldiers is made to rub some in bed on her husband, where most needed. There, slave, take away my truce! Now, quick hither with the wine-flagon, that I may fill up the drinking bowls!

CHORUS. I see a man, striding along apace, with knitted brows; he seems to us the bearer of terrible tidings.

HERALD. Oh! toils and battles! 'tis Lamachus!

LAMACHUS. What noise resounds around my dwelling, where shines the glint of arms.

HERALD. The Generals order you forthwith to take your battalions and your plumes, and, despite the snow, to go and guard our borders. They have learnt that a band of Boeotians intend taking advantage of the feast of Cups to invade our country.

LAMACHUS. Ah! the Generals! they are numerous, but not good for much! It's cruel, not to be able to enjoy the feast!

DICAEOPOLIS. Oh! warlike host of Lamachus!

LAMACHUS. Wretch! do you dare to jeer me?

DICAEOPOLIS. Do you want to fight this four-winged Geryon?

LAMACHUS. Oh! oh! what fearful tidings!

DICAEOPOLIS. Ah! ah! I see another herald running up; what news does he bring me?

HERALD. Dicaeopolis!

DICAEOPOLIS. What is the matter?

HERALD. Come quickly to the feast and bring your basket and your cup; 'tis the priest of Bacchus who invites you. But hasten, the guests have been waiting for you a long while. All is ready—couches, tables, cushions, chaplets, perfumes, dainties and courtesans to boot; biscuits, cakes, sesamé-bread, tarts, and—lovely dancing women, the sweetest charm of the festivity. But come with all haste.

LAMACHUS. Oh! hostile gods!

DICAEOPOLIS. This is not astounding; you have chosen this huge, great ugly Gorgon's head for your patron. You, shut the door, and let someone get ready the meal.

LAMACHUS. Slave! slave! my knapsack!

DICAEOPOLIS. Slave! slave! a basket!

LAMACHUS. Take salt and thyme, slave, and don't forget the onions.

DICAEOPOLIS. Get some fish for me; I cannot bear onions.

LAMACHUS. Slave, wrap me up a little stale salt meat in a fig-leaf.

DICAEOPOLIS. And for me some good greasy tripe in a fig-leaf; I will have it cooked here.

LAMACHUS. Bring me the plumes for my helmet.

DICAEOPOLIS. Bring me wild pigeons and thrushes.

LAMACHUS. How white and beautiful are these ostrich feathers!

DICAEOPOLIS. How fat and well browned is the flesh of this wood-pigeon!

LAMACHUS. Bring me the case for my triple plume.

DICAEOPOLIS. Pass me over that dish of hare.

LAMACHUS. *Oh!* the moths have eaten the hair of my crest!

DICAEOPOLIS. I shall always eat hare before dinner.

LAMACHUS. Hi! friend! try not to scoff at my armour.

DICAEOPOLIS. Hi! friend! will you kindly not stare at my thrushes.

LAMACHUS. Hi! friend! will you kindly not address me.

DICAEOPOLIS. I do not address you; I am scolding my slave. Shall we wager and submit the matter to Lamachus, which of the two is the best to eat, a locust or a thrush?

LAMACHUS. Insolent hound!

DICAEOPOLIS. He much prefers the locusts.

LAMACHUS. Slave, unhook my spear and bring it to me.

DICAEOPOLIS. Slave, slave, take the sausage from the fire and bring it to me.

LAMACHUS. Come, let me draw my spear from its sheath. Hold it, slave, hold it tight.

DICAEOPOLIS. And you, slave, grip, grip well hold of the skewer.

LAMACHUS. Slave, the bracings for my shield.

DICAEOPOLIS. Pull the loaves out of the oven and bring me these bracings of my stomach.

LAMACHUS. My round buckler with the Gorgon's head.

DICAEOPOLIS. My round cheese-cake.

LAMACHUS. What clumsy wit!

DICAEOPOLIS. What delicious cheese-cake!

LAMACHUS. Pour oil on the buckler. Hah! hah! I can see an old man who will be accused of cowardice.

DICAEOPOLIS. Pour honey on the cake. Hah! hah! I can see an old man who makes Lamachus of the Gorgon's head weep with rage.

LAMACHUS. Slave, full war armour.

DICAEOPOLIS. Slave, my beaker; that is my armour.

LAMACHUS. With this I hold my ground with any foe.

DICAEOPOLIS. And I with this with any tosspot.

LAMACHUS. Fasten the strappings to the buckler; personally I shall carry the knapsack.

DICAEOPOLIS. Pack the dinner well into the basket; personally I shall carry the cloak.

LAMACHUS. Slave, take up the buckler and let's be off. It is snowing! Ah! 'tis a question of facing the winter.

DICAEOPOLIS. Take up the basket, 'tis a question of getting to the feast.

CHORUS. We wish you both joy on your journeys, which differ so much. One goes to mount guard and freeze, while the other will drink, crowned with flowers, and then sleep with a young beauty, who will rub his tool for him.

I say it freely; may Zeus confound Antimachus, the poet-historian, the son of Psacas! When Choregus at the Lenaea, alas! alas! he dismissed me dinnerless. May I see him devouring with his eyes a cuttle-fish, just served, well cooked, hot and properly salted; and the moment that he stretches his hand to help himself, may a dog seize it and run off with it. Such is my first wish. I also hope for him a misfortune at night. That returning all-fevered from horse practice, he may meet an Orestes, mad with drink, who breaks open his head; that wishing to seize a stone, he, in the dark, may pick up a fresh stool, hurl his missile, miss aim and hit Cratinus.

SLAVE OF LAMACHUS. Slaves of Lamachus! Water, water in a little pot! Make it warm, get ready cloths, cerate, greasy wool and bandages for his ankle. In leaping a ditch, the master has hurt himself against a stake; he has dislocated and twisted his ankle, broken his head by falling on a stone, while his Gorgon shot far away from his buckler. His mighty braggadocio plume rolled on the ground; at this sight he uttered these doleful words, "Radiant star, I gaze on thee for the last time; my eyes close to all light, I die." Having said this, he falls into the water, gets out again, meets some runaways and pursues the robbers with his spear at their backsides. But here he comes, himself. Get the door open.

LAMACHUS. Oh! heavens! oh! heavens! What cruel pain! I faint, I tremble! Alas! I die! the foe's lance has struck me! But what would hurt me most would be for Dicaeopolis to see me wounded thus and laugh at my ill-fortune.

DICAEOPOLIS (*enters with two courtesans*). Oh! my gods! what bosoms! Hard as a quince! Come, my treasures, give me voluptuous kisses! Glue your lips to mine. Haha! I was the first to empty my cup.

LAMACHUS. Oh! cruel fate! how I suffer! accursed wounds!

DICAEOPOLIS. Hah! hah! hail! Knight Lamachus! (*Embraces Lamachus.*)

LAMACHUS. By the hostile gods! (*Bites Dicaeopolis.*)

DICAEOPOLIS. Ah! great gods!

LAMACHUS. Why do you embrace me?

DICAEOPOLIS. And why do you bite me?

LAMACHUS. 'Twas a cruel score I was paying back!

DICAEOPOLIS. Scores are not evened at the feast of Cups!

LAMACHUS. Oh! Paean, Paean!

DICAEOPOLIS. But to-day is not the feast of Paean.

LAMACHUS. Oh! support my leg, do; ah! hold it tenderly, my friends!

DICAEOPOLIS. And you, my darlings, take hold of my tool both of you!

LAMACHUS. This blow with the stone makes me dizzy; my sight grows dim.

DICAEOPOLIS. For myself, I want to get to bed; I am bursting with lustfulness, I want to be fucking in the dark.

LAMACHUS. Carry me to the surgeon Pittalus.

DICAEOPOLIS. Take me to the judges. Where is the king of the feast? The wine-skin is mine!

LAMACHUS. That spear has pierced my bones; what torture I endure!

DICAEOPOLIS. You see this empty cup! I triumph! I triumph!

CHORUS. Old man, I come at your bidding! You triumph! you triumph!

DICAEOPOLIS. Again I have brimmed my cup with unmixed wine and drained it at a draught!

CHORUS. You triumph then, brave champion; thine is the wine-skin!

DICAEOPOLIS. Follow me, singing "Triumph! Triumph!"

CHORUS. Aye! we will sing of thee, thee and thy sacred wine-skin, and we all, as we follow thee, will repeat in thine honour, "Triumph, Triumph!"

FINIS OF "THE ACHARNIANS"

Peace

Introduction

The 'Peace' was brought out four years after 'The Acharnians' (422 B.C.), when the War had already lasted ten years. The leading motive is the same as in the former play—the intense desire of the less excitable and more moderate-minded citizens for relief from the miseries of war.

Trygaeus, a rustic patriot, finding no help in men, resolves to ascend to heaven to expostulate personally with Zeus for allowing this wretched state of things to continue. With this object he has fed and trained a gigantic dung-beetle, which he mounts, and is carried, like Bellerophon on Pegasus, on an aerial journey. Eventually he reaches Olympus, only to find that the gods have gone elsewhere, and that the heavenly abode is occupied solely by the demon of War, who is busy pounding up the Greek States in a huge mortar. However, his benevolent purpose is not in vain; for learning from Hermes that the goddess Peace has been cast into a pit, where she is kept a fast prisoner, he calls upon the different peoples of Hellas to make a united effort and rescue her, and with their help drags her out and brings her back in triumph to earth. The play concludes with the restoration of the goddess to her ancient honours, the festivities of the rustic population and the nuptials of Trygaeus with Opora (Harvest), handmaiden of Peace, represented as a pretty courtesan.

Such references as there are to Cleon in this play are noteworthy. The great Demagogue was now dead, having fallen in the same action as the rival Spartan general, the renowned Brasidas, before Amphipolis, and whatever Aristophanes says here of his old enemy is conceived in the spirit of 'de mortuis nil nisi bonum.' In one scene Hermes is descanting on the evils which had nearly ruined Athens and declares that 'The Tanner' was the cause of them all. But Trygaeus interrupts him with the words:

"Hold—say not so, good master Hermes;   Let the man rest in peace where now he lies.   He is no longer of our world, but yours."

Here surely we have a trait of magnanimity on the author's part as admirable in its way as the wit and boldness of his former attacks had been in theirs.

Peace

DRAMATIS PERSONAE

TRYGAEUS.
TWO SERVANTS of TRYGAEUS.
MAIDENS, Daughters of TRYGAEUS.
HERMES.
WAR.
TUMULT.
HIEROCLES, a Soothsayer.
A SICKLE-MAKER.
A CREST-MAKER.
A TRUMPET-MAKER.
A HELMET-MAKER.
A SPEAR-MAKER.
SON OF LAMACHUS.
SON OF CLEONYMUS.
CHORUS OF HUSBANDMEN.

SCENE: A farmyard, two slaves busy beside a dungheap; afterwards, in Olympus.

FIRST SERVANT. Quick, quick, bring the dung-beetle his cake.

SECOND SERVANT. Coming, coming.

FIRST SERVANT. Give it to him, and may it kill him!

SECOND SERVANT. May he never eat a better.

FIRST SERVANT. Now give him this other one kneaded up with ass's dung.

SECOND SERVANT. There! I've done that too.

FIRST SERVANT. And where's what you gave him just now; surely he can't have devoured it yet!

SECOND SERVANT. Indeed he has; he snatched it, rolled it between his feet and boiled it.

FIRST SERVANT. Come, hurry up, knead up a lot and knead them stiffly.

SECOND SERVANT. Oh, scavengers, help me in the name of the gods, if you do not wish to see me fall down choked.

FIRST SERVANT. Come, come, another made of the stool of a young scapegrace catamite. 'Twill be to the beetle's taste; he likes it well ground.

SECOND SERVANT. There! I am free at least from suspicion; none will accuse me of tasting what I mix.

FIRST SERVANT. Faugh! come, now another! keep on mixing with all your might.

SECOND SERVANT. I' faith, no. I can stand this awful cesspool stench no longer, so I bring you the whole ill-smelling gear.

FIRST SERVANT. Pitch it down the sewer sooner, and yourself with it.

SECOND SERVANT. Maybe, one of you can tell me where I can buy a stopped-up nose, for there is no work more disgusting than to mix food for a beetle and to carry it to him. A pig or a dog will at least pounce upon our excrement without more ado, but this foul wretch affects the disdainful, the spoilt mistress, and won't eat unless I offer him a cake that has been kneaded for an entire day.... But let us open the door a bit ajar without his seeing it. Has he done eating? Come, pluck up courage, cram yourself till you burst! The cursed creature! It wallows in its food! It grips it between its claws like a wrestler clutching his opponent, and with head and feet together rolls up its paste like a ropemaker twisting a hawser. What an indecent, stinking, gluttonous beast! I know not what angry god let this monster loose upon us, but of a certainty it was neither Aphrodité nor the Graces.

FIRST SERVANT. Who was it then?

SECOND SERVANT. No doubt the Thunderer, Zeus.

FIRST SERVANT. But perhaps some spectator, some beardless youth, who thinks himself a sage, will say, "What is this? What does the beetle mean?" And then an Ionian, sitting next him, will add, "I think 'tis an allusion to Cleon, who so shamelessly feeds on filth all by himself."—But now I'm going indoors to fetch the beetle a drink.

SECOND SERVANT. As for me, I will explain the matter to you all, children, youths, grown-ups and old men, aye, even to the decrepit dotards. My master is mad, not as you are, but with another sort of madness, quite a new kind. The livelong day he looks open-mouthed towards heaven and never stops addressing Zeus. "Ah! Zeus," he cries, "what are thy intentions? Lay aside thy besom; do not sweep Greece away!"

TRYGAEUS. Ah! ah! ah!

FIRST SERVANT. Hush, hush! Methinks I hear his voice!

TRYGAEUS. Oh! Zeus, what art thou going to do for our people? Dost thou not see this, that our cities will soon be but empty husks?

FIRST SLAVE. As I told you, that is his form of madness. There you have a sample of his follies. When his trouble first began to seize him, he said to himself, "By what means could I go straight to Zeus?" Then he made himself very slender little ladders and so clambered up towards heaven; but he soon came hurtling down again and broke his head. Yesterday, to our misfortune, he went out and brought us back this thoroughbred, but from where I know not, this great beetle, whose groom he has forced me to become. He himself caresses it as though it were a horse, saying, "Oh! my little Pegasus, my noble aerial steed, may your wings soon bear me straight to Zeus!" But what is my master doing? I must stoop down to look through this hole. Oh! great gods! Here! neighbours, run here quick! here is my master flying off mounted on his beetle as if on horseback.

TRYGAEUS. Gently, gently, go easy, beetle; don't start off so proudly, or trust at first too greatly to your powers; wait till you have sweated, till the beating of your wings shall make your limb joints supple. Above all things, don't let off some foul smell, I adjure you; else I would rather have you stop in the stable altogether.

SECOND SERVANT. Poor master! Is he crazy?

TRYGAEUS. Silence! silence!

SECOND SERVANT (to Trygaeus). But why start up into the air on chance?

TRYGAEUS. 'Tis for the weal of all the Greeks; I am attempting a daring and novel feat.

SECOND SERVANT. But what is your purpose? What useless folly!

TRYGAEUS. No words of ill omen! Give vent to joy and command all men to keep silence, to close down their drains and privies with new tiles and to stop their own vent-holes.

FIRST SERVANT. No, I shall not be silent, unless you tell me where you are going.

TRYGAEUS. Why, where am I likely to be going across the sky, if it be not to visit Zeus?

FIRST SERVANT. For what purpose?

TRYGAEUS. I want to ask him what he reckons to do for all the Greeks.

SECOND SERVANT. And if he doesn't tell you?

TRYGAEUS. I shall pursue him at law as a traitor who sells Greece to the Medes.

SECOND SERVANT. Death seize me, if I let you go.

TRYGAEUS. It is absolutely necessary.

SECOND SERVANT. Alas! alas! dear little girls, your father is deserting you secretly to go to heaven. Ah! poor orphans, entreat him, beseech him.

LITTLE DAUGHTER. Father! father! what is this I hear? Is it true? What! you would leave me, you would vanish into the sky, you would go to the crows? 'Tis impossible! Answer, father, an you love me.

TRYGAEUS. Yes, I am going. You hurt me too sorely, my daughters, when you ask me for bread, calling me your daddy, and there is not the ghost of an obolus in the house; if I succeed and come back, you will have a barley loaf every morning—and a punch in the eye for sauce!

LITTLE DAUGHTER. But how will you make the journey? 'Tis not a ship that will carry you thither.

TRYGAEUS. No, but this winged steed will.

LITTLE DAUGHTER. But what an idea, daddy, to harness a beetle, on which to fly to the gods.

TRYGAEUS. We see from Aesop's fables that they alone can fly to the abode of the Immortals.

LITTLE DAUGHTER. Father, father, 'tis a tale nobody can believe! that such a stinking creature can have gone to the gods.

TRYGAEUS. It went to have vengeance on the eagle and break its eggs.

LITTLE DAUGHTER. Why not saddle Pegasus? you would have a more *tragic* appearance in the eyes of the gods.

TRYGAEUS. Eh! don't you see, little fool, that then twice the food would be wanted? Whereas my beetle devours again as filth what I have eaten myself.

LITTLE DAUGHTER. And if it fell into the watery depths of the sea, could it escape with its wings?

TRYGAEUS (*showing his penis*). I am fitted with a rudder in case of need, and my Naxos beetle will serve me as a boat.

LITTLE DAUGHTER. And what harbour will you put in at?

TRYGAEUS. Why, is there not the harbour of Cantharos at the Piraeus?

LITTLE DAUGHTER. Take care not to knock against anything and so fall off into space; once a cripple, you would be a fit subject for Euripides, who would put you into a tragedy.

TRYGAEUS. I'll see to it. Good-bye! (*To the Athenians.*) You, for love of whom I brave these dangers, do ye neither let wind nor go to stool for the space of three days, for, if, while cleaving the air, my steed should scent anything, he would fling me head foremost from the summit of my hopes. Now come, my Pegasus, get a-going with up-pricked ears and make your golden bridle resound gaily. Eh! what are you doing? What are you up to? Do you turn your nose towards the cesspools? Come, pluck up a spirit; rush upwards from the earth, stretch out your speedy wings and make straight for the palace of Zeus; for once give up foraging in your daily food.—Hi! you down there, what are you after now? Oh! my god! 'tis a man emptying his belly in the Piraeus, close to the house where the bad girls are. But is it my death you seek then, my death? Will you not bury that right away and pile a great heap of earth upon it and plant wild thyme therein and pour perfumes on it? If I were to fall from up here and misfortune happened to me, the town of Chioswould owe a fine of five talents for my death, all along of your cursed rump. Alas! how frightened I am! oh! I have no heart for jests. Ah! machinist, take great care of me. There is already a wind whirling round my navel; take great care or, from sheer fright, I shall form food for my beetle.... But I think I am no longer far from the gods; aye, that is the dwelling of Zeus, I perceive. Hullo! Hi! where is the doorkeeper? Will no one open?

The scene changes and heaven is presented.

HERMES. Meseems I can sniff a man. (*He perceives Trygaeus astride his beetle.*) Why, what plague is this?

TRYGAEUS. A horse-beetle.

HERMES. Oh! impudent, shameless rascal! oh! scoundrel! triple scoundrel! the greatest scoundrel in the world! how did you come here? Oh! scoundrel of all scoundrels! your name? Reply.

TRYGAEUS. Triple scoundrel.

HERMES. Your country?

TRYGAEUS. Triple scoundrel.

HERMES. Your father?

TRYGAEUS. My father? Triple scoundrel.

HERMES. By the Earth, you shall die, unless you tell me your name.

TRYGAEUS. I am Trygaeus of the Athmonian deme, a good vine-dresser, little addicted to quibbling and not at all an informer.

HERMES. Why do you come?

TRYGAEUS. I come to bring you this meat.

HERMES. Ah! my good friend, did you have a good journey?

TRYGAEUS. Glutton, be off! I no longer seem a triple scoundrel to you. Come, call Zeus.

HERMES. Ah! ah! you are a long way yet from reaching the gods, for they moved yesterday.

TRYGAEUS. To what part of the earth?

HERMES. Eh! of the earth, did you say?

TRYGAEUS. In short, where are they then?

HERMES. Very far, very far, right at the furthest end of the dome of heaven.

TRYGAEUS. But why have they left you all alone here?

HERMES. I am watching what remains of the furniture, the little pots and pans, the bits of chairs and tables, and odd wine-jars.

TRYGAEUS. And why have the gods moved away?

HERMES. Because of their wrath against the Greeks. They have located War in the house they occupied themselves and have given him full power to do with you exactly as he pleases; then they went as high up as ever they could, so as to see no more of your fights and to hear no more of your prayers.

TRYGAEUS. What reason have they for treating us so?

HERMES. Because they have afforded you an opportunity for peace more than once, but you have always preferred war. If the Laconians got the very slightest advantage, they would exclaim, "By the Twin Brethren! the Athenians shall smart for this." If, on the contrary, the latter triumphed and the Laconians came with peace proposals, you would say, "By Demeter, they want to deceive us. No, by Zeus, we will not hear a word; they will always be coming as long as we hold Pylos."

TRYGAEUS. Yes, that is quite the style our folk do talk in.

HERMES. So that I don't know whether you will ever see Peace again.

TRYGAEUS. Why, where has she gone to then?

HERMES. War has cast her into a deep pit.

TRYGAEUS. Where?

HERMES. Down there, at the very bottom. And you see what heaps of stones he has piled over the top, so that you should never pull her out again.

TRYGAEUS. Tell me, what is War preparing against us?

HERMES. All I know is that last evening he brought along a huge mortar.

TRYGAEUS. And what is he going to do with his mortar?

HERMES. He wants to pound up all the cities of Greece in it.... But I must say good-bye, for I think he is coming out; what an uproar he is making!

TRYGAEUS. Ah! great gods! let us seek safety; meseems I already hear the noise of this fearful war mortar.

WAR (*enters carrying a mortar*). Oh! mortals, mortals, wretched mortals, how your jaws will snap!

TRYGAEUS. Oh! divine Apollo! what a prodigious big mortar! Oh, what misery the very sight of War causes me! This then is the foe from whom I fly, who is so cruel, so formidable, so stalwart, so solid on his legs!

WAR. Oh! Prasiae! thrice wretched, five times, aye, a thousand times wretched! for thou shalt be destroyed this day.

TRYGAEUS. This does not yet concern us over much; 'tis only so much the worse for the Laconians.

WAR. Oh! Megara! Megara! how utterly are you going to be ground up! what fine mincemeat are you to be made into!

TRYGAEUS. Alas! alas! what bitter tears there will be among the Megarians!

WAR. Oh, Sicily! you too must perish! Your wretched towns shall be grated like this cheese. Now let us pour some Attic honey into the mortar.

TRYGAEUS. Oh! I beseech you! use some other honey; this kind is worth four obols; be careful, oh! be careful of our Attic honey.

WAR. Hi! Tumult, you slave there!

TUMULT. What do you want?

WAR. Out upon you! You stand there with folded arms. Take this cuff o' the head for your pains.

TUMULT. Oh! how it stings! Master, have you got garlic in your fist, I wonder?

WAR. Run and fetch me a pestle.

TUMULT. But we haven't got one; 'twas only yesterday we moved.

WAR. Go and fetch me one from Athens, and hurry, hurry!

TUMULT. Aye, I hasten there; if I return without one, I shall have no cause for laughing. [*Exit.*

TRYGAEUS. Ah! what is to become of us, wretched mortals that we are? See the danger that threatens if he returns with the pestle, for War will quietly amuse himself with pounding all the towns of Hellas to pieces. Ah! Bacchus! cause this herald of evil to perish on his road!

WAR. Well!

TUMULT (*who has returned*). Well, what?

WAR. You have brought back nothing?

TUMULT. Alas! the Athenians have lost their pestle—the tanner, who ground Greece to powder.

TRYGAEUS. Oh! Athené, venerable mistress! 'tis well for our city he is dead, and before he could serve us with this hash.

WAR. Then go and seek one at Sparta and have done with it!

TUMULT. Aye, aye, master!

WAR. Be back as quick as ever you can.

TRYGAEUS (*to the audience*). What is going to happen, friends? 'Tis a critical hour. Ah! if there is some initiate of Samothrace among you, 'tis surely the moment to wish this messenger some accident—some sprain or strain.

TUMULT (*who returns*). Alas! alas! thrice again, alas!

WAR. What is it? Again you come back without it?

TUMULT. The Spartans too have lost their pestle.

WAR. How, varlet?

TUMULT. They had lent it to their allies in Thrace, who have lost it for them.

TRYGAEUS. Long life to you, Thracians! My hopes revive, pluck up courage, mortals!

WAR. Take all this stuff away; I am going in to make a pestle for myself.

TRYGAEUS. 'Tis now the time to sing as Datis did, as he masturbated himself at high noon, "Oh pleasure! oh enjoyment! oh delights!" 'Tis now, oh Greeks! the moment when freed of quarrels and fighting, we should rescue sweet Peace and draw her out of this pit, before some other pestle prevents us. Come, labourers, merchants, workmen, artisans, strangers, whether you be domiciled or not, islanders, come here, Greeks of all countries, come hurrying here with picks and levers and ropes! 'Tis the moment to drain a cup in honour of the Good Genius.

CHORUS. Come hither, all! quick, quick, hasten to the rescue! All peoples of Greece, now is the time or never, for you to help each other. You see yourselves freed from battles and all their horrors of bloodshed. The day, hateful to Lamachus, has come. Come then, what must be done? Give your orders, direct us, for I swear to work this day without ceasing, until with the help of our levers and our engines we have drawn back into light the greatest of all goddesses, her to whom the olive is so dear.

TRYGAEUS. Silence! if War should hear your shouts of joy he would bound forth from his retreat in fury.

CHORUS. Such a decree overwhelms us with joy; how different to the edict, which bade us muster with provisions for three days.

TRYGAEUS. Let us beware lest the cursed Cerberus prevent us even from the nethermost hell from delivering the goddess by his furious howling, just as he did when on earth.

CHORUS. Once we have hold of her, none in the world will be able to take her from us. Huzza! huzza!

TRYGAEUS. You will work my death if you don't subdue your shouts. War will come running out and trample everything beneath his feet.

CHORUS. Well then! *Let* him confound, let him trample, let him overturn everything! We cannot help giving vent to our joy.

TRYGAEUS. Oh! cruel fate! My friends! in the name of the gods, what possesses you? Your dancing will wreck the success of a fine undertaking.

CHORUS. 'Tis not I who want to dance; 'tis my legs that bound with delight.

TRYGAEUS. Enough, an you love me, cease your gambols.

CHORUS. There! Tis over.

TRYGAEUS. You say so, and nevertheless you go on.

CHORUS. Yet one more figure and 'tis done.

TRYGAEUS. Well, just this one; then you must dance no more.

CHORUS. No, no more dancing, if we can help you.

TRYGAEUS. But look, you are not stopping even now.

CHORUS. By Zeus, I am only throwing up my right leg, that's all.

TRYGAEUS. Come, I grant you that, but pray, annoy me no further.

CHORUS. Ah! the left leg too will have its fling; well, 'tis but its right. I am so happy, so delighted at not having to carry my buckler any more. I sing and I laugh more than if I had cast my old age, as a serpent does its skin.

TRYGAEUS. No, 'tis no time for joy yet, for you are not sure of success. But when you have got the goddess, then rejoice, shout and laugh; thenceforward you will be able to sail or stay at home, to make love or sleep, to attend festivals and processions, to play at cottabos, live like true Sybarites and to shout, Io, io!

CHORUS. Ah! God grant we may see the blessed day. I have suffered so much; have so oft slept with Phormio on hard beds. You will no longer find me an acid, angry, hard judge as heretofore, but will find me turned indulgent and grown younger by twenty years through happiness. We have been killing ourselves long enough, tiring ourselves out with going to the Lyceum and returning laden with spear and buckler.—But what can we do to please you? Come, speak; for 'tis a good Fate, that has named you our leader.

TRYGAEUS. How shall we set about removing these stones?

HERMES. Rash reprobate, what do you propose doing?

TRYGAEUS. Nothing bad, as Cillicon said.

HERMES. You are undone, you wretch.

TRYGAEUS. Yes, if the lot had to decide my life, for Hermes would know how to turn the chance.

HERMES. You are lost, you are dead.

TRYGAEUS. On what day?

HERMES. This instant.

TRYGAEUS. But I have not provided myself with flour and cheese yet to start for death.

HERMES. You *are* kneaded and ground already, I tell you.

TRYGAEUS. Hah! I have not yet tasted that gentle pleasure.

HERMES. Don't you know that Zeus has decreed death for him who is surprised exhuming Peace?

TRYGAEUS. What! must I really and truly die?

HERMES. You must.

TRYGAEUS. Well then, lend me three drachmae to buy a young pig; I wish to have myself initiated before I die.

HERMES. Oh! Zeus, the Thunderer!

TRYGAEUS. I adjure you in the name of the gods, master, don't denounce us!

HERMES. I may not, I cannot keep silent.

TRYGAEUS. In the name of the meats which I brought you so good-naturedly.

HERMES. Why, wretched man, Zeus will annihilate me, if I do not shout out at the top of my voice, to inform him what you are plotting.

TRYGAEUS. Oh, no! don't shout, I beg you, dear little Hermes.... And what are you doing, comrades? You stand there as though you were stocks and stones. Wretched men, speak, entreat him at once; otherwise he will be shouting.

CHORUS. Oh! mighty Hermes! don't do it; no, don't do it! If ever you have eaten some young pig, sacrificed by us on your altars, with pleasure, may this offering not be without value in your sight to-day.

TRYGAEUS. Do you not hear them wheedling you, mighty god?

CHORUS. Be not pitiless toward our prayers; permit us to deliver the goddess. Oh! the most human, the most generous of the gods, be favourable toward us, if it be true that you detest the haughty crests and proud brows of Pisander; we shall never cease, oh master, offering you sacred victims and solemn prayers.

TRYGAEUS. Have mercy, mercy, let yourself be touched by their words; never was your worship so dear to them as to-day.

HERMES. I' truth, never have you been greater thieves.

TRYGAEUS. I will reveal a great, a terrible conspiracy against the gods to you.

HERMES. Hah! speak and perchance I shall let myself be softened.

TRYGAEUS. Know then, that the Moon and that infamous Sun are plotting against you, and want to deliver Greece into the hands of the Barbarians.

HERMES. What for?

TRYGAEUS. Because it is to you that we sacrifice, whereas the barbarians worship them; hence they would like to see you destroyed, that they alone might receive the offerings.

HERMES. 'Tis then for this reason that these untrustworthy charioteers have for so long been defrauding us, one of them robbing us of daylight and the other nibbling away at the other's disk.

TRYGAEUS. Yes, certainly. So therefore, Hermes, my friend, help us with your whole heart to find and deliver the captive and we will celebrate the great Panathenaea in your honour as well as all the festivals of the other gods; for Hermes shall be the Mysteries, the Dipolia, the Adonia; everywhere the towns, freed from their miseries, will sacrifice to Hermes, the Liberator; you will be loaded with benefits of every kind, and to start with, I offer you this cup for libations as your first present.

HERMES. Ah! how golden cups do influence me! Come, friends, get to work. To the pit quickly, pick in hand and drag away the stones.

CHORUS. We go, but you, the cleverest of all the gods, supervise our labours; tell us, good workman as you are, what we must do; we shall obey your orders with alacrity.

TRYGAEUS. Quick, reach me your cup, and let us preface our work by addressing prayers to the gods.

HERMES. Oh! sacred, sacred libations! Keep silence, oh! ye people! keep silence!

TRYGAEUS. Let us offer our libations and our prayers, so that this day may begin an era of unalloyed happiness for Greece and that he who has bravely pulled at the rope with us may never resume his buckler.

CHORUS. Aye, may we pass our lives in peace, caressing our mistresses and poking the fire.

TRYGAEUS. May he who would prefer the war, oh Dionysus, be ever drawing barbed arrows out of his elbows.

CHORUS. If there be a citizen, greedy for military rank and honours, who refuses, oh, divine Peace! to restore you to daylight, may he behave as cowardly as Cleonymus on the battlefield.

TRYGAEUS. If a lance-maker or a dealer in shields desires war for the sake of better trade, may he be taken by pirates and eat nothing but barley.

CHORUS. If some ambitious man does not help us, because he wants to become a General, or if a slave is plotting to pass over to the enemy, let his limbs be broken on the wheel, may he be beaten to death with rods! As for us, may Fortune favour us! Io! Paean, Io!

TRYGAEUS. Don't say Paean, but simply, Io.

CHORUS. Very well, then! Io! Io! I'll simply say, Io!

TRYGAEUS. To Hermes, the Graces, Hora, Aphrodité, Eros!

CHORUS. And not to Ares?

TRYGAEUS. No.

CHORUS. Nor doubtless to Enyalius?

TRYGAEUS. No.

CHORUS. Come, all strain at the ropes to tear away the stones. Pull!

HERMES. Heave away, heave, heave, oh!

CHORUS. Come, pull harder, harder.

HERMES. Heave away, heave, heave, oh!

CHORUS. Still harder, harder still.

HERMES. Heave away, heave! Heave away, heave, heave, oh!

TRYGAEUS. Come, come, there is no working together. Come! all pull at the same instant! you Boeotians are only pretending. Beware!

HERMES. Come, heave away, heave!

CHORUS. Hi! you two pull as well.

TRYGAEUS. Why, I am pulling, I am hanging on to the rope and straining till I am almost off my feet; I am working with all my might.

HERMES. Why does not the work advance then?

TRYGAEUS. Lamachus, this is too bad! You are in the way, sitting there. We have no use for your Medusa's head, friend.

HERMES. But hold, the Argives have not pulled the least bit; they have done nothing but laugh at us for our pains while they were getting gain with both hands.

TRYGAEUS. Ah! my dear sir, the Laconians at all events pull with vigour.

CHORUS. But look! only those among them who generally hold the plough-tail show any zeal, while the armourers impede them in their efforts.

HERMES. And the Megarians too are doing nothing, yet look how they are pulling and showing their teeth like famished curs; the poor wretches are dying of hunger!

TRYGAEUS. This won't do, friends. Come! all together! Everyone to the work and with a good heart for the business.

HERMES. Heave away, heave!

TRYGAEUS. Harder!

HERMES. Heave away, heave!

TRYGAEUS. Come on then, by heaven.

HERMES. Heave away, heave! Heave away, heave!

CHORUS. This will never do.

TRYGAEUS. Is it not a shame? some pull one way and others another. You, Argives there, beware of a thrashing!

HERMES. Come, put your strength into it.

TRYGAEUS. Heave away, heave!

CHORUS. There are many ill-disposed folk among us.

TRYGAEUS. Do you at least, who long for peace, pull heartily.

CHORUS. But there are some who prevent us.

HERMES. Off to the Devil with you, Megarians! The goddess hates you. She recollects that you were the first to rub her the wrong way. Athenians, you are not well placed for pulling. There you are too busy with law-suits; if you really want to free the goddess, get down a little towards the sea.

CHORUS. Come, friends, none but husbandmen on the rope.

HERMES. Ah! that will do ever so much better.

CHORUS. He says the thing is going well. Come, all of you, together and with a will.

TRYGAEUS. 'Tis the husbandmen who are doing all the work.

CHORUS. Come then, come, and all together! Hah! hah! at last there is some unanimity in the work. Don't let us give up, let us redouble our efforts. There! now we have it! Come then, all together! Heave away, heave! Heave away, heave! Heave away, heave! Heave away, heave! Heave away, heave! All together! (*Peace is drawn out of the pit.*)

TRYGAEUS. Oh! venerated goddess, who givest us our grapes, where am I to find the ten-thousand-gallon words wherewith to greet thee? I have none such at home. Oh! hail to thee, Opora, and thou, Theoria! How beautiful is thy face! How sweet thy breath! What gentle fragrance comes from thy bosom, gentle as freedom from military duty, as the most dainty perfumes!

HERMES. Is it then a smell like a soldier's knapsack?

CHORUS. Oh! hateful soldier! your hideous satchel makes me sick! it stinks like the belching of onions, whereas this lovable deity has the odour of sweet fruits, of festivals, of the Dionysia, of the harmony of flutes, of the comic poets, of the verses of Sophocles, of the phrases of Euripides...

TRYGAEUS. That's a foul calumny, you wretch! She detests that framer of subtleties and quibbles.

CHORUS. ... of ivy, of straining-bags for wine, of bleating ewes, of provision-laden women hastening to the kitchen, of the tipsy servant wench, of the upturned wine-jar, and of a whole heap of other good things.

HERMES. Then look how the reconciled towns chat pleasantly together, how they laugh; and yet they are all cruelly mishandled; their wounds are bleeding still.

TRYGAEUS. But let us also scan the mien of the spectators; we shall thus find out the trade of each.

HERMES. Ah! good gods! look at that poor crest-maker, tearing at his hair, and at that pike-maker, who has just broken wind in yon sword-cutler's face.

TRYGAEUS. And do you see with what pleasure this sickle-maker is making long noses at the spear-maker?

HERMES. Now ask the husbandmen to be off.

TRYGAEUS. Listen, good folk! Let the husbandmen take their farming tools and return to their fields as quick as possible, but without either sword, spear or javelin. All is as quiet as if Peace had been reigning for a century. Come, let everyone go till the earth, singing the Paean.

CHORUS. Oh, thou, whom men of standing desired and who art good to husbandmen, I have gazed upon thee with delight; and now I go to greet my vines, to caress after so long an absence the fig trees I planted in my youth.

TRYGAEUS. Friends, let us first adore the goddess, who has delivered us from crests and Gorgons; then let us hurry to our farms, having first bought a nice little piece of salt fish to eat in the fields.

HERMES. By Posidon! what a fine crew they make and dense as the crust of a cake; they are as nimble as guests on their way to a feast.

TRYGAEUS. See, how their iron spades glitter and how beautifully their three-pronged mattocks glisten in the sun! How regularly they will align the plants! I also burn myself to go into the country and to turn over the earth I have so long neglected.—Friends, do you remember the happy life that peace afforded us formerly; can you recall the splendid baskets of figs, both fresh and dried, the myrtles, the sweet wine, the violets blooming near the spring, and the olives, for which we have wept so much? Worship, adore the goddess for restoring you so many blessings.

CHORUS. Hail! hail! thou beloved divinity! thy return overwhelms us with joy. When far from thee, my ardent wish to see my fields again made me pine with regret. From thee came all blessings. Oh! much desired Peace! thou art the sole support of those who spend their lives tilling the earth. Under thy rule we had a thousand delicious enjoyments at our beck; thou wert the husbandman's wheaten cake and his safeguard. So that our vineyards, our young fig-tree woods and all our plantations hail thee with delight and smile at thy coming. But where was she then, I wonder, all the long time she spent away from us? Hermes, thou benevolent god, tell us!

HERMES. Wise husbandmen, hearken to my words, if you want to know why she was lost to you. The start of our misfortunes was the exile of Phidias;

Pericles feared he might share his ill-luck, he mistrusted your peevish nature and, to prevent all danger to himself, he threw out that little spark, the Megarian decree, set the city aflame, and blew up the conflagration with a hurricane of war, so that the smoke drew tears from all Greeks both here and over there. At the very outset of this fire our vines were a-crackle, our casks knocked together; it was beyond the power of any man to stop the disaster, and Peace disappeared.

TRYGAEUS. That, by Apollo! is what no one ever told me; I could not think what connection there could be between Phidias and Peace.

CHORUS. Nor I; I know it now. This accounts for her beauty, if she is related to him. There are so many things that escape us.

HERMES. Then, when the towns subject to you saw that you were angered one against the other and were showing each other your teeth like dogs, they hatched a thousand plots to pay you no more dues and gained over the chief citizens of Sparta at the price of gold. They, being as shamelessly greedy as they were faithless in diplomacy, chased off Peace with ignominy to let loose War. Though this was profitable to them, 'twas the ruin of the husbandmen, who were innocent of all blame; for, in revenge, your galleys went out to devour their figs.

TRYGAEUS. And 'twas with justice too; did they not break down my black fig tree, which I had planted and dunged with my own hands?

CHORUS. Yes, by Zeus! yes, 'twas well done; the wretches broke a chest for me with stones, which held six medimni of corn.

HERMES. Then the rural labourers flocked into the city and let themselves be bought over like the others. Not having even a grape-stone to munch and longing after their figs, they looked towards the orators. These well knew that the poor were driven to extremity and lacked even bread; but they nevertheless drove away the Goddess each time she reappeared in answer to the wish of the country with their loud shrieks, that were as sharp as pitchforks; furthermore, they attacked the well-filled purses of the richest among our allies on the pretence that they belonged to Brasidas' party. And then you would tear the poor accused wretch to pieces with your teeth; for the city, all pale with hunger and cowed with terror, gladly snapped up any calumny that was thrown it to devour. So the strangers, seeing what terrible blows the informers dealt, sealed their lips with gold. They grew rich, while you, alas! you could only see that Greece was going to ruin. 'Twas the tanner who was the author of all this woe.

TRYGAEUS. Enough said, Hermes, leave that man in Hades, whither he has gone; he no longer belongs to us, but rather to yourself. That he was a cheat, a braggart, a calumniator when alive, why, nothing could be truer; but anything you might say now would be an insult to one of your own folk. Oh! venerated Goddess! why art thou silent?

HERMES. And how could she speak to the spectators? She is too angry at all that they have made her suffer.

TRYGAEUS. At least let her speak a little to you, Hermes.

HERMES. Tell me, my dear, what are your feelings with regard to them? Come, you relentless foe of all bucklers, speak; I am listening to you. (*Peace whispers into Hermes' ear.*) Is that your grievance against them? Yes, yes, I understand. Hearken, you folk, this is her complaint. She says, that after the affair of Pylos she came to you unbidden to bring you a basket full of truces and that you thrice repulsed her by your votes in the assembly.

TRYGAEUS. Yes, we did wrong, but forgive us, for our mind was then entirely absorbed in leather.

HERMES. Listen again to what she has just asked me. Who was her greatest foe here? and furthermore, had she a friend who exerted himself to put an end to the fighting?

TRYGAEUS. Her most devoted friend was Cleonymus; it is undisputed.

HERMES. How then did Cleonymus behave in fights?

TRYGAEUS. Oh! the bravest of warriors! Only he was not born of the father he claims; he showed it quick enough in the army by throwing away his weapons.

HERMES. There is yet another question she has just put to me. Who rules now in the rostrum?

TRYGAEUS. 'Tis Hyperbolus, who now holds empire on the Pnyx. (*To Peace.*) What now? you turn away your head!

HERMES. She is vexed, that the people should give themselves a wretch of that kind for their chief.

TRYGAEUS Oh! we shall not employ him again; but the people, seeing themselves without a leader, took him haphazard, just as a man, who is naked, springs upon the first cloak he sees.

HERMES. She asks, what will be the result of such a choice of the city?

TRYGAEUS. We shall be more far-seeing in consequence.

HERMES. And why?

TRYGAEUS. Because he is a lamp-maker. Formerly we only directed our business by groping in the dark; now we shall only deliberate by lamplight.

HERMES. Oh! oh! what questions she does order me to put to you!

TRYGAEUS. What are they?

HERMES. She wants to have news of a whole heap of old-fashioned things she left here. First of all, how is Sophocles?

TRYGAEUS. Very well; but something very strange has happened to him.

HERMES. What then?

TRYGAEUS. He has turned from Sophocles into Simonides.

HERMES. Into Simonides? How so?

TRYGAEUS. Because, though old and broken-down as he is, he would put to sea on a hurdle to gain an obolus.

HERMES. And wise Cratinus, is he still alive?

TRYGAEUS. He died about the time of the Laconian invasion.

HERMES. How?

TRYGAEUS. Of a swoon. He could not bear the shock of seeing one of his casks full of wine broken. Ah! what a number of other misfortunes our city has suffered! So, dearest mistress, nothing can now separate us from thee.

HERMES. If that be so, receive Opora here for a wife; take her to the country, live with her, and grow fine grapes together.

TRYGAEUS. Come, my dear friend, come and accept my kisses. Tell me, Hermes, my master, do you think it would hurt me to fuck her a little, after so long an abstinence?

HERMES. No, not if you swallow a potion of penny-royal afterwards. But hasten to lead Theoria to the Senate; 'twas there she lodged before.

TRYGAEUS. Oh! fortunate Senate! Thanks to Theoria, what soups you will swallow for the space of three days! how you will devour meats and cooked tripe! Come, farewell, friend Hermes!

HERMES. And to you also, my dear sir, may you have much happiness, and don't forget me.

TRYGAEUS. Come, beetle, home, home, and let us fly on a swift wing.

HERMES. Oh! he is no longer here.

TRYGAEUS. Where has he gone to then?

HERMES. He is harnessed to the chariot of Zeus and bears the thunderbolts.

TRYGAEUS. But where will the poor wretch get his food?

HERMES. He will eat Ganymede's ambrosia.

TRYGAEUS. Very well then, but how am I going to descend?

HERMES. Oh! never fear, there is nothing simpler; place yourself beside the goddess.

TRYGAEUS. Come, my pretty maidens, follow me quickly; there are plenty of folk awaiting you with standing tools.

CHORUS. Farewell and good luck be yours! Let us begin by handing over all this gear to the care of our servants, for no place is less safe than a theatre; there is always a crowd of thieves prowling around it, seeking to find some mischief to do. Come, keep a good watch over all this. As for ourselves, let us explain to the spectators what we have in our minds, the purpose of our play.

Undoubtedly the comic poet who mounted the stage to praise himself in the parabasis would deserve to be handed over to the sticks of the beadles. Nevertheless, oh Muse, if it be right to esteem the most honest and illustrious of our comic writers at his proper value, permit our poet to say that he thinks he has deserved a glorious renown. First of all, 'tis he who has compelled his rivals no longer to scoff at rags or to war with lice; and as for those Heracles, always chewing and ever hungry, those poltroons and cheats who allow themselves to be beaten at will, he was the first to cover them with ridicule and to chase them from the stage; he has also dismissed that slave, whom one never failed to set a-weeping before you, so that his comrade might have the chance of jeering at his stripes and might ask, "Wretch, what has happened to your hide? Has the lash rained an army of its thongs on you and laid your back waste?" After having delivered us from all these wearisome ineptitudes and these low buffooneries, he has built up for us a great art, like a palace with high towers, constructed of fine phrases, great thoughts and of jokes not common on the streets. Moreover 'tis not obscure private persons or women that he stages in his comedies; but, bold as Heracles, 'tis the very greatest whom he attacks, undeterred by the fetid stink of leather or the threats of hearts of mud. He has the right to say, "I am the first ever dared to go straight for that beast with the sharp teeth and the terrible eyes that flashed lambent fire like those of Cynna, surrounded by a hundred lewd flatterers, who spittle-licked him to his heart's content; it had a voice like a roaring torrent, the stench of a seal, a foul Lamia's testicles and the rump of a camel."

I did not recoil in horror at the sight of such a monster, but fought him relentlessly to win your deliverance and that of the Islanders. Such are the services which should be graven in your recollection and entitle me to your thanks. Yet I have not been seen frequenting the wrestling school intoxicated with success and trying to tamper with young boys; but I took all my theatrical gear and returned straight home. I pained folk but little and caused them much amusement; my conscience rebuked me for nothing. Hence both grown men and youths should be on my side and I likewise invite the bald to give me their votes; for, if I triumph, everyone will say, both at table and at festivals, "Carry this to the bald man, give these cakes to the bald one, do not grudge the poet whose talent shines as bright as his own bare skull the share he deserves."

Oh, Muse! drive the War far from our city and come to preside over our dances, if you love me; come and celebrate the nuptials of the gods, the banquets of us mortals and the festivals of the fortunate; these are the themes that inspire thy most poetic songs. And should Carcinus come to beg thee for admission with his sons to thy chorus, refuse all traffic with them; remember they are but gelded birds, stork-necked dancers, mannikins about as tall as a pat of goat's dung, in fact machine-made poets. Contrary to all expectation, the father has at last managed to finish a piece, but he owns himself a cat strangled it one fine evening.

Such are the songs with which the Muse with the glorious hair inspires the able poet and which enchant the assembled populace, when the spring swallow twitters beneath the foliage; but the god spare us from the chorus of Morsimus and that of Melanthius! Oh! what a bitter discordancy grated upon my ears that day when the tragic chorus was directed by this same Melanthius and his brother, these two Gorgons, these two harpies, the plague of the seas, whose gluttonous bellies devour the entire race of fishes, these followers of old women, these goats with their stinking arm-pits. Oh! Muse, spit upon them abundantly and keep the feast gaily with me.

TRYGAEUS. Ah! 'tis a rough job getting to the gods! my legs are as good as broken through it. How small you were, to be sure, when seen from heaven! you had all the appearance too of being great rascals; but seen close, you look even worse.

SERVANT. Is that you, master?

TRYGAEUS. So I have been told.

SERVANT. What has happened to you?

TRYGAEUS. My legs pain me; it is such a plaguey long journey.

SERVANT. Oh! do tell me....

TRYGAEUS. What?

SERVANT. Did you see any other man besides yourself strolling about in heaven?

TRYGAEUS. No, only the souls of two or three dithyrambic poets.

SERVANT. What were they doing up there?

TRYGAEUS. They were seeking to catch some lyric exordia as they flew by immersed in the billows of the air.

SERVANT. Is it true, what they tell us, that men are turned into stars after death?

TRYGAEUS. Quite true.

SERVANT. Then who is that star I see over yonder?

TRYGAEUS. That is Ion of Chios, the author of an ode beginning "Morning"; as soon as ever he got to heaven, they called him "the Morning Star."

SERVANT. And those stars like sparks, that plough up the air as they dart across the sky?

TRYGAEUS. They are the rich leaving the feast with a lantern and a light inside it. But hurry up, show this young girl into my house, clean out the bath, heat some water and prepare the nuptial couch for herself and me. When 'tis done, come back here; meanwhile I am off to present this one to the Senate.

SERVANT. But where then did you get these pretty chattels?

TRYGAEUS. Where? why in heaven.

SERVANT. I would not give more than an obolus for gods who have got to keeping brothels like us mere mortals.

TRYGAEUS. They are not all so, but there are some up there too who live by this trade.

SERVANT. Come, that's rich! But I bethink me, shall I give her something to eat?

TRYGAEUS. No, for she would neither touch bread nor cake; she is used to licking ambrosia at the table of the gods.

SERVANT. Well, we can give her something to lick down here too.

CHORUS. Here is a truly happy old man, as far as I can judge.

TRYGAEUS. Ah! but what shall I be, when you see me presently dressed for the wedding?

CHORUS. Made young again by love and scented with perfumes, your lot will be one we all shall envy.

TRYGAEUS. And when I lie beside her and caress her bosoms?

CHORUS. Oh! then you will be happier than those spinning-tops who call Carcinus their father.

TRYGAEUS. And I well deserve it; have I not bestridden a beetle to save the Greeks, who now, thanks to me, can make love at their ease and sleep peacefully on their farms?

SERVANT. The girl has quitted the bath; she is charming from head to foot, both belly and buttocks; the cake is baked and they are kneading the sesame-biscuit; nothing is lacking but the bridegroom's penis.

TRYGAEUS. Let us first hasten to lodge Theoria in the hands of the Senate.

SERVANT. But tell me, who is this woman?

TRYGAEUS. Why, 'tis Theoria, with whom we used formerly to go to Brauron, to get tipsy and frolic. I had the greatest trouble to get hold of her.

SERVANT. Ah! you charmer! what pleasure your pretty bottom will afford me every four years!

TRYGAEUS. Let us see, who of you is steady enough to be trusted by the Senate with the care of this charming wench? Hi! you, friend! what are you drawing there?

SERVANT. I am drawing the plan of the tent I wish to erect for myself on the isthmus.

TRYGAEUS. Come, who wishes to take the charge of her? No one? Come, Theoria, I am going to lead you into the midst of the spectators and confide you to their care.

SERVANT. Ah! there is one who makes a sign to you.

TRYGAEUS. Who is it?

SERVANT. 'Tis Ariphrades. He wishes to take her home at once.

TRYGAEUS. No, I'm sure he shan't. He would soon have her done for, licking up all her life juice. Come, Theoria, put down all this gear.—Senate, Prytanes, look upon Theoria and see what precious blessings I place in your hands. Hasten to raise its limbs and to immolate the victim. Admire the fine chimney, it is quite black with smoke, for 'twas here that the Senate did their cooking before the War. Now that you have found Theoria again, you can start the most charming games from to-morrow, wrestling with her on the ground, either on your hands and feet, or you can lay her on her side, or stand before her with bent knees, or, well rubbed with oil, you can boldly enter the lists, as in the Pancratium, belabouring your foe with blows from your fist or otherwise. The next day you will celebrate equestrian games, in which the riders will ride side by side, or else the chariot teams, thrown one on top of another, panting and whinnying, will roll and knock against each other on the ground, while other rivals, thrown out of their seats, will fall before reaching the goal, utterly exhausted by their efforts.—Come, Prytanes, take Theoria. Oh! look how graciously yonder fellow has received her; you would not have been in such a hurry to introduce her to the Senate, if nothing were coming to you through it; you would not have failed to plead some holiday as an excuse.

CHORUS. Such a man as you assures the happiness of all his fellow-citizens.

TRYGAEUS. When you are gathering your vintages you will prize me even better.

CHORUS. E'en from to-day we hail you as the deliverer of mankind.

TRYGAEUS. Wait until you have drunk a beaker of new wine, before you appraise my true merits.

CHORUS. Excepting the gods, there is none greater than yourself, and that will ever be our opinion.

TRYGAEUS. Yea, Trygaeus of Athmonia has deserved well of you, he has freed both husbandman and craftsman from the most cruel ills; he has vanquished Hyperbolus.

CHORUS. Well then, what must we do now?

TRYGAEUS. You must offer pots of green-stuff to the goddess to consecrate her altars.

CHORUS. Pots of green-stuff as we do to poor Hermes—and even he thinks the fare but mean?

TRYGAEUS. What will you offer then? A fatted bull?

CHORUS. Oh, no! I don't want to start bellowing the battle-cry.

TRYGAEUS. A great fat swine then?

CHORUS. No, no.

TRYGAEUS. Why not?

CHORUS. We don't want any of the swinishness of Theagenes.

TRYGAEUS. What other victim do you prefer then?

CHORUS. A sheep.

TRYGAEUS. A sheep?

CHORUS. Yes.

TRYGAEUS. But you must give the word the Ionic form.

CHORUS. Purposely. So that if anyone in the assembly says, "We must go to war," all may start bleating in alarm, "Oï, oï."

TRYGAEUS. A brilliant idea.

CHORUS. And we shall all be lambs one toward the other, yea, and milder still toward the allies.

TRYGAEUS. Then go for the sheep and haste to bring it back with you; I will prepare the altar for the sacrifice.

CHORUS. How everything succeeds to our wish, when the gods are willing and Fortune favours us! how opportunely everything falls out.

TRYGAEUS. Nothing could be truer, for look! here stands the altar all ready at my door.

CHORUS. Hurry, hurry, for the winds are fickle; make haste, while the divine will is set on stopping this cruel war and is showering on us the most striking benefits.

TRYGAEUS. Here is the basket of barley-seed mingled with salt, the chaplet and the sacred knife; and there is the fire; so we are only waiting for the sheep.

CHORUS. Hasten, hasten, for, if Chaeris sees you, he will come without bidding, he and his flute; and when you see him puffing and panting and out of breath, you will have to give him something.

TRYGAEUS. Come, seize the basket and take the lustral water and hurry to circle round the altar to the right.

SERVANT. There! 'tis done. What is your next bidding?

TRYGAEUS. Hold! I take this fire-brand first and plunge it into the water.

SERVANT. Be quick! be quick! Sprinkle the altar.

TRYGAEUS. Give me some barley-seed, purify yourself and hand me the basin; then scatter the rest of the barley among the audience.

SERVANT. 'Tis done.

TRYGAEUS. You have thrown it?

SERVANT. Yes, by Hermes! and all the spectators have had their share.

TRYGAEUS. But not the women?

SERVANT. Oh! their husbands will give it them this evening.

TRYGAEUS. Let us pray! Who is here? Are there any good men?

SERVANT. Come, give, so that I may sprinkle these. Faith! they are indeed good, brave men.

TRYGAEUS. You believe so?

SERVANT. I am sure, and the proof of it is that we have flooded them with lustral water and they have not budged an inch.

TRYGAEUS. Come then, to prayers; to prayers, quick!—Oh! Peace, mighty queen, venerated goddess, thou, who presidest over choruses and at nuptials, deign to accept the sacrifices we offer thee.

SERVANT. Receive it, greatly honoured mistress, and behave not like the coquettes, who half open the door to entice the gallants, draw back when they are stared at, to return once more if a man passes on. But do not act like this to us.

TRYGAEUS. No, but like an honest woman, show thyself to thy worshippers, who are worn with regretting thee all these thirteen years. Hush the noise of battle, be a true Lysimacha to us. Put an end to this tittle-tattle, to this idle babble, that set us defying one another. Cause the Greeks once more to taste the pleasant beverage of friendship and temper all hearts with the gentle feeling of forgiveness. Make excellent commodities flow to our markets, fine heads of garlic, early cucumbers, apples, pomegranates and nice little cloaks for the slaves; make them bring geese, ducks, pigeons and larks from Boeotia and baskets of eels from Lake Copaïs; we shall all rush to buy them, disputing their possession with Morychus, Teleas, Glaucetes and every other glutton. Melanthius will arrive on the market last of all; 'twill be, "no more eels, all sold!" and then he'll start a-groaning and exclaiming as in his monologue of Medea, "I am dying, I am dying! Alas! I have let those hidden in the beet escape me!" And won't we laugh? These are the wishes, mighty goddess, which we pray thee to grant.

SERVANT. Take the knife and slaughter the sheep like a finished cook.

TRYGAEUS. No, the goddess does not wish it.

SERVANT. And why not?

TRYGAEUS. Blood cannot please Peace, so let us spill none upon her altar. Therefore go and sacrifice the sheep in the house, cut off the legs and bring them here; thus the carcase will be saved for the choragus.

CHORUS. You, who remain here, get chopped wood and everything needed for the sacrifice ready.

TRYGAEUS. Don't I look like a diviner preparing his mystic fire?

CHORUS. Undoubtedly. Will anything that it behoves a wise man to know escape you? Don't you know all that a man should know, who is distinguished for his wisdom and inventive daring?

TRYGAEUS. There! the wood catches. Its smoke blinds poor Stilbides. I am now going to bring the table and thus be my own slave.

CHORUS. You have braved a thousand dangers to save your sacred town. All honour to you! your glory will be ever envied.

SERVANT. Hold! here are the legs, place them upon the altar. For myself, I mean to go back to the entrails and the cakes.

TRYGAEUS. I'll see to those; I want you here.

SERVANT. Well then, here I am. Do you think I have been long?

TRYGAEUS. Just get this roasted. Ah! who is this man, crowned with laurel, who is coming to me?

SERVANT. He has a self-important look; is he some diviner?

TRYGAEUS. No, i' faith! 'tis Hierocles.

SERVANT. Ah! that oracle-monger from Oreus. What is he going to tell us?

TRYGAEUS. Evidently he is coming to oppose the peace.

SERVANT. No, 'tis the odour of the fat that attracts him.

TRYGAEUS. Let us appear not to see him.

SERVANT. Very well.

HIEROCLES. What sacrifice is this? to what god are you offering it?

TRYGAEUS (*to the servant*). Silence!—(*Aloud.*) Look after the roasting and keep your hands off the meat.

HIEROCLES. To whom are you sacrificing? Answer me. Ah! the tail is showing favourable omens.

SERVANT. Aye, very favourable, oh, loved and mighty Peace!

HIEROCLES. Come, cut off the first offering and make the oblation.

TRYGAEUS. 'Tis not roasted enough.

HIEROCLES. Yea, truly, 'tis done to a turn.

TRYGAEUS. Mind your own business, friend! (*To the servant.*) Cut away. Where is the table? Bring the libations.

HIEROCLES. The tongue is cut separately.

TRYGAEUS. We know all that. But just listen to one piece of advice.

HIEROCLES. And that is?

TRYGAEUS. Don't talk, for 'tis divine Peace to whom we are sacrificing.

HIEROCLES. Oh! wretched mortals, oh, you idiots!

TRYGAEUS. Keep such ugly terms for yourself.

HIEROCLES. What! you are so ignorant you don't understand the will of the gods and you make a treaty, you, who are men, with apes, who are full of malice!

TRYGAEUS. Ha, ha, ha!

HIEROCLES. What are you laughing at?

TRYGAEUS. Ha, ha! your apes amuse me!

HIEROCLES. You simple pigeons, you trust yourselves to foxes, who are all craft, both in mind and heart.

TRYGAEUS. Oh, you trouble-maker! may your lungs get as hot as this meat!

HIEROCLES. Nay, nay! if only the Nymphs had not fooled Bacis, and Bacis mortal men; and if the Nymphs had not tricked Bacis a second time....

TRYGAEUS. May the plague seize you, if you won't stop wearying us with your Bacis!

HIEROCLES. ... it would not have been written in the book of Fate that the bonds of Peace must be broken; but first....

TRYGAEUS. The meat must be dusted with salt.

HIEROCLES. ... it does not please the blessed gods that we should stop the War until the wolf uniteth with the sheep.

TRYGAEUS. How, you cursed animal, could the wolf ever unite with the sheep?

HIEROCLES. As long as the wood-bug gives off a fetid odour, when it flies; as long as the noisy bitch is forced by nature to litter blind pups, so long shall peace be forbidden.

TRYGAEUS. Then what should be done? Not to stop the War would be to leave it to the decision of chance which of the two people should suffer the most, whereas by uniting under a treaty, we share the empire of Greece.

HIEROCLES. You will never make the crab walk straight.

TRYGAEUS. You shall no longer be fed at the Prytaneum; the war done, oracles are not wanted.

HIEROCLES. You will never smooth the rough spikes of the hedgehog.

TRYGAEUS. Will you never stop fooling the Athenians?

HIEROCLES. What oracle ordered you to burn these joints of mutton in honour of the gods?

TRYGAEUS. This grand oracle of Homer's: "Thus vanished the dark war-clouds and we offered a sacrifice to new-born Peace. When the flame had consumed the thighs of the victim and its inwards had appeased our hunger, we poured out the libations of wine." 'Twas I who arranged the sacred rites, but none offered the shining cup to the diviner.

HIEROCLES. I care little for that. 'Tis not the Sibyl who spoke it.

TRYGAEUS. Wise Homer has also said: "He who delights in the horrors of civil war has neither country nor laws nor home." What noble words!

HIEROCLES. Beware lest the kite turn your brain and rob....

TRYGAEUS. Look out, slave! This oracle threatens our meat. Quick, pour the libation, and give me some of the inwards.

HIEROCLES. I too will help myself to a bit, if you like.

TRYGAEUS. The libation! the libation!

HIEROCLES. Pour out also for me and give me some of this meat.

TRYGAEUS. No, the blessed gods won't allow it yet; let us drink; and as for you, get you gone, for 'tis their will. Mighty Peace! stay ever in our midst.

HIEROCLES. Bring the tongue hither.

TRYGAEUS. Relieve us of your own.

HIEROCLES. The libation.

TRYGAEUS. Here! and this into the bargain (*strikes him*).

HIEROCLES. You will not give me any meat?

TRYGAEUS. We cannot give you any until the wolf unites with the sheep.

HIEROCLES. I will embrace your knees.

TRYGAEUS. 'Tis lost labour, good fellow; you will never smooth the rough spikes of the hedgehog.... Come, spectators, join us in our feast.

HIEROCLES. And what am I to do?

TRYGAEUS. You? go and eat the Sibyl.

HIEROCLES. No, by the Earth! no, you shall not eat without me; if you do not give, I take; 'tis common property.

TRYGAEUS (*to the servant*). Strike, strike this Bacis, this humbugging soothsayer.

HIEROCLES. I take to witness....

TRYGAEUS. And I also, that you are a glutton and an impostor. Hold him tight and beat the impostor with a stick.

SERVANT. You look to that; I will snatch the skin from him, which he has stolen from us. Are you going to let go that skin, you priest from hell! do you hear! Oh! what a fine crow has come from Oreus! Stretch your wings quickly for Elymnium.

CHORUS. Oh! joy, joy! no more helmet, no more cheese nor onions! No, I have no passion for battles; what I love, is to drink with good comrades in the corner by the fire when good dry wood, cut in the height of the summer, is crackling; it is to cook pease on the coals and beechnuts among the embers; 'tis to kiss our pretty Thracian while my wife is at the bath. Nothing is more pleasing, when the rain is sprouting our sowings, than to chat with some friend, saying, "Tell me, Comarchides, what shall we do? I would willingly drink myself, while the heavens are watering our fields. Come, wife, cook three measures of beans, adding to them a little wheat, and give us some figs. Syra! call Manes off the fields, 'tis impossible to prune the vine or to align the ridges, for the ground is too wet to-day. Let someone bring me the thrush and those two chaffinches; there were also some curds and four pieces of hare, unless the cat stole them last evening, for I know not what the infernal noise was that I heard in the house. Serve up three of the pieces for me, slave, and give the fourth to my father. Go and ask Aeschinades for some myrtle branches with berries on them, and then, for 'tis the same road, you will invite Charinades to come and drink with me to the honour of the gods who watch over our crops."

When the grasshopper sings its dulcet tune, I love to see the Lemnian vines beginning to ripen, for 'tis the earliest plant of all. I love likewise to watch the fig filling out, and when it has reached maturity I eat with appreciation and exclaim, "Oh! delightful season!" Then too I bruise some thyme and infuse it in water. Indeed I grow a great deal fatter passing the summer this way than in watching a cursed captain with his three plumes and his military cloak of a startling crimson (he calls it true Sardian purple), which he takes care to dye himself with Cyzicus saffron in a battle; then he is the first to run away, shaking his plumes like a great yellow prancing cock, while I am left to watch the nets. Once back again in Athens, these brave fellows behave abominably; they write down these, they scratch through others, and this backwards and forwards two or three times at random. The departure is set for to-morrow, and some citizen has brought no provisions, because he didn't know he had to go; he stops in front of the statue of Pandion, reads his name, is dumbfounded and starts away at a run, weeping bitter tears. The townsfolk are less ill-used, but that is how the husbandmen are treated by these men of war, the hated of the gods and of men, who know nothing but how to throw away their shield. For this reason, if it please heaven, I propose to call these rascals to account, for they are lions in times of peace, but sneaking foxes when it comes to fighting.

TRYGAEUS. Oh! oh! what a crowd for the nuptial feast! Here! dust the tables with this crest, which is good for nothing else now. Halloa! produce the cakes, the thrushes, plenty of good jugged hare and the little loaves.

A SICKLE-MAKER. Trygaeus, where is Trygaeus?

TRYGAEUS. I am cooking the thrushes.

SICKLE-MAKER. Trygaeus, my best of friends, what a fine stroke of business you have done for me by bringing back Peace! Formerly my sickles would not have sold at an obolus apiece, to-day I am being paid fifty drachmas for every one. And here is a neighbour who is selling his casks for the country at three drachmae each. So come, Trygaeus, take as many sickles and casks as you will for nothing. Accept them for nothing; 'tis because of our handsome profits on our sales that we offer you these wedding presents.

TRYGAEUS. Thanks. Put them all down inside there, and come along quick to the banquet. Ah! do you see that armourer yonder coming with a wry face?

A CREST-MAKER. Alas! alas! Trygaeus, you have ruined me utterly.

TRYGAEUS. What! won't the crests go any more, friend?

CREST-MAKER. You have killed my business, my livelihood, and that of this poor lance-maker too.

TRYGAEUS. Come, come, what are you asking for these two crests?

CREST-MAKER. What do you bid for them?

TRYGAEUS. What do I bid? Oh! I am ashamed to say. Still, as the clasp is of good workmanship, I would give two, even three measures of dried figs; I could use 'em for dusting the table.

CREST-MAKER. All right, tell them to bring me the dried figs; 'tis always better than nothing.

TRYGAEUS. Take them away, be off with your crests and get you gone; they are moulting, they are losing all their hair; I would not give a single fig for them.

A BREASTPLATE-MAKER. Good gods, what am I going to do with this fine ten-minae breast-plate, which is so splendidly made?

TRYGAEUS. Oh, you will lose nothing over it.

BREASTPLATE-MAKER. I will sell it you at cost price.

TRYGAEUS. 'Twould be very useful as a night-stool....

BREASTPLATE-MAKER. Cease your insults, both to me and my wares.

TRYGAEUS. ... if propped on three stones. Look, 'tis admirable.

BREASTPLATE-MAKER. But how can you wipe, idiot?

TRYGAEUS. I can pass one hand through here, and the other there, and so....

BREASTPLATE-MAKER. What! do you wipe with both hands?

TRYGAEUS. Aye, so that I may not be accused of robbing the State, by blocking up an oar-hole in the galley.

BREASTPLATE-MAKER. So you would pay ten minae for a night-stool?

TRYGAEUS. Undoubtedly, you rascal. Do you think I would sell my rump for a thousand drachmae?

BREASTPLATE-MAKER. Come, have the money paid over to me.

TRYGAEUS. No, friend; I find it hurts me to sit on. Take it away, I won't buy.

A TRUMPET-MAKER. What is to be done with this trumpet, for which I gave sixty drachmae the other day?

TRYGAEUS. Pour lead into the hollow and fit a good, long stick to the top; and you will have a balanced cottabos.

TRUMPET-MAKER. Ha! would you mock me?

TRYGAEUS. Well, here's another notion. Pour in lead as I said, add here a dish hung on strings, and you will have a balance for weighing the figs which you give your slaves in the fields.

A HELMET-MAKER. Cursed fate! I am ruined. Here are helmets, for which I gave a mina each. What am I to do with them? who will buy them?

TRYGAEUS. Go and sell them to the Egyptians; they will do for measuring loosening medicines.

A SPEAR-MAKER. Ah! poor helmet-maker, things are indeed in a bad way.

TRYGAEUS. That man has no cause for complaint.

SPEAR-MAKER. But helmets will be no more used.

TRYGAEUS. Let him learn to fit a handle to them and he can sell them for more money.

SPEAR-MAKER. Let us be off, comrade.

TRYGAEUS. No, I want to buy these spears.

SPEAR-MAKER. What will you give?

TRYGAEUS. If they could be split in two, I would take them at a drachma per hundred to use as vine-props.

SPEAR-MAKER. The insolent dog! Let us go, friend.

TRYGAEUS. Ah! here come the guests, children from the table to relieve themselves; I fancy they also want to hum over what they will be singing presently. Hi! child! what do you reckon to sing? Stand there and give me the opening line.

THE SON OF LAMACHUS. "Glory to the young warriors...."

TRYGAEUS. Oh! leave off about your young warriors, you little wretch; we are at peace and you are an idiot and a rascal.

SON OF LAMACHUS. "The skirmish begins, the hollow bucklers clash against each other."

TRYGAEUS. Bucklers! Leave me in peace with your bucklers.

SON OF LAMACHUS. "And then there came groanings and shouts of victory."

TRYGAEUS. Groanings! ah! by Bacchus! look out for yourself, you cursed squaller, if you start wearying us again with your groanings and hollow bucklers.

SON OF LAMACHUS. Then what should I sing? Tell me what pleases you.

TRYGAEUS. "'Tis thus they feasted on the flesh of oxen," or something similar, as, for instance, "Everything that could tickle the palate was placed on the table."

SON OF LAMACHUS. "'Tis thus they feasted on the flesh of oxen and, tired of warfare, unharnessed their foaming steeds."

TRYGAEUS. That's splendid; tired of warfare, they seat themselves at table; sing, sing to us how they still go on eating after they are satiated.

SON OF LAMACHUS. "The meal over, they girded themselves ..."

TRYGAEUS. With good wine, no doubt?

SON OF LAMACHUS. "... with armour and rushed forth from the towers, and a terrible shout arose."

TRYGAEUS. Get you gone, you little scapegrace, you and your battles! You sing of nothing but warfare. Who is your father then?

SON OF LAMACHUS. My father?

TRYGAEUS. Why yes, your father.

SON OF LAMACHUS. I am Lamachus' son.

TRYGAEUS. Oh! oh! I could indeed have sworn, when I was listening to you, that you were the son of some warrior who dreams of nothing but wounds and bruises, of some Boulomachus or Clausimachus; go and sing your plaguey songs to the spearmen.... Where is the son of Cleonymus? Sing me something before going back to the feast. I am at least certain he will not sing of battles, for his father is far too careful a man.

SON OF CLEONYMUS. "An inhabitant of Saïs is parading with the spotless shield which I regret to say I have thrown into a thicket."

TRYGAEUS. Tell me, you little good-for-nothing, are you singing that for your father?

SON or CLEONYMUS. "But I saved my life."

TRYGAEUS. And dishonoured your family. But let us go in; I am very certain, that being the son of such a father, you will never forget this song of the buckler. You, who remain to the feast, 'tis your duty to devour dish after dish and not to ply empty jaws. Come, put heart into the work and eat with your mouths full. For, believe me, poor friends, white teeth are useless furniture, if they chew nothing.

CHORUS. Never fear; thanks all the same for your good advice.

TRYGAEUS. You, who yesterday were dying of hunger, come, stuff yourselves with this fine hare-stew; 'tis not every day that we find cakes lying neglected. Eat, eat, or I predict you will soon regret it.

CHORUS. Silence! Keep silence! Here is the bride about to appear! Take nuptial torches and let all rejoice and join in our songs. Then, when we have danced, clinked our cups and thrown Hyperbolus through the doorway, we will carry back all our farming tools to the fields and shall pray the gods to give wealth to the Greeks and to cause us all to gather in an abundant barley harvest, enjoy a noble vintage, to grant that we may choke with good figs, that our wives may prove fruitful, that in fact we may recover all our lost blessings, and that the sparkling fire may be restored to the hearth.

TRYGAEUS. Come, wife, to the fields and seek, my beauty, to brighten and enliven my nights. Oh! Hymen! oh! Hymenaeus!

CHORUS. Oh! Hymen! oh! Hymenaeus! oh! thrice happy man, who so well deserve your good fortune!

TRYGAEUS. Oh! Hymen! oh! Hymenaeus!

CHORUS. Oh! Hymen! oh! Hymenaeus!

FIRST SEMI-CHORUS. What shall we do to her?

SECOND SEMI-CHORUS. What shall we do to her?

FIRST SEMI-CHORUS. We will gather her kisses.

SECOND SEMI-CHORUS. We will gather her kisses.

CHORUS. Come, comrades, we who are in the first row, let us pick up the bridegroom and carry him in triumph. Oh! Hymen! oh! Hymenaeus!

TRYGAEUS. Oh! Hymen! oh! Hymenaeus!

CHORUS. You shall have a fine house, no cares and the finest of figs. Oh! Hymen! oh! Hymenaeus!

TRYGAEUS. Oh! Hymen! oh! Hymenaeus!

CHORUS. The bridegroom's fig is great and thick; the bride's is very soft and tender.

TRYGAEUS. While eating and drinking deep draughts of wine, continue to repeat: Oh! Hymen! oh! Hymenaeus!

CHORUS. Oh! Hymen! oh! Hymenaeus!

TRYGAEUS. Farewell, farewell, my friends. All who come with me shall have cakes galore.

FINIS OF "PEACE"

Lysistrata

Introduction

The 'Lysistrata,' the third and concluding play of the War and Peace series, was not produced till ten years later than its predecessor, the 'Peace,' viz. in 411 B.C. It is now the twenty-first year of the War, and there seems as little prospect of peace as ever. A desperate state of things demands a desperate remedy, and the Poet proceeds to suggest a burlesque solution of the difficulty.

The women of Athens, led by Lysistrata and supported by female delegates from the other states of Hellas, determine to take matters into their own hands and force the men to stop the War. They meet in solemn conclave, and Lysistrata expounds her scheme, the rigorous application to husbands and lovers of a self-denying ordinance—"we must refrain from the male organ altogether." Every wife and mistress is to refuse all sexual favours whatsoever, till the men have come to terms of peace. In cases where the women _must_ yield 'par force majeure,' then it is to be with an ill grace and in such a way as to afford the minimum of gratification to their partner; they are to lie passive and take no more part in the amorous game than they are absolutely obliged to. By these means Lysistrata assures them they will very soon gain their end. "If we sit indoors prettily dressed out in our best transparent silks and prettiest gewgaws, and with our 'mottes' all nicely depilated, their tools will stand up so stiff that they will be able to deny us nothing." Such is the burden of her advice.

After no little demur, this plan of campaign is adopted, and the assembled women take a solemn oath to observe the compact faithfully. Meantime as a precautionary measure they seize the Acropolis, where the State treasure is kept; the old men of the city assault the doors, but are repulsed by "the terrible regiment" of women. Before long the device of the bold Lysistrata proves entirely effective, Peace is concluded, and the play ends with the hilarious festivities of the Athenian and Spartan plenipotentiaries in celebration of the event.

This drama has a double Chorus—of women and of old men, and much excellent fooling is got out of the fight for possession of the citadel between the two hostile bands; while the broad jokes and decidedly suggestive situations arising out of the general idea of the plot outlined above may be "better imagined than described."

Lysistrata

DRAMATIS PERSONAE

LYSISTRATA.
CALONICÉ.
MYRRHINÉ.
LAMPITO.
STRATYLLIS.
A MAGISTRATE.
CINESIAS.
A CHILD.
HERALD OF THE LACEDAEMONIANS.
ENVOYS OF THE LACEDAEMONIANS.
POLYCHARIDES.
MARKET LOUNGERS.
A SERVANT.
AN ATHENIAN CITIZEN.
CHORUS OF OLD MEN.
CHORUS OF WOMEN.

SCENE: In a public square at Athens; afterwards before the gates of the Acropolis, and finally within the precincts of the citadel.

LYSISTRATA (*alone*). Ah! if only they had been invited to a Bacchic revelling, or a feast of Pan or Aphrodité or Genetyllis, why! the streets would have been impassable for the thronging tambourines! Now there's never a woman here-ah! except my neighbour Calonicé, whom I see approaching yonder.... Good day, Calonicé.

CALONICÉ. Good day, Lysistrata; but pray, why this dark, forbidding face, my dear? Believe me, you don't look a bit pretty with those black lowering brows.

LYSISTRATA. Oh! Calonicé, my heart is on fire; I blush for our sex. Men *will* have it we are tricky and sly....

CALONICÉ. And they are quite right, upon my word!

LYSISTRATA. Yet, look you, when the women are summoned to meet for a matter of the last importance, they lie abed instead of coming.

CALONICÉ. Oh! they will come, my dear; but 'tis not easy, you know, for women to leave the house. One is busy pottering about her husband; another is getting the servant up; a third is putting her child asleep, or washing the brat or feeding it.

LYSISTRATA. But I tell you, the business that calls them here is far and away more urgent.

CALONICÉ. And why *do* you summon us, dear Lysistrata? What is it all about?

LYSISTRATA. About a big affair.

CALONICÉ. And is it thick too?

LYSISTRATA. Yes indeed, both big and great.

CALONICÉ. And we are not all on the spot!

LYSISTRATA. Oh! if it were what you suppose, there would be never an absentee. No, no, it concerns a thing I have turned about and about this way and that of many sleepless nights.

CALONICÉ. It must be something mighty fine and subtle for you to have turned it about so!

LYSISTRATA. So fine, it means just this, Greece saved by the women!

CALONICÉ. By women! Why, its salvation hangs on a poor thread then!

LYSISTRATA. Our country's fortunes depend on us—it is with us to undo utterly the Peloponnesians....

CALONICÉ. That would be a noble deed truly!

LYSISTRATA. To exterminate the Boeotians to a man!

CALONICÉ. But surely you would spare the eels.

LYSISTRATA. For Athens' sake I will never threaten so fell a doom; trust me for that. However, if the Boeotian and Peloponnesian women join us, Greece is saved.

CALONICÉ. But how should women perform so wise and glorious an achievement, we women who dwell in the retirement of the household, clad in diaphanous garments of yellow silk and long flowing gowns, decked out with flowers and shod with dainty little slippers?

LYSISTRATA. Nay, but those are the very sheet-anchors of our salvation—those yellow tunics, those scents and slippers, those cosmetics and transparent robes.

CALONICÉ. How so, pray?

LYSISTRATA. There is not a man will wield a lance against another ...

CALONICÉ. Quick, I will get me a yellow tunic from the dyer's.

LYSISTRATA. ... or want a shield.

CALONICÉ. I'll run and put on a flowing gown.

LYSISTRATA. ... or draw a sword.

CALONICÉ. I'll haste and buy a pair of slippers this instant.

LYSISTRATA. Now tell me, would not the women have done best to come?

CALONICÉ. Why, they should have *flown* here!

LYSISTRATA. Ah! my dear, you'll see that like true Athenians, they will do everything too late.... Why, there's not a woman come from the shoreward parts, not one from Salamis.

CALONICÉ. But I know for certain they embarked at daybreak.

LYSISTRATA. And the dames from Acharnae! why, I thought they would have been the very first to arrive.

CALONICÉ. Theagenes wife at any rate is sure to come; she has actually been to consult Hecaté.... But look! here are some arrivals—and there are more behind. Ah! ha! now what countrywomen may they be?

LYSISTRATA. They are from Anagyra.

CALONICÉ. Yes! upon my word, 'tis a levy *en masse* of all the female population of Anagyra!

MYRRHINÉ. Are we late, Lysistrata? Tell us, pray; what, not a word?

LYSISTRATA. I cannot say much for you, Myrrhiné! you have not bestirred yourself overmuch for an affair of such urgency.

MYRRHINÉ I could not find my girdle in the dark. However, if the matter is so pressing, here we are; so speak.

LYSISTRATA. No, but let us wait a moment more, till the women of Boeotia arrive and those from the Peloponnese.

MYRRHINÉ Yes, that is best.... Ah! here comes Lampito.

LYSISTRATA. Good day, Lampito, dear friend from Lacedaemon. How well and handsome you look! what a rosy complexion! and how strong you seem; why, you could strangle a bull surely!

LAMPITO. Yes, indeed, I really think I could. 'Tis because I do gymnastics and practise the kick dance.

LYSISTRATA. And what superb bosoms!

LAMPITO. La! you are feeling me as if I were a beast for sacrifice.

LYSISTRATA. And this young woman, what countrywoman is she?

LAMPITO. She is a noble lady from Boeotia.

LYSISTRATA. Ah! my pretty Boeotian friend, you are as blooming as a garden.

CALONICÉ. Yes, on my word! and the garden is so prettily weeded too!

LYSISTRATA. And who is this?

LAMPITO. 'Tis an honest woman, by my faith! she comes from Corinth.

LYSISTRATA. Oh! honest, no doubt then—as honesty goes at Corinth.

LAMPITO. But who has called together this council of women, pray?

LYSISTRATA. I have.

LAMPITO. Well then, tell us what you want of us.

LYSISTRATA. With pleasure, my dear.

MYRRHINÉ. What is the most important business you wish to inform us about?

LYSISTRATA. I will tell you. But first answer me one question.

MYRRHINÉ. What is that?

LYSISTRATA. Don't you feel sad and sorry because the fathers of your children are far away from you with the army? For I'll undertake, there is not one of you whose husband is not abroad at this moment.

CALONICÉ. Mine has been the last five months in Thrace—looking after Eucrates.

LYSISTRATA. 'Tis seven long months since mine left me for Pylos.

LAMPITO. As for mine, if he ever does return from service, he's no sooner back than he takes down his shield again and flies back to the wars.

LYSISTRATA. And not so much as the shadow of a lover! Since the day the Milesians betrayed us, I have never once seen an eight-inch-long *godemiche* even, to be a leathern consolation to us poor widows.... Now tell me, if I have discovered a means of ending the war, will you all second me?

MYRRHINÉ. Yes verily, by all the goddesses, I swear I will, though I have to put my gown in pawn, and drink the money the same day.

CALONICÉ. And so will I, though I must be split in two like a flat-fish, and have half myself removed.

LAMPITO. And I too; why, to secure Peace, I would climb to the top of Mount Taygetus.

LYSISTRATA. Then I will out with it at last, my mighty secret! Oh! sister women, if we would compel our husbands to make peace, we must refrain....

MYRRHINÉ. Refrain from what? tell us, tell us!

LYSISTRATA. But will you do it?

MYRRHINÉ. We will, we will, though we should die of it.

LYSISTRATA. We must refrain from the male organ altogether.... Nay, why do you turn your backs on me? Where are you going? So, you bite your lips, and shake your heads, eh? Why these pale, sad looks? why these tears? Come, will you do it—yes or no? Do you hesitate?

MYRRHINÉ. No, I will not do it; let the War go on.

LYSISTRATA. And you, my pretty flat-fish, who declared just now they might split you in two?

CALONICÉ. Anything, anything but that! Bid me go through the fire, if you will; but to rob us of the sweetest thing in all the world, my dear, dear Lysistrata!

LYSISTRATA. And you?

MYRRHINÉ. Yes, I agree with the others; I too would sooner go through the fire.

LYSISTRATA. Oh, wanton, vicious sex! the poets have done well to make tragedies upon us; we are good for nothing then but love and lewdness! But you, my dear, you from hardy Sparta, if *you* join me, all may yet be well; help me, second me, I conjure you.

LAMPITO. 'Tis a hard thing, by the two goddesses it is! for a woman to sleep alone without ever a standing weapon in her bed. But there, Peace must come first.

LYSISTRATA. Oh, my dear, my dearest, best friend, you are the only one deserving the name of woman!

CALONICÉ. But if—which the gods forbid—we do refrain altogether from what you say, should we get peace any sooner?

LYSISTRATA. Of course we should, by the goddesses twain! We need only sit indoors with painted cheeks, and meet our mates lightly clad in transparent gowns of Amorgos silk, and with our "mottes" nicely plucked smooth; then their tools will stand like mad and they will be wild to lie with us. That will be the time to refuse, and they will hasten to make peace, I am convinced of that!

LAMPITO. Yes, just as Menelaus, when he saw Helen's naked bosom, threw away his sword, they say.

CALONICÉ. But, poor devils, suppose our husbands go away and leave us.

LYSISTRATA. Then, as Pherecrates says, we must "flay a skinned dog," that's all.

CALONICÉ. Bah! these proverbs are all idle talk.... But if our husbands drag us by main force into the bedchamber?

LYSISTRATA. Hold on to the door posts.

CALONICÉ. But if they beat us?

LYSISTRATA. Then yield to their wishes, but with a bad grace; there is no pleasure for them, when they do it by force. Besides, there are a thousand ways of tormenting them. Never fear, they'll soon tire of the game; there's no satisfaction for a man, unless the woman shares it.

CALONICÉ. Very well, if you *will* have it so, we agree.

LAMPITO. For ourselves, no doubt we shall persuade our husbands to conclude a fair and honest peace; but there is the Athenian populace, how are we to cure these folk of their warlike frenzy?

LYSISTRATA. Have no fear; we undertake to make our own people hear reason.

LAMPITO. Nay, impossible, so long as they have their trusty ships and the vast treasures stored in the temple of Athené.

LYSISTRATA. Ah! but we have seen to that; this very day the Acropolis will be in our hands. That is the task assigned to the older women; while we are here in council, they are going, under pretence of offering sacrifice, to seize the citadel.

LAMPITO. Well said indeed! so everything is going for the best.

LYSISTRATA. Come, quick, Lampito, and let us bind ourselves by an inviolable oath.

LAMPITO. Recite the terms; we will swear to them.

LYSISTRATA. With pleasure. Where is our Usheress? Now, what are you staring at, pray? Lay this shield on the earth before us, its hollow upwards, and someone bring me the victim's inwards.

CALONICÉ. Lysistrata, say, what oath are we to swear?

LYSISTRATA. What oath? Why, in Aeschylus, they sacrifice a sheep, and swear over a buckler; we will do the same.

CALONICÉ. No, Lysistrata, one cannot swear peace over a buckler, surely.

LYSISTRATA. What other oath do you prefer?

CALONICÉ. Let's take a white horse, and sacrifice it, and swear on its entrails.

LYSISTRATA. But where get a white horse from?

CALONICÉ. Well, what oath shall we take then?

LYSISTRATA. Listen to me. Let's set a great black bowl on the ground; let's sacrifice a skin of Thasian wine into it, and take oath not to add one single drop of water.

LAMPITO. Ah! that's an oath pleases me more than I can say.

LYSISTRATA. Let them bring me a bowl and a skin of wine.

CALONICÉ. Ah! my dears, what a noble big bowl! what a delight 'twill be to empty it!

LYSISTRATA. Set the bowl down on the ground, and lay your hands on the victim.... Almighty goddess, Persuasion, and thou, bowl, boon comrade of joy and merriment, receive this our sacrifice, and be propitious to us poor women!

CALONICÉ. Oh! the fine red blood! how well it flows!

LAMPITO. And what a delicious savour, by the goddesses twain!

LYSISTRATA. Now, my dears, let me swear first, if you please.

CALONICÉ. No, by the goddess of love, let us decide that by lot.

LYSISTRATA. Come then, Lampito, and all of you, put your hands to the bowl; and do you, Calonicé, repeat in the name of all the solemn terms I am going to recite. Then you must all swear, and pledge yourselves by the same promises.—"*I will have naught to do whether with lover or husband....*"

CALONICÉ. *I will have naught to do whether with lover or husband....*

LYSISTRATA. *Albeit he come to me with stiff and standing tool....*

CALONICÉ. *Albeit he come to me with stiff and standing tool....* Oh! Lysistrata, I cannot bear it!

LYSISTRATA. *I will live at home in perfect chastity....*

CALONICÉ. *I will live at home in perfect chastity....*

LYSISTRATA. *Beautifully dressed and wearing a saffron-coloured gown....*

CALONICÉ. *Beautifully dressed and wearing a saffron-coloured gown....*

LYSISTRATA. *To the end I may inspire my husband with the most ardent longings.*

CALONICÉ. *To the end I may inspire my husband with the most ardent longings.*

LYSISTRATA. *Never will I give myself voluntarily....*

CALONICÉ. *Never will I give myself voluntarily....*

LYSISTRATA. *And if he has me by force....*

CALONICÉ. *And if he has me by force....*

LYSISTRATA. *I will be cold as ice, and never stir a limb....*

CALONICÉ. *I will be cold as ice, and never stir a limb....*

LYSISTRATA. *I will not lift my legs in air....*

CALONICÉ. *I will not lift my legs in air....*

LYSISTRATA. *Nor will I crouch with bottom upraised, like carven lions on a knife-handle.*

CALONICÉ. *Nor will I crouch with bottom upraised, like carven lions on a knife-handle.*

LYSISTRATA. *An if I keep my oath, may I be suffered to drink of this wine.*

CALONICÉ. *An if I keep my oath, may I be suffered to drink of this wine.*

LYSISTRATA. *But if I break it, let my bowl be filled with water.*

CALONICÉ. *But if I break it, let my bowl be filled with water.*

LYSISTRATA. Will ye all take this oath?

MYRRHINÉ. Yes, yes!

LYSISTRATA. Then lo! I immolate the victim. (*She drinks.*)

CALONICÉ. Enough, enough, my dear; now let us all drink in turn to cement our friendship.

LAMPITO. Hark! what do those cries mean?

LYSISTRATA. 'Tis what I was telling you; the women have just occupied the Acropolis. So now, Lampito, do you return to Sparta to organize the plot, while your comrades here remain as hostages. For ourselves, let us away to join the rest in the citadel, and let us push the bolts well home.

CALONICÉ. But don't you think the men will march up against us?

LYSISTRATA. I laugh at them. Neither threats nor flames shall force our doors; they shall open only on the conditions I have named.

CALONICÉ. Yes, yes, by the goddess of love! let us keep up our old-time repute for obstinacy and spite.

CHORUS OF OLD MEN. Go easy, Draces, go easy; why, your shoulder is all chafed by these plaguey heavy olive stocks. But forward still, forward, man, as needs must. What unlooked-for things do happen, to be sure, in a long life! Ah! Strymodorus, who would ever have thought it? Here we have the women, who used, for our misfortune, to eat our bread and live in our houses, daring nowadays to lay hands on the holy image of the goddess, to seize the Acropolis and draw bars and bolts to keep any from entering! Come, Philurgus man, let's hurry thither; let's lay our faggots all about the citadel, and on the blazing pile burn with our hands these vile conspiratresses, one and all—and Lycon's wife, Lysistrata, first and foremost! Nay, by Demeter, never will I let 'em laugh at me, whiles I have a breath left in my body. Cleomenes himself, the first who ever seized our citadel, had to quit it to his sore dishonour; spite his Lacedaemonian pride, he had to deliver me up his arms and slink off with a single garment to his back. My word! but he was filthy and ragged! and what an unkempt beard, to be sure! He had not had a bath for six long years! Oh! but that was a mighty siege! Our men were ranged seventeen deep before the gate, and never left their posts, even to sleep. These women, these enemies of Euripides and all the gods, shall I do nothing to hinder their inordinate insolence? else let them tear down my trophies of Marathon. But look ye, to finish our toilsome climb, we have only this last steep bit left to mount. Verily 'tis no easy job without beasts of burden, and how these logs do bruise my shoulder! Still let us on, and blow up our fire and see it does not go out just as we reach our destination. Phew! phew! (*blows the fire*). Oh! dear! what a dreadful smoke! it bites my eyes like a mad dog. It is Lemnos fire for sure, or it would never devour my eyelids like this. Come on, Laches, let's hurry, let's bring succour to the goddess; it's now or never! Phew! phew! (*blows the fire*). Oh! dear! what a confounded smoke!—There now, there's our fire all bright and burning, thank the gods! Now, why not first put down our loads here, then take a vine-branch, light it at the brazier and hurl it at the gate by way of battering-ram? If they don't answer our summons by pulling back the bolts, then we set fire to the woodwork, and the smoke will choke 'em. Ye gods! what a smoke! Pfaugh! Is there never a Samos general will help me unload my burden?—Ah! it shall not gall my shoulder any more. (*Tosses down his wood.*) Come, brazier, do your duty, make the embers flare, that I may kindle a brand; I want to be the first to hurl one. Aid me, heavenly Victory; let us punish for their insolent audacity the women who have seized our citadel, and may we raise a trophy of triumph for success!

CHORUS OF WOMEN. Oh! my dears, methinks I see fire and smoke; can it be a conflagration? Let us hurry all we can. Fly, fly, Nicodicé, ere Calycé and Crityllé perish in the fire, or are stifled in the smoke raised by these accursed old men and their pitiless laws. But, great gods, can it be I come too late? Rising at dawn, I had the utmost trouble to fill this vessel at the fountain. Oh! what a crowd there was, and what a din! What a rattling of water-pots! Servants and slave-girls pushed and thronged me! However, here I have it full at last; and I am running to carry the water to my fellow townswomen, whom our foes are plotting to burn alive. News has been brought us that a company of old, doddering greybeards, loaded with enormous faggots, as if they wanted to heat a furnace, have taken the field, vomiting dreadful threats, crying that they must reduce to ashes these horrible women. Suffer them not, oh! goddess, but, of thy grace, may I see Athens and Greece cured of their warlike folly. 'Tis to this end, oh! thou guardian deity of our city, goddess of the golden crest, that they have seized thy sanctuary. Be their friend and ally, Athené, and if any man hurl against them lighted firebrands, aid us to carry water to extinguish them.

STRATYLLIS. Let me be, I say. Oh! oh! (*She calls for help.*)

CHORUS OF WOMEN. What is this I see, ye wretched old men? Honest and pious folk ye cannot be who act so vilely.

CHORUS OF OLD MEN. Ah, ha! here's something new! a swarm of women stand posted outside to defend the gates!

CHORUS OF WOMEN. Ah! ah! we frighten you, do we; we seem a mighty host, yet you do not see the ten-thousandth part of our sex.

CHORUS OF OLD MEN. Ho, Phaedrias! shall we stop their cackle? Suppose one of us were to break a stick across their backs, eh?

CHORUS OF WOMEN. Let us set down our water-pots on the ground, to be out of the way, if they should dare to offer us violence.

CHORUS OF OLD MEN. Let someone knock out two or three teeth for them, as they did to Bupalus; they won't talk so loud then.

CHORUS OF WOMEN. Come on then; I wait you with unflinching foot, and I will snap off your testicles like a bitch.

CHORUS OF OLD MEN. Silence! ere my stick has cut short your days.

CHORUS OF WOMEN. Now, just you dare to touch Stratyllis with the tip of your finger!

CHORUS OF OLD MEN. And if I batter you to pieces with my fists, what will you do?

CHORUS OF WOMEN. I will tear out your lungs and entrails with my teeth.

CHORUS OF OLD MEN. Oh! what a clever poet is Euripides! how well he says that woman is the most shameless of animals.

CHORUS OF WOMEN. Let's pick up our water-jars again, Rhodippé.

CHORUS OF OLD MEN. Ah! accursed harlot, what do you mean to do here with your water?

CHORUS OF WOMEN. And you, old death-in-life, with your fire? Is it to cremate yourself?

CHORUS OF OLD MEN. I am going to build you a pyre to roast your female friends upon.

CHORUS OF WOMEN. And I,—I am going to put out your fire.

CHORUS OF OLD MEN. You put out my fire—you!

CHORUS OF WOMEN. Yes, you shall soon see.

CHORUS OF OLD MEN. I don't know what prevents me from roasting you with this torch.

CHORUS OF WOMEN. I am getting you a bath ready to clean off the filth.

CHORUS OF OLD MEN. A bath for me, you dirty slut, you!

CHORUS OF WOMEN. Yes, indeed, a nuptial bath—he, he!

CHORUS OF OLD MEN. Do you hear that? What insolence!

CHORUS OF WOMEN. I am a free woman, I tell you.

CHORUS OF OLD MEN. I will make you hold your tongue, never fear!

CHORUS OF WOMEN. Ah, ha! you shall never sit more amongst the heliasts.

CHORUS OF OLD MEN. Burn off her hair for her!

CHORUS OF WOMEN. Water, do your office! (*The women pitch the water in their water-pots over the old men.*)

CHORUS OF OLD MEN. Oh, dear! oh, dear! oh, dear!

CHORUS OF WOMEN. Was it hot?

CHORUS OF OLD MEN. Hot, great gods! Enough, enough!

CHORUS OF WOMEN. I'm watering you, to make you bloom afresh.

CHORUS OF OLD MEN. Alas! I am too dry! Ah, me! how I am trembling with cold!

MAGISTRATE. These women, have they made din enough, I wonder, with their tambourines? bewept Adonis enough upon their terraces? I was listening to the speeches last assembly day, and Demostratus, whom heaven confound! was saying we must all go over to Sicily—and lo! his wife was dancing round repeating: Alas! alas! Adonis, woe is me for Adonis!

Demostratus was saying we must levy hoplites at Zacynthus—and lo! his wife, more than half drunk, was screaming on the house-roof: "Weep, weep for Adonis!"—while that infamous *Mad Ox* was bellowing away on his side.—Do ye not blush, ye women, for your wild and uproarious doings?

CHORUS OF OLD MEN. But you don't know all their effrontery yet! They abused and insulted us; then soused us with the water in their water-pots, and have set us wringing out our clothes, for all the world as if we had bepissed ourselves.

MAGISTRATE. And 'tis well done too, by Poseidon! We men must share the blame of their ill conduct; it is we who teach them to love riot and dissoluteness and sow the seeds of wickedness in their hearts. You see a husband go into a shop: "Look you, jeweller," says he, "you remember the necklace you made for my wife. Well, t'other evening, when she was dancing, the catch came open. Now, I am bound to start for Salamis; will you make it convenient to go up to-night to make her fastening secure?" Another will go to a cobbler, a great, strong fellow, with a great, long tool, and tell him: "The strap of one of my wife's sandals presses her little toe, which is extremely sensitive; come in about midday to supple the thing and stretch it." Now see the results. Take my own case—as a Magistrate I have enlisted rowers; I want money to pay 'em, and lo! the women clap to the door in my face. But why do we stand here with arms crossed? Bring me a crowbar; I'll chastise their insolence!—Ho! there, my fine fellow! (*addressing one of his attendant officers*) what are you gaping at the crows about? looking for a tavern, I suppose, eh? Come, crowbars here, and force open the gates. I will put a hand to the work myself.

LYSISTRATA. No need to force the gates; I am coming out—here I am. And why bolts and bars? What we want here is not bolts and bars and locks, but common sense.

MAGISTRATE. Really, my fine lady! Where is my officer? I want him to tie that woman's hands behind her back.

LYSISTRATA. By Artemis, the virgin goddess! if he touches me with the tip of his finger, officer of the public peace though he be, let him look out for himself!

MAGISTRATE (*to the officer*). How now, are you afraid? Seize her, I tell you, round the body. Two of you at her, and have done with it!

FIRST WOMAN. By Pandrosos! if you lay a hand on her, I'll trample you underfoot till you shit your guts!

MAGISTRATE. Oh, there! my guts! Where is my other officer? Bind that minx first, who speaks so prettily!

SECOND WOMAN. By Phoebé, if you touch her with one finger, you'd better call quick for a surgeon!

MAGISTRATE. What do you mean? Officer, where are you got to? Lay hold of her. Oh! but I'm going to stop your foolishness for you all!

THIRD WOMAN. By the Tauric Artemis, if you go near her, I'll pull out your hair, scream as you like.

MAGISTRATE. Ah! miserable man that I am! My own officers desert me. What ho! are we to let ourselves be bested by a mob of women? Ho! Scythians mine, close up your ranks, and forward!

LYSISTRATA. By the holy goddesses! you'll have to make acquaintance with four companies of women, ready for the fray and well armed to boot.

MAGISTRATE. Forward, Scythians, and bind them!

LYSISTRATA. Forward, my gallant companions; march forth, ye vendors of grain and eggs, garlic and vegetables, keepers of taverns and bakeries, wrench and strike and tear; come, a torrent of invective and insult! (*They beat the officers.*) Enough, enough! now retire, never rob the vanquished!

MAGISTRATE. Here's a fine exploit for my officers!

LYSISTRATA. Ah, ha! so you thought you had only to do with a set of slave-women! you did not know the ardour that fills the bosom of free-born dames.

MAGISTRATE. Ardour! yes, by Apollo, ardour enough—especially for the wine-cup!

CHORUS OF OLD MEN. Sir, sir! what use of words? they are of no avail with wild beasts of this sort. Don't you know how they have just washed us down—and with no very fragrant soap!

CHORUS OF WOMEN. What would you have? You should never have laid rash hands on us. If you start afresh, I'll knock your eyes out. My delight is to stay at home as coy as a young maid, without hurting anybody or moving any more than a milestone; but 'ware the wasps, if you go stirring up the wasps' nest!

CHORUS OF OLD MEN. Ah! great gods! how get the better of these ferocious creatures? 'tis past all bearing! But come, let us try to find out the reason of the dreadful scourge. With what end in view have they seized the citadel of Cranaus, the sacred shrine that is raised upon the inaccessible rock of the Acropolis? Question them; be cautious and not too credulous. 'Twould be culpable negligence not to pierce the mystery, if we may.

MAGISTRATE (*addressing the women*). I would ask you first why ye have barred our gates.

LYSISTRATA. To seize the treasury; no more money, no more war.

MAGISTRATE. Then money is the cause of the War?

LYSISTRATA. And of all our troubles. 'Twas to find occasion to steal that Pisander and all the other agitators were for ever raising revolutions. Well and good! but they'll never get another drachma here.

MAGISTRATE. What do you propose to do then, pray?

LYSISTRATA. You ask me that! Why, we propose to administer the treasury ourselves.

MAGISTRATE. *You* do?

LYSISTRATA. What is there in that to surprise you? Do we not administer the budget of household expenses?

MAGISTRATE. But that is not the same thing.

LYSISTRATA How so—not the same thing?

MAGISTRATE. It is the treasury supplies the expenses of the War.

LYSISTRATA. That's our first principle—no War!

MAGISTRATE. What! and the safety of the city?

LYSISTRATA. We will provide for that.

MAGISTRATE You?

LYSISTRATA Yes, just we.

MAGISTRATE. What a sorry business!

LYSISTRATA. Yes, we're going to save you, whether you will or no.

MAGISTRATE. Oh! the impudence of the creatures!

LYSISTRATA. You seem annoyed! but there, you've got to come to it.

MAGISTRATE. But 'tis the very height of iniquity!

LYSISTRATA. We're going to save you, my man.

MAGISTRATE. But if I don't want to be saved?

LYSISTRATA. Why, all the more reason!

MAGISTRATE. But what a notion, to concern yourselves with questions of Peace and War!

LYSISTRATA. We will explain our idea.

MAGISTRATE. Out with it then; quick, or ... (*threatening her*).

LYSISTRATA. Listen, and never a movement, please!

MAGISTRATE. Oh! it is too much for me! I cannot keep my temper!

A WOMAN. Then look out for yourself; you have more to fear than we have.

MAGISTRATE. Stop your croaking, old crow, you! (*To Lysistrata.*) Now you, say your say.

LYSISTRATA. Willingly. All the long time the War has lasted, we have endured in modest silence all you men did; we never allowed ourselves to open our lips. We were far from satisfied, for we knew how things were going; often in our homes we would hear you discussing, upside down and inside out, some important turn of affairs. Then with sad hearts, but smiling lips, we would ask you: Well, in to-day's Assembly did they vote Peace?—But, "Mind your own business!" the husband would growl, "Hold your tongue, do!" And I would say no more.

A WOMAN. I would not have held my tongue though, not I!

MAGISTRATE. You would have been reduced to silence by blows then.

LYSISTRATA. Well, for my part, I would say no more. But presently I would come to know you had arrived at some fresh decision more fatally foolish than ever. "Ah! my dear man," I would say, "what madness next!" But he would only look at me askance and say: "Just weave your web, do; else your cheeks will smart for hours. War is men's business!"

MAGISTRATE. Bravo! well said indeed!

LYSISTRATA. How now, wretched man? not to let us contend against your follies, was bad enough! But presently we heard you asking out loud in the open street: "Is there never a man left in Athens?" and, "No, not one, not one," you were assured in reply. Then, then we made up our minds without more delay to make common cause to save Greece. Open your ears to our wise counsels and hold your tongues, and we may yet put things on a better footing.

MAGISTRATE. *You* put things indeed! Oh! 'tis too much! The insolence of the creatures! Silence, I say.

LYSISTRATA. Silence yourself!

MAGISTRATE. May I die a thousand deaths ere I obey one who wears a veil!

LYSISTRATA. If that's all that troubles you, here, take my veil, wrap it round your head, and hold your tongue. Then take this basket; put on a girdle, card wool, munch beans. The War shall be women's business.

CHORUS OF WOMEN. Lay aside your water-pots, we will guard them, we will help our friends and companions. For myself, I will never weary of the dance; my knees will never grow stiff with fatigue. I will brave everything with my dear allies, on whom Nature has lavished virtue, grace, boldness, cleverness, and whose wisely directed energy is going to save the State. Oh! my good, gallant Lysistrata, and all my friends, be ever like a bundle of nettles; never let your anger slacken; the winds of fortune blow our way.

LYSISTRATA. May gentle Love and the sweet Cyprian Queen shower seductive charms on our bosoms and all our person. If only we may stir so amorous a lust among the men that their tools stand stiff as sticks, we shall indeed deserve the name of peace-makers among the Greeks.

MAGISTRATE. How will that be, pray?

LYSISTRATA. To begin with, we shall not see you any more running like mad fellows to the Market holding lance in fist.

A WOMAN. That will be something gained, anyway, by the Paphian goddess, it will!

LYSISTRATA. Now we see 'em, mixed up with saucepans and kitchen stuff, armed to the teeth, looking like wild Corybantes!

MAGISTRATE. Why, of course; that's how brave men should do.

LYSISTRATA. Oh! but what a funny sight, to behold a man wearing a Gorgon's-head buckler coming along to buy fish!

A WOMAN. 'Tother day in the Market I saw a phylarch with flowing ringlets; he was a-horseback, and was pouring into his helmet the broth he had just bought at an old dame's stall. There was a Thracian warrior too, who was brandishing his lance like Tereus in the play; he had scared a good woman selling figs into a perfect panic, and was gobbling up all her ripest fruit.

MAGISTRATE. And how, pray, would you propose to restore peace and order in all the countries of Greece?

LYSISTRATA. 'Tis the easiest thing in the world!

MAGISTRATE. Come, tell us how; I am curious to know.

LYSISTRATA. When we are winding thread, and it is tangled, we pass the spool across and through the skein, now this way, now that way; even so, to finish off the War, we shall send embassies hither and thither and everywhere, to disentangle matters.

MAGISTRATE. And 'tis with your yarn, and your skeins, and your spools, you think to appease so many bitter enmities, you silly women?

LYSISTRATA. If only you had common sense, you would always do in politics the same as we do with our yarn.

MAGISTRATE. Come, how is that, eh?

LYSISTRATA. First we wash the yarn to separate the grease and filth; do the same with all bad citizens, sort them out and drive them forth with rods—'tis the refuse of the city. Then for all such as come crowding up in search of employments and offices, we must card them thoroughly; then, to bring them all to the same standard, pitch them pell-mell into the same basket, resident aliens or no, allies, debtors to the State, all mixed up together. Then as for our Colonies, you must think of them as so many isolated hanks; find the ends of the separate threads, draw them to a centre here, wind them into one, make one great hank of the lot, out of which the Public can weave itself a good, stout tunic.

MAGISTRATE. Is it not a sin and a shame to see them carding and winding the State, these women who have neither art nor part in the burdens of the War?

LYSISTRATA. What! wretched man! why, 'tis a far heavier burden to us than to you. In the first place, we bear sons who go off to fight far away from Athens.

MAGISTRATE. Enough said! do not recall sad and sorry memories!

LYSISTRATA. Then secondly, instead of enjoying the pleasures of love and making the best of our youth and beauty, we are left to languish far from our husbands, who are all with the army. But say no more of ourselves; what afflicts me is to see our girls growing old in lonely grief.

MAGISTRATE. Don't the men grow old too?

LYSISTRATA. That is not the same thing. When the soldier returns from the wars, even though he has white hair, he very soon finds a young wife. But a woman has only one summer; if she does not make hay while the sun shines, no one will afterwards have anything to say to her, and she spends her days consulting oracles, that never send her a husband.

MAGISTRATE. But the old man who can still erect his organ ...

LYSISTRATA. But you, why don't you get done with it and die? You are rich; go buy yourself a bier, and I will knead you a honey-cake for Cerberus. Here, take this garland. (*Drenching him with water.*)

FIRST WOMAN. And this one too. (*Drenching him with water.*)

SECOND WOMAN. And these fillets. (*Drenching him with water.*)

LYSISTRATA. What do you lack more? Step aboard the boat; Charon is waiting for you, you're keeping him from pushing off.

MAGISTRATE. To treat me so scurvily! What an insult! I will go show myself to my fellow-magistrates just as I am.

LYSISTRATA. What! are you blaming us for not having exposed you according to custom? Nay, console yourself; we will not fail to offer up the third-day sacrifice for you, first thing in the morning.

CHORUS OF OLD MEN. Awake, friends of freedom; let us hold ourselves aye ready to act. I suspect a mighty peril; I foresee another Tyranny like Hippias'. I am sore afraid the Laconians assembled here with Cleisthenes have, by a stratagem of war, stirred up these women, enemies of the gods, to seize upon our treasury and the funds whereby I lived. Is it not a sin and a shame for them to interfere in advising the citizens, to prate of shields and lances, and to ally themselves with Laconians, fellows I trust no more than I would so many famished wolves? The whole thing, my friends, is nothing else but an attempt to re-establish Tyranny. But I will never submit; I will be on my guard for the future; I will always carry a blade hidden under myrtle boughs; I will post myself in the Public Square under arms, shoulder to shoulder with Aristogiton; and now, to make a start, I must just break a few of that cursed old jade's teeth yonder.

CHORUS OF WOMEN. Nay, never play the brave man, else when you go back home, your own mother won't know you. But, dear friends and allies, first let us lay our burdens down; then, citizens all, hear what I have to say. I have useful counsel to give our city, which deserves it well at my hands for the brilliant distinctions it has lavished on my girlhood. At seven years of age, I was bearer of the sacred vessels; at ten, I pounded barley for the altar of Athené; next, clad in a robe of yellow silk, I was *little bear* to Artemis at the Brauronia; presently, grown a tall, handsome maiden, they put a necklace of dried figs about my neck, and I was Basket-Bearer. So surely I am bound to give my best advice to Athens. What matters that I was born a woman, if I can cure your misfortunes? I pay my share of tolls and taxes, by giving men to the State. But you, you miserable greybeards, you contribute nothing to the public charges; on the contrary, you have wasted the treasure of our forefathers, as it was called, the treasure amassed in the days of the Persian Wars. You pay nothing at all in return; and into the bargain you endanger our lives and liberties by your mistakes. Have you one word to say for yourselves? ... Ah! don't irritate me, you there, or I'll lay my slipper across your jaws; and it's pretty heavy.

CHORUS OF OLD MEN. Outrage upon outrage! things are going from bad to worse. Let us punish the minxes, every one of us that has a man's appendages to boast of. Come, off with our tunics, for a man must savour of manhood; come, my friends, let us strip naked from head to foot. Courage, I say, we who in our day garrisoned Lipsydrion; let us be young again, and shake off eld. If we give them the least hold over us, 'tis all up! their audacity will know no bounds! We shall see them building ships, and fighting sea-fights, like Artemisia; nay, if they want to mount and ride as cavalry, we had best cashier the knights, for indeed women excel in riding, and have a fine, firm seat for the gallop. Just think of all those squadrons of Amazons Micon has painted for us engaged in hand-to-hand combat with men. Come then, we must e'en fit collars to all these willing necks.

CHORUS OF WOMEN. By the blessed goddesses, if you anger me, I will let loose the beast of my evil passions, and a very hailstorm of blows will set you yelling for help. Come, dames, off tunics, and quick's the word; women must scent the savour of women in the throes of passion.... Now just you dare to measure strength with me, old greybeard, and I warrant you you'll never eat garlic or black beans more. No, not a word! my anger is at boiling point, and I'll do with you what the beetle did with the eagle's eggs. I laugh at your threats, so long as I have on my side Lampito here, and the noble Theban, my dear Ismenia.... Pass decree on decree, you can do us no hurt, you wretch abhorred of all your fellows. Why, only yesterday, on occasion of the feast of Hecaté, I asked my neighbours of Boeotia for one of their daughters for whom my girls have a lively liking—a fine, fat eel to wit; and if they did not refuse, all along of your silly decrees! We shall never cease to suffer the like, till someone gives you a neat trip-up and breaks your neck for you!

CHORUS OF WOMEN (addressing Lysistrata). You, Lysistrata, you who are leader of our glorious enterprise, why do I see you coming towards me with so gloomy an air?

LYSISTRATA. 'Tis the behaviour of these naughty women, 'tis the female heart and female weakness so discourages me.

CHORUS OF WOMEN. Tell us, tell us, what is it?

LYSISTRATA. I only tell the simple truth.

CHORUS OF WOMEN. What has happened so disconcerting; come, tell your friends.

LYSISTRATA. Oh! the thing is so hard to tell—yet so impossible to conceal.

CHORUS OF WOMEN. Nay, never seek to hide any ill that has befallen our cause.

LYSISTRATA. To blurt it out in a word—we are in heat!

CHORUS OF WOMEN. Oh! Zeus, oh! Zeus!

LYSISTRATA. What use calling upon Zeus? The thing is even as I say. I cannot stop them any longer from lusting after the men. They are all for deserting. The first I caught was slipping out by the postern gate near the cave of Pan; another was letting herself down by a rope and pulley; a third was busy preparing her escape; while a fourth, perched on a bird's back, was just taking wing for Orsilochus' house, when I seized her by the hair. One and all, they are inventing excuses to be off home. Look! there goes one, trying to get out! Halloa there! whither away so fast?

FIRST WOMAN. I want to go home; I have some Miletus wool in the house, which is getting all eaten up by the worms.

LYSISTRATA. Bah! you and your worms! go back, I say!

FIRST WOMAN. I will return immediately, I swear I will by the two goddesses! I only have just to spread it out on the bed.

LYSISTRATA. You shall not do anything of the kind! I say, you shall not go.

FIRST WOMAN. Must I leave my wool to spoil then?

LYSISTRATA. Yes, if need be.

SECOND WOMAN. Unhappy woman that I am! Alas for my flax! I've left it at home unstript!

LYSISTRATA. So, here's another trying to escape to go home and strip her flax forsooth!

SECOND WOMAN. Oh! I swear by the goddess of light, the instant I have put it in condition I will come straight back.

LYSISTRATA. You shall do nothing of the kind! If once you began, others would want to follow suit.

THIRD WOMAN. Oh! goddess divine, Ilithyia, patroness of women in labour, stay, stay the birth, till I have reached a spot less hallowed than Athene's Mount!

LYSISTRATA. What mean you by these silly tales?

THIRD WOMAN. I am going to have a child—now, this minute.

LYSISTRATA. But you were not pregnant yesterday!

THIRD WOMAN. Well, I am to-day. Oh! let me go in search of the midwife, Lysistrata, quick, quick!

LYSISTRATA. What is this fable you are telling me? Ah! what have you got there so hard?

THIRD WOMAN. A male child.

LYSISTRATA. No, no, by Aphrodité! nothing of the sort! Why, it feels like something hollow—a pot or a kettle. Oh! you baggage, if you have not got the sacred helmet of Pallas—and you said you were with child!

THIRD WOMAN. And so I am, by Zeus, I am!

LYSISTRATA. Then why this helmet, pray?

THIRD WOMAN. For fear my pains should seize me in the Acropolis; I mean to lay my eggs in this helmet, as the doves do.

LYSISTRATA. Excuses and pretences every word! the thing's as clear as daylight. Anyway, you must stay here now till the fifth day, your day of purification.

THIRD WOMAN. I cannot sleep any more in the Acropolis, now I have seen the snake that guards the Temple.

FOURTH WOMAN. Ah! and those confounded owls with their dismal hooting! I cannot get a wink of rest, and I'm just dying of fatigue.

LYSISTRATA. You wicked women, have done with your falsehoods! You want your husbands, that's plain enough. But don't you think they want you just as badly? They are spending dreadful nights, oh! I know that well enough. But hold out, my dears, hold out! A little more patience, and the victory will be ours. An Oracle promises us success, if only we remain united. Shall I repeat the words?

FIRST WOMAN. Yes, tell us what the Oracle declares.

LYSISTRATA. Silence then! Now—"Whenas the swallows, fleeing before the hoopoes, shall have all flocked together in one place, and shall refrain them from all amorous commerce, then will be the end of all the ills of life; yea, and Zeus, which doth thunder in the skies, shall set above what was erst below...."

CHORUS OF WOMEN. What! shall the men be underneath?

LYSISTRATA. "But if dissension do arise among the swallows, and they take wing from the holy Temple, 'twill be said there is never a more wanton bird in all the world."

CHORUS OF WOMEN. Ye gods! the prophecy is clear. Nay, never let us be cast down by calamity! let us be brave to bear, and go back to our posts. 'Twere shameful indeed not to trust the promises of the Oracle.

CHORUS OF OLD MEN. I want to tell you a fable they used to relate to me when I was a little boy. This is it: Once upon a time there was a young man called Melanion, who hated the thought of marriage so sorely that he fled away to the wilds. So he dwelt in the mountains, wove himself nets, kept a dog and caught hares. He never, never came back, he had such a horror of women. As chaste as Melanion, we loathe the jades just as much as he did.

AN OLD MAN. You dear old woman, I would fain kiss you.

A WOMAN. I will set you crying without onions.

OLD MAN. ... And give you a sound kicking.

OLD WOMAN. Ah, ha! what a dense forest you have there! (*Pointing.*)

OLD MAN. So was Myronides one of the best-bearded of men o' this side; his backside was all black, and he terrified his enemies as much as Phormio.

CHORUS OF WOMEN. I want to tell you a fable too, to match yours about Melanion. Once there was a certain man called Timon, a tough customer, and a whimsical, a true son of the Furies, with a face that seemed to glare out of a thorn-bush. He withdrew from the world because he couldn't abide bad men, after vomiting a thousand curses at 'em. He had a holy horror of ill-conditioned fellows, but he was mighty tender towards women.

A WOMAN. Suppose I up and broke your jaw for you!

AN OLD MAN. I am not a bit afraid of you.

A WOMAN. Suppose I let fly a good kick at you?

OLD MAN. I should see your backside then.

WOMAN. You would see that, for all my age, it is very well attended to, and all fresh singed smooth.

LYSISTRATA. Ho there! come quick, come quick!

FIRST WOMAN. What is it? Why these cries?

LYSISTRATA. A man! a man! I see him approaching all afire with the flames of love. Oh! divine Queen of Cyprus, Paphos and Cythera, I pray you still be propitious to our emprise.

FIRST WOMAN. Where is he, this unknown foe?

LYSISTRATA. Yonder—beside the Temple of Demeter.

FIRST WOMAN. Yes, indeed, I see him; but who is it?

LYSISTRATA. Look, look! does any of you recognize him?

FIRST WOMAN. I do, I do! 'tis my husband Cinesias.

LYSISTRATA. To work then! Be it your task to inflame and torture and torment him. Seductions, caresses, provocations, refusals, try every means! Grant every favour,—always excepting what is forbidden by our oath on the wine-bowl.

MYRRHINÉ. Have no fear, I undertake the work.

LYSISTRATA. Well, I will stay here to help you cajole the man and set his passions aflame. The rest of you, withdraw.

CINESIAS. Alas! alas! how I am tortured by spasm and rigid convulsion! Oh! I am racked on the wheel!

LYSISTRATA. Who is this that dares to pass our lines?

CINESIAS. It is I.

LYSISTRATA. What, a man?

CINESIAS. Yes, no doubt about it, a man!

LYSISTRATA. Begone!

CINESIAS. But who are you that thus repulses me?

LYSISTRATA. The sentinel of the day.

CINESIAS. By all the gods, call Myrrhiné hither.

LYSISTRATA. Call Myrrhiné hither, quotha? And pray, who are you?

CINESIAS. I am her husband, Cinesias, son of Peon.

LYSISTRATA. Ah! good day, my dear friend. Your name is not unknown amongst us. Your wife has it for ever on her lips; and she never touches an egg or an apple without saying: "'Twill be for Cinesias."

CINESIAS. Really and truly?

LYSISTRATA. Yes, indeed, by Aphrodité! And if we fall to talking of men, quick your wife declares: "Oh! all the rest, they're good for nothing compared with Cinesias."

CINESIAS. Oh! I beseech you, go and call her to me.

LYSISTRATA. And what will you give me for my trouble?

CINESIAS.

This, if you like (*handling his tool*). I will give you what I have there!

LYSISTRATA. Well, well, I will tell her to come.

CINESIAS. Quick, oh! be quick! Life has no more charms for me since she left my house. I am sad, sad, when I go indoors; it all seems so empty; my victuals have lost their savour. Desire is eating out my heart!

MYRRHINÉ. I love him, oh! I love him; but he won't let himself be loved. No! I shall not come.

CINESIAS. Myrrhiné, my little darling Myrrhiné, what are you saying? Come down to me quick.

MYRRHINÉ. No indeed, not I.

CINESIAS. I call you, Myrrhiné, Myrrhiné; will you not come?

MYRRHINÉ. Why should you call me? You do not want me.

CINESIAS. Not want you! Why, my weapon stands stiff with desire!

MYRRHINÉ. Good-bye.

CINESIAS. Oh! Myrrhiné, Myrrhiné, in our child's name, hear me; at any rate hear the child! Little lad, call your mother.

CHILD. Mammy, mammy, mammy!

CINESIAS. There, listen! Don't you pity the poor child? It's six days now you've never washed and never fed the child.

MYRRHINÉ. Poor darling, your father takes mighty little care of you!

CINESIAS. Come down, dearest, come down for the child's sake.

MYRRHINÉ. Ah! what a thing it is to be a mother! Well, well, we must come down, I suppose.

CINESIAS. Why, how much younger and prettier she looks! And how she looks at me so lovingly! Her cruelty and scorn only redouble my passion.

MYRRHINÉ. You are as sweet as your father is provoking! Let me kiss you, my treasure, mother's darling!

CINESIAS. Ah! what a bad thing it is to let yourself be led away by other women! Why give me such pain and suffering, and yourself into the bargain?

MYRRHINÉ. Hands off, sir!

CINESIAS. Everything is going to rack and ruin in the house.

MYRRHINÉ. I don't care.

CINESIAS. But your web that's all being pecked to pieces by the cocks and hens, don't you care for that?

MYRRHINÉ. Precious little.

CINESIAS. And Aphrodite, whose mysteries you have not celebrated for so long? Oh! won't you come back home?

MYRRHINÉ. No, at least, not till a sound Treaty put an end to the War.

CINESIAS. Well, if you wish it so much, why, we'll make it, your Treaty.

MYRRHINÉ. Well and good! When that's done, I will come home. Till then, I am bound by an oath.

CINESIAS. At any rate, let's have a short time together.

MYRRHINÉ. No, no, no! ... all the same I cannot say I don't love you.

CINESIAS. You love me? Then why refuse what I ask, my little girl, my sweet Myrrhiné.

MYRRHINÉ. You must be joking! What, before the child!

CINESIAS. Manes, carry the lad home. There, you see, the child is gone; there's nothing to hinder us; let us to work!

MYRRHINÉ. But, miserable man, where, where are we to do it?

CINESIAS. In the cave of Pan; nothing could be better.

MYRRHINÉ. But how to purify myself, before going back into the citadel?

CINESIAS. Nothing easier! you can wash at the Clepsydra.

MYRRHINÉ. But my oath? Do you want me to perjure myself?

CINESIAS. I take all responsibility; never make yourself anxious.

MYRRHINÉ. Well, I'll be off, then, and find a bed for us.

CINESIAS. Oh! 'tis not worth while; we can lie on the ground surely.

MYRRHINÉ. No, no! bad man as you are, I don't like your lying on the bare earth.

CINESIAS. Ah! how the dear girl loves me!

MYRRHINÉ (*coming back with a bed*). Come, get to bed quick; I am going to undress. But, plague take it, we must get a mattress.

CINESIAS. A mattress! Oh! no, never mind!

MYRRHINÉ. No, by Artemis! lie on the bare sacking, never! That were too squalid.

CINESIAS. A kiss!

MYRRHINÉ. Wait a minute!

CINESIAS. Oh! by the great gods, be quick back!

MYRRHINÉ (*coming back with a mattress*). Here is a mattress. Lie down, I am just going to undress. But, but you've got no pillow.

CINESIAS. I don't want one, no, no.

MYRRHINÉ. But I do.

CINESIAS. Oh! dear, oh, dear! they treat my poor penis for all the world like Heracles.

MYRRHINÉ (*coming back with a pillow*). There, lift your head, dear!

CINESIAS. That's really everything.

MYRRHINÉ. Is it everything, I wonder.

CINESIAS. Come, my treasure.

MYRRHINÉ. I am just unfastening my girdle. But remember what you promised me about making Peace; mind you keep your word.

CINESIAS. Yes, yes, upon my life I will.

MYRRHINÉ. Why, you have no blanket.

CINESIAS. Great Zeus! what matter of that? 'tis you I want to fuck.

MYRRHINÉ Never fear—directly, directly! I'll be back in no time.

CINESIAS. The woman will kill me with her blankets!

MYRRHINÉ (*coming back with a blanket*). Now, get up for one moment.

CINESIAS. But I tell you, our friend here is up—all stiff and ready!

MYRRHINÉ. Would you like me to scent you?

CINESIAS. No, by Apollo, no, please!

MYRRHINÉ. Yes, by Aphrodité, but I will, whether you wish it or no.

CINESIAS. Ah! great Zeus, may she soon be done!

MYRRHINÉ (*coming back with a flask of perfume*). Hold out your hand; now rub it in.

CINESIAS. Oh! in Apollo's name, I don't much like the smell of it; but perhaps 'twill improve when it's well rubbed in. It does not somehow smack of the marriage bed!

MYRRHINÉ. There, what a scatterbrain I am; if I have not brought Rhodian perfumes!

CINESIAS. Never mind, dearest, let be now.

MYRRHINÉ. You are joking!

CINESIAS. Deuce take the man who first invented perfumes, say I!

MYRRHINÉ (*coming back with another flask*). Here, take this bottle.

CINESIAS. I have a better all ready for your service, darling. Come, you provoking creature, to bed with you, and don't bring another thing.

MYRRHINÉ. Coming, coming; I'm just slipping off my shoes. Dear boy, will you vote for peace?

CINESIAS. I'll think about it. (*Myrrhiné runs away.*) I'm a dead man, she is killing me! She has gone, and left me in torment! I must have someone to fuck, I must! Ah me! the loveliest of women has choused and cheated me. Poor little lad (*addressing his penis*), how am I to give you what you want so badly? Where is Cynalopex? quick, man, get him a nurse, do!

CHORUS OF OLD MEN. Poor, miserable wretch, baulked in your amorousness! what tortures are yours! Ah! you fill me with pity. Could any man's back and loins stand such a strain? His organ stands stiff and rigid, and there's never a wench to help him!

CINESIAS. Ye gods in heaven, what pains I suffer!

CHORUS OF OLD MEN. Well, there it is; 'tis her doing, that abandoned hussy!

CINESIAS. Nay, nay! rather say that sweetest, dearest darling.

CHORUS OF OLD MEN. That dearest darling? no, no, that hussy, say I! Zeus, thou god of the skies, canst not let loose a hurricane, to sweep them all up into the air, and whirl 'em round, then drop 'em down crash! and impale them on the point of his weapon!

A HERALD. Say, where shall I find the Senate and the Prytanes? I am bearer of despatches.

MAGISTRATE. But are you a man or a Priapus, pray?

HERALD. Oh! but he's mighty simple. I am a herald, of course, I swear I am, and I come from Sparta about making peace.

MAGISTRATE. But look, you are hiding a lance under your clothes, surely.

HERALD. No, nothing of the sort.

MAGISTRATE. Then why do you turn away like that, and hold your cloak out from your body? Have you gotten swellings in the groin with your journey?

HERALD. By the twin brethren! the man's an old maniac.

MAGISTRATE. Ah, ha! my fine lad, why I can see it standing, oh fie!

HERALD. I tell you no! but enough of this foolery.

MAGISTRATE. Well, what is it you have there then?

HERALD. A Lacedaemonian 'skytalé.'

MAGISTRATE. Oh, indeed, a 'skytalé,' is it? Well, well, speak out frankly; I know all about these matters. How are things going at Sparta now?

HERALD. Why, everything is turned upside down at Sparta; and all the allies are half dead with lusting. We simply must have Pellené.

MAGISTRATE. What is the reason of it all? Is it the god Pan's doing?

HERALD. No, but Lampito's and the Spartan women's, acting at her instigation; they have denied the men all access to their cunts.

MAGISTRATE. But whatever do you do?

HERALD. We are at our wits' end; we walk bent double, just as if we were carrying lanterns in a wind. The jades have sworn we shall not so much as touch their cunts till we have all agreed to conclude peace.

MAGISTRATE. Ha, ha! So I see now, 'tis a general conspiracy embracing all Greece. Go you back to Sparta and bid them send Envoys with plenary powers to treat for peace. I will urge our Senators myself to name Plenipotentiaries from us; and to persuade them, why, I will show them this. (*Pointing to his erect penis.*)

HERALD. What could be better? I fly at your command.

CHORUS OF OLD MEN. No wild beast is there, no flame of fire, more fierce and untameable than woman; the panther is less savage and shameless.

CHORUS OF WOMEN. And yet you dare to make war upon me, wretch, when you might have me for your most faithful friend and ally.

CHORUS OF OLD MEN. Never, never can my hatred cease towards women.

CHORUS OF WOMEN. Well, please yourself. Still I cannot bear to leave you all naked as you are; folks would laugh at me. Come, I am going to put this tunic on you.

CHORUS OF OLD MEN. You are right, upon my word! it was only in my confounded fit of rage I took it off.

CHORUS OF WOMEN. Now at any rate you look like a man, and they won't make fun of you. Ah! if you had not offended me so badly, I would take out that nasty insect you have in your eye for you.

CHORUS OF OLD MEN. Ah! so that's what was annoying me so! Look, here's a ring, just remove the insect, and show it me. By Zeus! it has been hurting my eye this ever so long.

CHORUS OF WOMEN. Well, I agree, though your manners are not over and above pleasant. Oh! what a huge great gnat! just look! It's from Tricorysus, for sure.

CHORUS OF OLD MEN. A thousand thanks! the creature was digging a regular well in my eye; now it's gone, my tears flow freely.

CHORUS OF WOMEN. I will wipe them for you—bad, naughty man though you are. Now, just one kiss.

CHORUS OF OLD MEN. No—a kiss, certainly not!

CHORUS OF WOMEN. Just one, whether you like it or not.

CHORUS OF OLD MEN. Oh! those confounded women! how they do cajole us! How true the saying: "'Tis impossible to live with the baggages, impossible to live without 'em"! Come, let us agree for the future not to regard each other any more as enemies; and to clinch the bargain, let us sing a choric song.

CHORUS OF WOMEN. We desire, Athenians, to speak ill of no man; but on the contrary to say much good of everyone, and to *do* the like. We have had enough of misfortunes and calamities. Is there any, man or woman, wants a bit of money—two or three minas or so; well, our purse is full. If only peace is concluded, the borrower will not have to pay back. Also I'm inviting to supper a few Carystian friends, who are excellently well qualified. I have still a drop of good soup left, and a young porker I'm going to kill, and the flesh will be sweet and tender. I shall expect you at my house to-day; but first away to the baths with you, you and your children; then come all of you, ask no one's leave, but walk straight up, as if you were at home; never fear, the door will be ... shut in your faces!

CHORUS OF OLD MEN. Ah! here come the Envoys from Sparta with their long flowing beards; why, you would think they wore a cage between their thighs. (*Enter the Lacedaemonian Envoys.*) Hail to you, first of all, Laconians; then tell us how you fare.

A LACONIAN. No need for many words; you see what a state we are in.

CHORUS OF OLD MEN. Alas! the situation grows more and more strained! the intensity of the thing is just frightful.

LACONIAN. 'Tis beyond belief. But to work! summon your Commissioners, and let us patch up the best peace we may.

CHORUS OF OLD MEN. Ah! our men too, like wrestlers in the arena, cannot endure a rag over their bellies; 'tis an athlete's malady, which only exercise can remedy.

AN ATHENIAN. Can anybody tell us where Lysistrata is? Surely she will have some compassion on our condition.

CHORUS OF OLD MEN. Look! 'tis the very same complaint. (*Addressing the Athenian.*) Don't you feel of mornings a strong nervous tension?

ATHENIAN. Yes, and a dreadful, dreadful torture it is! Unless peace is made very soon, we shall find no resource but to fuck Clisthenes.

CHORUS OF OLD MEN. Take my advice, and put on your clothes again; one of the fellows who mutilated the Hermae might see you.

ATHENIAN. You are right.

LACONIAN. Quite right. There, I will slip on my tunic.

ATHENIAN. Oh! what a terrible state we are in! Greeting to you, Laconian fellow-sufferers.

LACONIAN (*addressing one of his countrymen*). Ah! my boy, what a thing it would have been if these fellows had seen us just now when our tools were on full stand!

ATHENIAN. Speak out, Laconians, what is it brings you here?

LACONIAN. We have come to treat for peace.

ATHENIAN. Well said; we are of the same mind. Better call Lysistrata then; she is the only person will bring us to terms.

LACONIAN. Yes, yes—and Lysistratus into the bargain, if you will.

CHORUS OF OLD MEN. Needless to call her; she has heard your voices, and here she comes.

ATHENIAN. Hail, boldest and bravest of womankind! The time is come to show yourself in turn uncompromising and conciliatory, exacting and yielding, haughty and condescending. Call up all your skill and artfulness. Lo! the foremost men in Hellas, seduced by your fascinations, are agreed to entrust you with the task of ending their quarrels.

LYSISTRATA. 'Twill be an easy task—if only they refrain from mutual indulgence in masculine love; if they do, I shall know the fact at once. Now, where is the gentle goddess Peace? Lead hither the Laconian Envoys. But, look you, no roughness or violence; our husbands always behaved so boorishly. Bring them to me with smiles, as women should. If any refuse to give you his hand, then catch him by the penis and draw him politely forward. Bring up the Athenians too; you may take them just how you will. Laconians, approach; and you, Athenians, on my other side. Now hearken all! I am but a woman; but I have good common sense; Nature has dowered me with discriminating judgment, which I have yet further developed, thanks to the wise teachings of my father and the elders of the city. First I must bring a reproach against you that applies equally to both sides. At Olympia, and Thermopylae, and Delphi, and a score of other places too numerous to mention, you celebrate before the same altars ceremonies common to all Hellenes; yet you go cutting each other's throats, and sacking Hellenic cities, when all the while the Barbarian is yonder threatening you! That is my first point.

ATHENIAN. Ah, ah! concupiscence is killing me!

LYSISTRATA. Now 'tis to you I address myself, Laconians. Have you forgotten how Periclides, your own countryman, sat a suppliant before our altars? How pale he was in his purple robes! He had come to crave an army of us; 'twas the time when Messenia was pressing you sore, and the Sea-god was shaking the earth. Cimon marched to your aid at the head of four thousand hoplites, and saved Lacedaemon. And, after such a service as that, you ravage the soil of your benefactors!

ATHENIAN. They do wrong, very wrong, Lysistrata.

LACONIAN. We do wrong, very wrong. Ah! great gods! what lovely thighs she has!

LYSISTRATA. And now a word to the Athenians. Have you no memory left of how, in the days when ye wore the tunic of slaves, the Laconians came, spear in hand, and slew a host of Thessalians and partisans of Hippias the Tyrant? They, and they only, fought on your side on that eventful day; they delivered you from despotism, and thanks to them our Nation could change the short tunic of the slave for the long cloak of the free man.

LACONIAN. I have never seen a woman of more gracious dignity.

ATHENIAN. I have never seen a woman with a finer cunt!

LYSISTRATA. Bound by such ties of mutual kindness, how can you bear to be at war? Stop, stay the hateful strife, be reconciled; what hinders you?

LACONIAN. We are quite ready, if they will give us back our rampart.

LYSISTRATA. What rampart, my dear man?

LACONIAN. Pylos, which we have been asking for and craving for ever so long.

ATHENIAN. In the Sea-god's name, you shall never have it!

LYSISTRATA. Agree, my friends, agree.

ATHENIAN. But then what city shall we be able to stir up trouble in?

LYSISTRATA. Ask for another place in exchange.

ATHENIAN. Ah! that's the ticket! Well, to begin with, give us Echinus, the Maliac gulf adjoining, and the two legs of Megara.

LACONIAN. Oh! surely, surely not all that, my dear sir.

LYSISTRATA. Come to terms; never make a difficulty of two legs more or less!

ATHENIAN. Well, I'm ready now to off coat and cultivate my land.

LACONIAN. And I too, to dung it to start with.

LYSISTRATA. That's just what you shall do, once peace is signed. So, if you really want to make it, go consult your allies about the matter.

ATHENIAN. What allies, I should like to know? Why, we are *all* on the stand; not one but is mad to be fucking. What we all want, is to be abed with our wives; how should our allies fail to second our project?

LACONIAN. And ours the same, for certain sure!

ATHENIANS. The Carystians first and foremost, by the gods!

LYSISTRATA. Well said, indeed! Now be off to purify yourselves for entering the Acropolis, where the women invite you to supper; we will empty our provision baskets to do you honour. At table, you will exchange oaths and pledges; then each man will go home with his wife.

ATHENIAN. Come along then, and as quick as may be.

LACONIAN. Lead on; I'm your man.

ATHENIAN. Quick, quick's the word, say I.

CHORUS OF WOMEN. Embroidered stuffs, and dainty tunics, and flowing gowns, and golden ornaments, everything I have, I offer them you with all my heart; take them all for your children, for your girls, against they are chosen "basket-bearers" to the goddess. I invite you every one to enter, come in and choose whatever you will; there is nothing so well fastened, you cannot break the seals, and carry away the contents. Look about you everywhere ... you won't find a blessed thing, unless you have sharper eyes than mine. And if any of you lacks corn to feed his slaves and his young and numerous family, why, I have a few grains of wheat at home; let him take what I have to give, a big twelve-pound loaf included. So let my poorer neighbours all come with bags and wallets; my man, Manes, shall give them corn; but I warn them not to come near my door, or—beware the dog!

A MARKET-LOUNGER. I say, you, open the door!

A SLAVE. Go your way, I tell you. Why, bless me, they're sitting down now; I shall have to singe 'em with my torch to make 'em stir! What an impudent lot of fellows!

MARKET-LOUNGER. I don't mean to budge.

SLAVE. Well, as you *must* stop, and I don't want to offend you—but you'll see some queer sights.

MARKET-LOUNGER. Well and good, I've no objection.

SLAVE. No, no, you must be off—or I'll tear your hair out, I will; be off, I say, and don't annoy the Laconian Envoys; they're just coming out from the banquet-hall.

AN ATHENIAN. Such a merry banquet I've never seen before! The Laconians were simply charming. After the drink is in, why, we're all wise men, all. It's only natural, to be sure, for sober, we're all fools. Take my advice, my fellow-countrymen, our Envoys should always be drunk. We go to Sparta; we enter the city sober; why, we must be picking a quarrel directly. We don't understand what they say to us, we imagine a lot they don't say at all, and we report home all wrong, all topsy-turvy. But, look you, to-day it's quite different; we're enchanted whatever happens; instead of Clitagoras, they might sing us Telamon, and we should clap our hands just the same. A perjury or two into the bargain, la! what does that matter to merry companions in their cups?

SLAVE. But here they are back again! Will you begone, you loafing scoundrels.

MARKET-LOUNGER. Ah ha! here's the company coming out already.

A LACONIAN. My dear, sweet friend, come, take your flute in hand; I would fain dance and sing my best in honour of the Athenians and our noble selves.

AN ATHENIAN. Yes, take your flute, i' the gods' name. What a delight to see him dance!

CHORUS OF LACONIANS. Oh Mnemosyné! inspire these men, inspire my muse who knows our exploits and those of the Athenians. With what a godlike ardour did they swoop down at Artemisium on the ships of the Medes! What a glorious victory was that! For the soldiers of Leonidas, they were like fierce wild-boars whetting their tushes. The sweat ran down their faces, and drenched all their limbs, for verily the Persians were as many as the sands of the seashore. Oh! Artemis, huntress queen, whose arrows pierce the denizens of the woods, virgin goddess, be thou favourable to the Peace we here conclude; through thee may our hearts be long united! May this treaty draw close for ever the bonds of a happy friendship! No more wiles and stratagems! Aid us, oh! aid us, maiden huntress!

LYSISTRATA. All is for the best; and now, Laconians, take your wives away home with you, and you, Athenians, yours. May husband live happily with wife, and wife with husband. Dance, dance, to celebrate our bliss, and let us be heedful to avoid like mistakes for the future.

CHORUS OF ATHENIANS Appear, appear, dancers, and the Graces with you! Let us invoke, one and all, Artemis, and her heavenly brother, gracious Apollo, patron of the dance, and Dionysus, whose eye darts flame, as he steps forward surrounded by the Maenad maids, and Zeus, who wields the flashing lightning, and his august, thrice-blessed spouse, the Queen of Heaven! These let us invoke, and all the other gods, calling all the inhabitants of the skies to witness the noble Peace now concluded under the fond auspices of Aphrodité. Io Paean! Io Paean! dance, leap, as in honour of a victory won. Evoé! Evoé! And you, our Laconian guests, sing us a new and inspiring strain!

CHORUS OF LACONIANS. Leave once more, oh! leave once more the noble height of Taygetus, oh! Muse of Lacedaemon, and join us in singing the praises of Apollo of Amyclae, and Athena of the Brazen House, and the gallant twin sons of Tyndarus, who practise arms on the banks of Eurotas river. Haste, haste hither with nimble-footed pace, let us sing Sparta, the city that delights in choruses divinely sweet and graceful dances, when our maidens bound lightly by the river side, like frolicsome fillies, beating the ground with rapid steps and shaking their long locks in the wind, as Bacchantes wave their wands in the wild revels of the Wine-god. At their head, oh! chaste and beauteous goddess, daughter of Latona, Artemis, do thou lead the song and dance. A fillet binding thy waving tresses, appear in thy loveliness; leap like a fawn; strike thy divine hands together to animate the dance, and aid us to renown the valiant goddess of battles, great Athené of the Brazen House!

FINIS OF "LYSISTRATA"

The Clouds

Introduction

The satire in this, one of the best known of all Aristophanes' comedies, is directed against the new schools of philosophy, or perhaps we should rather say dialectic, which had lately been introduced, mostly from abroad, at Athens. The doctrines held up to ridicule are those of the 'Sophists'—such men as Thrasymachus from Chalcedon in Bithynia, Gorgias from Leontini in Sicily, Protagoras from Abdera in Thrace, and other foreign scholars and rhetoricians who had flocked to Athens as the intellectual centre of the Hellenic world. Strange to say, Socrates of all people, the avowed enemy and merciless critic of these men and their methods, is taken as their representative, and personally attacked with pitiless raillery. Presumably this was merely because he was the most prominent and noteworthy teacher and thinker of the day, while his grotesque personal appearance and startling eccentricities of behaviour gave a ready handle to caricature. Neither the author nor his audience took the trouble, or were likely to take the trouble, to discriminate nicely; there was, of course, a general resemblance between the Socratic 'elenchos' and the methods of the new practitioners of dialectic; and this was enough for stage purposes. However unjustly, Socrates is taken as typical of the newfangled sophistical teachers, just as in 'The Acharnians' Lamachus, with his Gorgon shield, is introduced as representative of the War party, though that general was not specially responsible for the continuance of hostilities more than anybody else.

Aristophanes' point of view, as a member of the aristocratical party and a fine old Conservative, is that these Sophists, as the professors of the new education had come to be called, and Socrates as their protagonist, were insincere and dangerous innovators, corrupting morals, persuading young men to despise the old-fashioned, home-grown virtues of the State and teaching a system of false and pernicious tricks of verbal fence whereby anything whatever could be proved, and the worse be made to seem the better—provided always sufficient payment were forthcoming. True, Socrates refused to take money from his pupils, and made it his chief reproach against the lecturing Sophists that they received fees; but what of that? The

Comedian cannot pay heed to such fine distinctions, but belabours the whole tribe with indiscriminate raillery and scurrility.

The play was produced at the Great Dionysia in 423 B.C., but proved unsuccessful, Cratinus and Amipsias being awarded first and second prize. This is said to have been due to the intrigues and influence of Alcibiades, who resented the caricature of himself presented in the sporting Phidippides. A second edition of the drama was apparently produced some years later, to which the 'Parabasis' of the play as we possess it must belong, as it refers to events subsequent to the date named.

The plot is briefly as follows: Strepsiades, a wealthy country gentleman, has been brought to penury and deeply involved in debt by the extravagance and horsy tastes of his son Phidippides. Having heard of the wonderful new art of argument, the royal road to success in litigation, discovered by the Sophists, he hopes that, if only he can enter the 'Phrontisterion,' or Thinking-Shop, of Socrates, he will learn how to turn the tables on his creditors and avoid paying the debts which are dragging him down. He joins the school accordingly, but is found too old and stupid to profit by the lessons. So his son Phidippides is substituted as a more promising pupil. The latter takes to the new learning like a duck to water, and soon shows what progress he has made by beating his father and demonstrating that he is justified by all laws, divine and human, in what he is doing. This opens the old man's eyes, who sets fire to the 'Phrontisterion,' and the play ends in a great conflagration of this home of humbug.

The Clouds

DRAMATIS PERSONAE

STREPSIADES.
PHIDIPPIDES.
SERVANT OF STREPSIADES.
SOCRATES.
DISCIPLES OF SOCRATES.
JUST DISCOURSE.
UNJUST DISCOURSE. PASIAS, a Money-lender.
PASIAS' WITNESS. AMYNIAS, another Money-lender.
CHAEREPHON.
CHORUS OF CLOUDS.

SCENE: A sleeping-room in Strepsiades' house; then in front of Socrates' house.

STREPSIADES. Great gods! will these nights never end? will daylight never come? I heard the cock crow long ago and my slaves are snoring still! Ah! 'twas not so formerly. Curses on the War! has it not done me ills enough? Now I may not even chastise my own slaves. Again there's this brave lad, who never wakes the whole long night, but, wrapped in his five coverlets, farts away to his heart's content. Come! let me nestle in well and snore too, if it be possible ... oh! misery, 'tis vain to think of sleep with all these expenses, this stable, these debts, which are devouring me, thanks to this fine cavalier, who only knows how to look after his long locks, to show himself off in his chariot and to dream of horses! And I, I am nearly dead, when I see the moon bringing the third decade in her train and my liability falling due.... Slave! light the lamp and bring me my tablets. Who are all my creditors? Let me see and reckon up the interest. What is it I owe? ... Twelve minae to Pasias.... What! twelve minae to Pasias? ... Why did I borrow these? Ah! I know! 'Twas to buy that thoroughbred, which cost me so dear. How I should have prized the stone that had blinded him!

PHIDIPPIDES (*in his sleep*). That's not fair, Philo! Drive your chariot straight, I say.

STREPSIADES. 'Tis this that is destroying me. He raves about horses, even in his sleep.

PHIDIPPIDES (*still sleeping*). How many times round the track is the race for the chariots of war?

STREPSIADES. 'Tis your own father you are driving to death ... to ruin. Come! what debt comes next, after that of Pasias? ... Three minae to Amynias for a chariot and its two wheels.

PHIDIPPIDES (*still asleep*). Give the horse a good roll in the dust and lead him home.

STREPSIADES. Ah! wretched boy! 'tis my money that you are making roll. My creditors have distrained on my goods, and here are others again, who demand security for their interest.

PHIDIPPIDES (*awaking*). What is the matter with you, father, that you groan and turn about the whole night through?

STREPSIADES. I have a bum-bailiff in the bedclothes biting me.

PHIDIPPIDES. For pity's sake, let me have a little sleep.

STREPSIADES. Very well, sleep on! but remember that all these debts will fall back on your shoulders. Oh! curses on the go-between who made me marry your mother! I lived so happily in the country, a commonplace, everyday life, but a good and easy one—had not a trouble, not a care, was rich in bees, in sheep and in olives. Then forsooth I must marry the niece of Megacles, the son of Megacles; I belonged to the country, she was from the town; she was a haughty, extravagant woman, a true Coesyra. On the nuptial day, when I lay beside her, I was reeking of the dregs of the wine-cup, of cheese and of wool; she was redolent with essences, saffron, tender kisses, the love of spending, of good cheer and of wanton delights. I will not say she did nothing; no, she worked hard ... to ruin me, and pretending all the while merely to be showing her the cloak she had woven for me, I said, "Wife, you go too fast about your work, your threads are too closely woven and you use far too much wool."

A SLAVE. There is no more oil in the lamp.

STREPSIADES. Why then did you light such a guzzling lamp? Come here, I am going to beat you!

SLAVE. What for?

STREPSIADES. Because you have put in too thick a wick.... Later, when we had this boy, what was to be his name? 'Twas the cause of much quarrelling with my loving wife. She insisted on having some reference to a horse in his name, that he should be called Xanthippus, Charippus or Callippides. I wanted to name him Phidonides after his grandfather. We disputed long, and finally agreed to style him Phidippides.... She used to fondle and coax him, saying, "Oh! what a joy it will be to me when you have grown up, to see you, like my father, Megacles, clothed in purple and standing up straight in your chariot driving your steeds toward the town." And I would say to him, "When, like your father, you will go, dressed in a skin, to fetch back your goats from Phelleus." Alas! he never listened to me and his madness for horses has shattered my fortune. But by dint of thinking the livelong night, I have discovered a road to salvation, both miraculous and divine. If he will but follow it, I shall be out of my trouble! First, however, he must be awakened, but let it be done as gently as possible. How shall I manage it? Phidippides! my little Phidippides!

PHIDIPPIDES. What is it, father!

STREPSIADES. Kiss me and give me your hand.

PHIDIPPIDES. There! What's it all about?

STREPSIADES. Tell me! do you love me?

PHIDIPPIDES. By Posidon, the equestrian Posidon! yes, I swear I do.

STREPSIADES. Oh, do not, I pray you, invoke this god of horses; 'tis he who is the cause of all my cares. But if you really love me, and with your whole heart, my boy, believe me.

PHIDIPPIDES. Believe you? about what?

STREPSIADES. Alter your habits forthwith and go and learn what I tell you.

PHIDIPPIDES. Say on, what are your orders?

STREPSIADES. Will you obey me ever so little?

PHIDIPPIDES. By Bacchus, I will obey you.

STREPSIADES. Very well then! Look this way. Do you see that little door and that little house?

PHIDIPPIDES. Yes, father. But what are you driving at?

STREPSIADES. That is the school of wisdom. There, they prove that we are coals enclosed on all sides under a vast extinguisher, which is the sky. If well paid, these men also teach one how to gain law-suits, whether they be just or not.

PHIDIPPIDES. What do they call themselves?

STREPSIADES. I do not know exactly, but they are deep thinkers and most admirable people.

PHIDIPPIDES. Bah! the wretches! I know them; you mean those quacks with livid faces, those barefoot fellows, such as that miserable Socrates and Chaerephon.

STREPSIADES. Silence! say nothing foolish! If you desire your father not to die of hunger, join their company and let your horses go.

PHIDIPPIDES. No, by Bacchus! even though you gave me the pheasants that Leogoras rears.

STREPSIADES. Oh! my beloved son, I beseech you, go and follow their teachings.

PHIDIPPIDES. And what is it I should learn?

STREPSIADES. 'Twould seem they have two courses of reasoning, the true and the false, and that, thanks to the false, the worst law-suits can be gained. If then you learn this science, which is false, I shall not pay an obolus of all the debts I have contracted on your account.

PHIDIPPIDES. No, I will not do it. I should no longer dare to look at our gallant horsemen, when I had so tarnished my fair hue of honour.

STREPSIADES. Well then, by Demeter! I will no longer support you, neither you, nor your team, nor your saddle-horse. Go and hang yourself, I turn you out of house and home.

PHIDIPPIDES. My uncle Megacles will not leave me without horses; I shall go to him and laugh at your anger.

STREPSIADES. One rebuff shall not dishearten me. With the help of the gods I will enter this school and learn myself. But at my age, memory has gone and the mind is slow to grasp things. How can all these fine distinctions, these subtleties be learned? Bah! why should I dally thus instead of rapping at the door? Slave, slave! (*He knocks and calls.*)

A DISCIPLE. A plague on you! Who are you?

STREPSIADES. Strepsiades, the son of Phido, of the deme of Cicynna.

DISCIPLE. 'Tis for sure only an ignorant and illiterate fellow who lets drive at the door with such kicks. You have brought on a miscarriage—of an idea!

STREPSIADES. Pardon me, pray; for I live far away from here in the country. But tell me, what was the idea that miscarried?

DISCIPLE. I may not tell it to any but a disciple.

STREPSIADES. Then tell me without fear, for I have come to study among you.

DISCIPLE. Very well then, but reflect, that these are mysteries. Lately, a flea bit Chaerephon on the brow and then from there sprang on to the head of Socrates. Socrates asked Chaerephon, "How many times the length of its legs does a flea jump?"

STREPSIADES. And how ever did he set about measuring it?

DISCIPLE. Oh! 'twas most ingenious! He melted some wax, seized the flea and dipped its two feet in the wax, which, when cooled, left them shod with true Persian buskins. These he slipped off and with them measured the distance.

STREPSIADES. Ah! great Zeus! what a brain! what subtlety!

DISCIPLE. I wonder what then would you say, if you knew another of Socrates' contrivances?

STREPSIADES. What is it? Pray tell me.

DISCIPLE. Chaerephon of the deme of Sphettia asked him whether he thought a gnat buzzed through its proboscis or through its rear.

STREPSIADES. And what did he say about the gnat?

DISCIPLE. He said that the gut of the gnat was narrow, and that, in passing through this tiny passage, the air is driven with force towards the breech; then after this slender channel, it encountered the rump, which was distended like a trumpet, and there it resounded sonorously.

STREPSIADES. So the rear of a gnat is a trumpet. Oh! what a splendid discovery! Thrice happy Socrates! 'Twould not be difficult to succeed in a law-suit, knowing so much about the gut of a gnat!

DISCIPLE. Not long ago a lizard caused him the loss of a sublime thought.

STREPSIADES. In what way, an it please you?

DISCIPLE. One night, when he was studying the course of the moon and its revolutions and was gazing open-mouthed at the heavens, a lizard shitted upon him from the top of the roof.

STREPSIADES. This lizard, that relieved itself over Socrates, tickles me.

DISCIPLE. Yesternight we had nothing to eat.

STREPSIADES. Well! What did he contrive, to secure you some supper?

DISCIPLE. He spread over the table a light layer of cinders, bending an iron rod the while; then he took up a pair of compasses and at the same moment unhooked a piece of the victim which was hanging in the palaestra.

STREPSIADES. And we still dare to admire Thales! Open, open this home of knowledge to me quickly! Haste, haste to show me Socrates; I long to become his disciple. But do, do open the door. (*The disciple admits Strepsiades.*) Ah! by Heracles! what country are those animals from?

DISCIPLE. Why, what are you astonished at? What do you think they resemble?

STREPSIADES. The captives of Pylos. But why do they look so fixedly on the ground?

DISCIPLE. They are seeking for what is below the ground.

STREPSIADES. Ah! 'tis onions they are seeking. Do not give yourselves so much trouble; I know where there are some, fine and large ones. But what are those fellows doing, who are bent all double?

DISCIPLE. They are sounding the abysses of Tartarus.

STREPSIADES. And what is their rump looking at in the heavens?

DISCIPLE. It is studying astronomy on its own account. But come in; so that the master may not find us here.

STREPSIADES. Not yet, not yet; let them not change their position. I want to tell them my own little matter.

DISCIPLE. But they may not stay too long in the open air and away from school.

STREPSIADES. In the name of all the gods, what is that? Tell me. (*Pointing to a celestial globe.*)

DISCIPLE. That is astronomy.

STREPSIADES. And that? (*Pointing to a map.*)

DISCIPLE. Geometry.

STREPSIADES. What is that used for?

DISCIPLE. To measure the land.

STREPSIADES. But that is apportioned by lot.

DISCIPLE. No, no, I mean the entire earth.

STREPSIADES. Ah! what a funny thing! How generally useful indeed is this invention!

DISCIPLE. There is the whole surface of the earth. Look! Here is Athens.

STREPSIADES. Athens! you are mistaken; I see no courts sitting.

DISCIPLE. Nevertheless it is really and truly the Attic territory.

STREPSIADES. And where are my neighbours of Cicynna?

DISCIPLE. They live here. This is Euboea; you see this island, that is so long and narrow.

STREPSIADES. I know. 'Tis we and Pericles, who have stretched it by dint of squeezing it. And where is Lacedaemon?

DISCIPLE. Lacedaemon? Why, here it is, look.

STREPSIADES. How near it is to us! Think it well over, it must be removed to a greater distance.

DISCIPLE. But, by Zeus, that is not possible.

STREPSIADES. Then, woe to you! And who is this man suspended up in a basket?

DISCIPLE. 'Tis *he himself.*

STREPSIADES. Who himself?

DISCIPLE. Socrates.

STREPSIADES. Socrates! Oh! I pray you, call him right loudly for me.

DISCIPLE. Call him yourself; I have no time to waste.

STREPSIADES. Socrates! my little Socrates!

SOCRATES. Mortal, what do you want with me?

STREPSIADES. First, what are you doing up there? Tell me, I beseech you.

SOCRATES. I traverse the air and contemplate the sun.

STREPSIADES. Thus 'tis not on the solid ground, but from the height of this basket, that you slight the gods, if indeed....

SOCRATES. I have to suspend my brain and mingle the subtle essence of my mind with this air, which is of the like nature, in order to clearly penetrate the things of heaven. I should have discovered nothing, had I remained on the ground to consider from below the things that are above; for the earth by its force attracts the sap of the mind to itself. 'Tis just the same with the water-cress.

STREPSIADES. What? Does the mind attract the sap of the water-cress? Ah! my dear little Socrates, come down to me! I have come to ask you for lessons.

SOCRATES. And for what lessons?

STREPSIADES. I want to learn how to speak. I have borrowed money, and my merciless creditors do not leave me a moment's peace; all my goods are at stake.

SOCRATES. And how was it you did not see that you were getting so much into debt?

STREPSIADES. My ruin has been the madness for horses, a most rapacious evil; but teach me one of your two methods of reasoning, the one whose object is not to repay anything, and, may the gods bear witness, that I am ready to pay any fee you may name.

SOCRATES. By which gods will you swear? To begin with, the gods are not a coin current with us.

STREPSIADES. But what do you swear by then? By the iron money of Byzantium?

SOCRATES. Do you really wish to know the truth of celestial matters?

STREPSIADES. Why, truly, if 'tis possible.

SOCRATES. ... and to converse with the clouds, who are our genii?

STREPSIADES. Without a doubt.

SOCRATES. Then be seated on this sacred couch.

STREPSIADES. I am seated.

SOCRATES. Now take this chaplet.

STREPSIADES. Why a chaplet? Alas! Socrates, would you sacrifice me, like Athamas?

SOCRATES. No, these are the rites of initiation.

STREPSIADES. And what is it I am to gain?

SOCRATES. You will become a thorough rattle-pate, a hardened old stager, the fine flour of the talkers.... But come, keep quiet.

STREPSIADES. By Zeus! You lie not! Soon I shall be nothing but wheat-flour, if you powder me in this fashion.

SOCRATES. Silence, old man, give heed to the prayers.... Oh! most mighty king, the boundless air, that keepest the earth suspended in space, thou bright Aether and ye venerable goddesses, the Clouds, who carry in your loins the thunder and the lightning, arise, ye sovereign powers and manifest yourselves in the celestial spheres to the eyes of the sage.

STREPSIADES. Not yet! Wait a bit, till I fold my mantle double, so as not to get wet. And to think that I did not even bring my travelling cap! What a misfortune!

SOCRATES. Come, oh! Clouds, whom I adore, come and show yourselves to this man, whether you be resting on the sacred summits of Olympus, crowned with hoar-frost, or tarrying in the gardens of Ocean, your father, forming sacred choruses with the Nymphs; whether you be gathering the waves of the Nile in golden vases or dwelling in the Maeotic marsh or on the snowy rocks of Mimas, hearken to my prayer and accept my offering. May these sacrifices be pleasing to you.

CHORUS. Eternal Clouds, let us appear, let us arise from the roaring depths of Ocean, our father; let us fly towards the lofty mountains, spread our damp wings over their forest-laden summits, whence we will dominate the distant valleys, the harvest fed by the sacred earth, the murmur of the divine streams and the resounding waves of the sea, which the unwearying orb lights up with its glittering beams. But let us shake off the rainy fogs, which hide our immortal beauty and sweep the earth from afar with our gaze.

SOCRATES. Oh, venerated goddesses, yes, you are answering my call! (*To Strepsiades.*) Did you hear their voices mingling with the awful growling of the thunder?

STREPSIADES. Oh! adorable Clouds, I revere you and I too am going to let off *my* thunder, so greatly has your own affrighted me. Faith! whether permitted or not, I must, I must shit!

SOCRATES. No scoffing; do not copy those accursed comic poets. Come, silence! a numerous host of goddesses approaches with songs.

CHORUS. Virgins, who pour forth the rains, let us move toward Attica, the rich country of Pallas, the home of the brave; let us visit the dear land of Cecrops, where the secret rites are celebrated, where the mysterious sanctuary flies open to the initiate.... What victims are offered there to the deities of heaven! What glorious temples! What statues! What holy prayers to the rulers of Olympus! At every season nothing but sacred festivals, garlanded victims, are to be seen. Then Spring brings round again the joyous feasts of Dionysus, the harmonious contests of the choruses and the serious melodies of the flute.

STREPSIADES. By Zeus! Tell me, Socrates, I pray you, who are these women, whose language is so solemn; can they be demigoddesses?

SOCRATES. Not at all. They are the Clouds of heaven, great goddesses for the lazy; to them we owe all, thoughts, speeches, trickery, roguery, boasting, lies, sagacity.

STREPSIADES. Ah! that was why, as I listened to them, my mind spread out its wings; it burns to babble about trifles, to maintain worthless arguments, to voice its petty reasons, to contradict, to tease some opponent. But are they not going to show themselves? I should like to see them, were it possible.

SOCRATES. Well, look this way in the direction of Parnes; I already see those who are slowly descending.

STREPSIADES. But where, where? Show them to me.

SOCRATES. They are advancing in a throng, following an oblique path across the dales and thickets.

STREPSIADES. 'Tis strange! I can see nothing.

SOCRATES. There, close to the entrance.

STREPSIADES. Hardly, if at all, can I distinguish them.

SOCRATES. You *must* see them clearly now, unless your eyes are filled with gum as thick as pumpkins.

STREPSIADES. Aye, undoubtedly! Oh! the venerable goddesses! Why, they fill up the entire stage.

SOCRATES. And you did not know, you never suspected, that they were goddesses?

STREPSIADES. No, indeed; methought the Clouds were only fog, dew and vapour.

SOCRATES. But what you certainly do not know is that they are the support of a crowd of quacks, both the diviners, who were sent to Thurium, the notorious physicians, the well-combed fops, who load their fingers with rings down to the nails, and the baggarts, who write dithyrambic verses, all these are idlers whom the Clouds provide a living for, because they sing them in their verses.

STREPSIADES. 'Tis then for this that they praise "the rapid flight of the moist clouds, which veil the brightness of day" and "the waving locks of the hundred-headed Typho" and "the impetuous tempests, which float through the heavens, like birds of prey with aerial wings, loaded with mists" and "the rains, the dew, which the clouds outpour." As a reward for these fine phrases they bolt well-grown, tasty mullet and delicate thrushes.

SOCRATES. Yes, thanks to these. And is it not right and meet?

STREPSIADES. Tell me then why, if these really are the Clouds, they so very much resemble mortals. This is not their usual form.

SOCRATES. What are they like then?

STREPSIADES. I don't know exactly; well, they are like great packs of wool, but not like women—no, not in the least.... And these have noses.

SOCRATES. Answer my questions.

STREPSIADES. Willingly! Go on, I am listening.

SOCRATES. Have you not sometimes seen clouds in the sky like a centaur, a leopard, a wolf or a bull?

STREPSIADES. Why, certainly I have, but what then?

SOCRATES. They take what metamorphosis they like. If they see a debauchee with long flowing locks and hairy as a beast, like the son of Xenophantes, they take the form of a Centaur in derision of his shameful passion.

STREPSIADES. And when they see Simon, that thiever of public money, what do they do then?

SOCRATES. To picture him to the life, they turn at once into wolves.

STREPSIADES. So that was why yesterday, when they saw Cleonymus, who cast away his buckler because he is the veriest poltroon amongst men, they changed into deer.

SOCRATES. And to-day they have seen Clisthenes; you see ... they are women.

STREPSIADES. Hail, sovereign goddesses, and if ever you have let your celestial voice be heard by mortal ears, speak to me, oh! speak to me, ye all-powerful queens.

CHORUS. Hail! veteran of the ancient times, you who burn to instruct yourself in fine language. And you, great high-priest of subtle nonsense, tell us your desire. To you and Prodicus alone of all the hollow orationers of to-day have we lent an ear—to Prodicus, because of his knowledge and his great wisdom, and to you, because you walk with head erect, a confident look, barefooted, resigned to everything and proud of our protection.

STREPSIADES. Oh! Earth! What august utterances! how sacred! how wondrous!

SOCRATES. That is because these are the only goddesses; all the rest are pure myth.

STREPSIADES. But by the Earth! is our Father, Zeus, the Olympian, not a god?

SOCRATES. Zeus! what Zeus? Are you mad? There is no Zeus.

STREPSIADES. What are you saying now? Who causes the rain to fall? Answer me that!

SOCRATES. Why, 'tis these, and I will prove it. Have you ever seen it raining without clouds? Let Zeus then cause rain with a clear sky and without their presence!

STREPSIADES. By Apollo! that is powerfully argued! For my own part, I always thought it was Zeus pissing into a sieve. But tell me, who is it makes the thunder, which I so much dread?

SOCRATES. 'Tis these, when they roll one over the other.

STREPSIADES. But how can that be? you most daring among men!

SOCRATES. Being full of water, and forced to move along, they are of necessity precipitated in rain, being fully distended with moisture from the regions where they have been floating; hence they bump each other heavily and burst with great noise.

STREPSIADES. But is it not Zeus who forces them to move?

SOCRATES. Not at all; 'tis aerial Whirlwind.

STREPSIADES. The Whirlwind! ah! I did not know that. So Zeus, it seems, has no existence, and 'tis the Whirlwind that reigns in his stead? But you have not yet told me what makes the roll of the thunder?

SOCRATES. Have you not understood me then? I tell you, that the Clouds, when full of rain, bump against one another, and that, being inordinately swollen out, they burst with a great noise.

STREPSIADES. How can you make me credit that?

SOCRATES. Take yourself as an example. When you have heartily gorged on stew at the Panathenaea, you get throes of stomach-ache and then suddenly your belly resounds with prolonged growling.

STREPSIADES. Yes, yes, by Apollo! I suffer, I get colic, then the stew sets a-growling like thunder and finally bursts forth with a terrific noise. At first, 'tis but a little gurgling *pappax, pappax!* then it increases, *papapappax!* and when I seek relief, why, 'tis thunder indeed, *papapappax! pappax!! papapappax!!!* just like the clouds.

SOCRATES. Well then, reflect what a noise is produced by your belly, which is but small. Shall not the air, which is boundless, produce these mighty claps of thunder?

STREPSIADES. But tell me this. Whence comes the lightning, the dazzling flame, which at times consumes the man it strikes, at others hardly singes him. Is it not plain, that 'tis Zeus hurling it at the perjurers?

SOCRATES. Out upon the fool! the driveller! he still savours of the golden age! If Zeus strikes at the perjurers, why has he not blasted Simon, Cleonymus and Theorus? Of a surety, greater perjurers cannot exist. No, he strikes his own Temple, and Sunium, the promontory of Athens, and the towering oaks. Now, why should he do that? An oak is no perjurer.

STREPSIADES. I cannot tell, but it seems to me well argued. What is the thunder then?

SOCRATES. When a dry wind ascends to the Clouds and gets shut into them, it blows them out like a bladder; finally, being too confined, it bursts them, escapes with fierce violence and a roar to flash into flame by reason of its own impetuosity.

STREPSIADES. Forsooth, 'tis just what happened to me one day. 'Twas at the feast of Zeus! I was cooking a sow's belly for my family and I had forgotten to slit it open. It swelled out and, suddenly bursting, discharged itself right into my eyes and burnt my face.

CHORUS. Oh, mortal! you, who desire to instruct yourself in our great wisdom, the Athenians, the Greeks will envy you your good fortune. Only you must have the memory and ardour for study, you must know how to stand the tests, hold your own, go forward without feeling fatigue, caring but little for food, abstaining from wine, gymnastic exercises and other similar follies, in fact, you must believe as every man of intellect should, that the greatest of all blessings is to live and think more clearly than the vulgar herd, to shine in the contests of words.

STREPSIADES. If it be a question of hardiness for labour, of spending whole nights at work, of living sparingly, of fighting my stomach and only eating chick-pease, rest assured, I am as hard as an anvil.

SOCRATES. Henceforward, following our example, you will recognize no other gods but Chaos, the Clouds and the Tongue, these three alone.

STREPSIADES. I would not speak to the others, even if I should meet them in the street; not a single sacrifice, not a libation, not a grain of incense for them!

CHORUS. Tell us boldly then what you want of us; you cannot fail to succeed, if you honour and revere us and if you are resolved to become a clever man.

STREPSIADES. Oh, sovereign goddesses, 'tis but a very small favour that I ask of you; grant that I may distance all the Greeks by a hundred stadia in the art of speaking.

CHORUS. We grant you this, and henceforward no eloquence shall more often succeed with the people than your own.

STREPSIADES. May the god shield me from possessing great eloquence! 'Tis not what I want. I want to be able to turn bad lawsuits to my own advantage and to slip through the fingers of my creditors.

CHORUS. It shall be as you wish, for your ambitions are modest. Commit yourself fearlessly to our ministers, the sophists.

STREPSIADES. This will I do, for I trust in you. Moreover there is no drawing back, what with these cursed horses and this marriage, which has eaten up my vitals. So let them do with me as they will; I yield my body to them. Come blows, come hunger, thirst, heat or cold, little matters it to me; they may flay me, if I only escape my debts, if only I win the reputation of being a bold rascal, a fine speaker, impudent, shameless, a braggart, and adept at stringing lies, an old stager at quibbles, a complete table of the laws, a thorough rattle, a fox to slip through any hole; supple as a leathern strap, slippery as an eel, an artful fellow, a blusterer, a villain; a knave with a hundred faces, cunning, intolerable, a gluttonous dog. With such epithets do I seek to be greeted; on these terms, they can treat me as they choose, and, if they wish, by Demeter! they can turn me into sausages and serve me up to the philosophers.

CHORUS. Here have we a bold and well-disposed pupil indeed. When we shall have taught you, your glory among the mortals will reach even to the skies.

STREPSIADES. Wherein will that profit me?

CHORUS. You will pass your whole life among us and will be the most envied of men.

STREPSIADES. Shall I really ever see such happiness?

CHORUS. Clients will be everlastingly besieging your door in crowds, burning to get at you, to explain their business to you and to consult you about their suits, which, in return for your ability, will bring you in great sums. But, Socrates, begin the lessons you want to teach this old man; rouse his mind, try the strength of his intelligence.

SOCRATES. Come, tell me the kind of mind you have; 'tis important I know this, that I may order my batteries against you in a new fashion.

STREPSIADES. Eh, what! in the name of the gods, are you purposing to assault me then?

SOCRATES. No. I only wish to ask you some questions. Have you any memory?

STREPSIADES. That depends: if anything is owed me, my memory is excellent, but if I owe, alas! I have none whatever.

SOCRATES. Have you a natural gift for speaking?

STREPSIADES. For speaking, no; for cheating, yes.

SOCRATES. How will you be able to learn then?

STREPSIADES. Very easily, have no fear.

SOCRATES. Thus, when I throw forth some philosophical thought anent things celestial, you will seize it in its very flight?

STREPSIADES. Then I am to snap up wisdom much as a dog snaps up a morsel?

SOCRATES. Oh! the ignoramus! the barbarian! I greatly fear, old man, 'twill be needful for me to have recourse to blows. Now, let me hear what you do when you are beaten.

STREPSIADES. I receive the blow, then wait a moment, take my witnesses and finally summon my assailant at law.

SOCRATES. Come, take off your cloak.

STREPSIADES. Have I robbed you of anything?

SOCRATES. No, but 'tis usual to enter the school without your cloak.

STREPSIADES. But I am not come here to look for stolen goods.

SOCRATES. Off with it, fool!

STREPSIADES. Tell me, if I prove thoroughly attentive and learn with zeal, which of your disciples shall I resemble, do you think?

SOCRATES. You will be the image of Chaerephon.

STREPSIADES. Ah! unhappy me! I shall then be but half alive?

SOCRATES. A truce to this chatter! follow me and no more of it.

STREPSIADES. First give me a honey-cake, for to descend down there sets me all a-tremble; meseems 'tis the cave of Trophonius.

SOCRATES. But get in with you! What reason have you for thus dallying at the door?

CHORUS. Good luck! you have courage; may you succeed, you, who, though already so advanced in years, wish to instruct your mind with new studies and practise it in wisdom!

CHORUS (Parabasis). Spectators! By Bacchus, whose servant I am, I will frankly tell you the truth. May I secure both victory and renown as certainly as I hold you for adept critics and as I regard this comedy as my best. I wished to give you the first view of a work, which had cost me much trouble, but I withdrew, unjustly beaten by unskilful rivals. 'Tis you, oh, enlightened public, for whom I have prepared my piece, that I reproach with this. Nevertheless I shall never willingly cease to seek the approval of the discerning. I have not forgotten the day, when men, whom one is happy to have for an audience, received my 'Young Man' and my 'Debauchee' with so much favour in this very place. Then as yet virgin, my Muse had not attained the legal age for maternity; she had to expose her first-born for another to adopt, and it has since grown up under your generous patronage. Ever since you have as good as sworn me your faithful alliance. Thus, like Electra of the poets, my comedy has come to seek you to-day, hoping again to encounter such enlightened spectators. As far away as she can discern her Orestes, she will be able to recognize him by his curly head. And note her modest demeanour! She has not sewn on a piece of hanging leather, thick and reddened at the end, to cause laughter among the children; she does not rail at the bald, neither does she dance the cordax; no old man is seen, who, while uttering his lines, batters his questioner with a stick to make his poor jests pass muster. She does not rush upon the scene carrying a torch and screaming, 'La, la! la, la!' No, she relies upon herself and her verses.... My value is so well known, that I take no further pride in it. I do not seek to deceive you, by reproducing the same subjects two or three times; I always invent fresh themes to present before you, themes that have no relation to each other and that are all clever. I attacked Cleon to his face and when he was all-powerful; but he has fallen, and now I have no desire to kick him when he is down. My rivals, on the contrary, once that this wretched Hyperbolus has given them the cue, have never ceased setting upon both him and his mother. First Eupolis presented his 'Maricas'; this was simply my 'Knights,' whom this plagiarist had clumsily furbished up again by adding to the piece an old drunken woman, so that she might dance the cordax. 'Twas an old idea, taken from Phrynichus, who caused his old hag to be devoured by a monster of the deep. Then Hermippus fell foul of Hyperbolus and now all the others fall upon him and repeat my comparison of the eels. May those who find amusement in their pieces not be pleased with mine, but as for you, who love and applaud my inventions, why, posterity will praise your good taste.

Oh, ruler of Olympus, all-powerful king of the gods, great Zeus, it is thou whom I first invoke; protect this chorus; and thou too, Posidon, whose dread trident upheaves at the will of thy anger both the bowels of the earth and the salty waves of the ocean. I invoke my illustrious father, the divine Aether, the universal sustainer of life, and Phoebus, who, from the summit of his chariot, sets the world aflame with his dazzling rays, Phoebus, a mighty deity amongst the gods and adored amongst mortals.

Most wise spectators, lend us all your attention. Give heed to our just reproaches. There exist no gods to whom this city owes more than it does to us, whom alone you forget. Not a sacrifice, not a libation is there for those who protect you! Have you decreed some mad expedition? Well! we thunder or we fall down in rain. When you chose that enemy of heaven, the Paphlagonian tanner, for a general, we knitted our brow, we caused our wrath to break out; the lightning shot forth, the thunder pealed, the moon deserted her course and the sun at once veiled his beam threatening no longer to give you light, if Cleon became general. Nevertheless you elected him; 'tis said, Athens never resolves upon some fatal step but the gods turn these errors into her greatest gain. Do you wish that this election should even now be a success for you? 'Tis a very simple thing to do; condemn this rapacious gull named Cleon for bribery and extortion, fit a wooden collar tight round his neck, and your error will be rectified and the commonweal will at once regain its old prosperity.

Aid me also, Phoebus, god of Delos, who reignest on the cragged peaks of Cynthia; and thou, happy virgin, to whom the Lydian damsels offer pompous sacrifice in a temple of gold; and thou, goddess of our country, Athené, armed with the aegis, the protectress of Athens; and thou, who, surrounded by the Bacchanals of Delphi, roamest over the rocks of Parnassus shaking the flame of thy resinous torch, thou, Bacchus, the god of revel and joy.

As we were preparing to come here, we were hailed by the Moon and were charged to wish joy and happiness both to the Athenians and to their allies; further, she said that she was enraged and that you treated her very shamefully, her, who does not pay you in words alone, but who renders you all real benefits. Firstly, thanks to her, you save at least a drachma each month for lights, for each, as he is leaving home at night, says, "Slave, buy no torches, for the moonlight is beautiful,"—not to name a thousand other benefits. Nevertheless you do not reckon the days correctly and your calendar is naught but confusion. Consequently the gods load her with threats each time they get home and are disappointed of their meal, because the festival has not been kept in the regular order of time. When you should be sacrificing, you are putting to the torture or administering justice. And often, we others, the gods, are fasting in token of mourning for the death of Memnon or Sarpedon, while you are devoting yourselves to joyous libations. 'Tis for this, that last year, when the lot would have invested Hyperbolus with the duty of Amphictyon, we took his crown from him, to teach him that time must be divided according to the phases of the moon.

SOCRATES. By Respiration, the Breath of Life! By Chaos! By the Air! I have never seen a man so gross, so inept, so stupid, so forgetful. All the little quibbles, which I teach him, he forgets even before he has learnt them. Yet I will not give it up, I will make him come out here into the open air. Where are you, Strepsiades? Come, bring your couch out here.

STREPSIADES. But the bugs will not allow me to bring it.

SOCRATES. Have done with such nonsense! place it there and pay attention.

STREPSIADES. Well, here I am.

SOCRATES. Good! Which science of all those you have never been taught, do you wish to learn first? The measures, the rhythms or the verses?

STREPSIADES. Why, the measures; the flour dealer cheated me out of two *choenixes* the other day.

SOCRATES. 'Tis not about that I ask you, but which, according to you, is the best measure, the trimeter or the tetrameter?

STREPSIADES. The one I prefer is the semisextarius.

SOCRATES. You talk nonsense, my good fellow.

STREPSIADES. I will wager your tetrameter is the semisextarius.

SOCRATES. Plague seize the dunce and the fool! Come, perchance you will learn the rhythms quicker.

STREPSIADES. Will the rhythms supply me with food?

SOCRATES. First they will help you to be pleasant in company, then to know what is meant by oenoplian rhythm and what by the dactylic.

STREPSIADES. Of the dactyl? I know that quite well.

SOCRATES. What is it then?

STREPSIADES. Why, 'tis this finger; formerly, when a child, I used this one.

SOCRATES. You are as low-minded as you are stupid.

STREPSIADES. But, wretched man, I do not want to learn all this.

SOCRATES. Then what *do* you want to know?

STREPSIADES. Not that, not that, but the art of false reasoning.

SOCRATES. But you must first learn other things. Come, what are the male quadrupeds?

STREPSIADES. Oh! I know the males thoroughly. Do you take me for a fool then? The ram, the buck, the bull, the dog, the pigeon.

SOCRATES. Do you see what you are doing; is not the female pigeon called the same as the male?

STREPSIADES. How else? Come now?

SOCRATES. How else? With you then 'tis pigeon and pigeon!

STREPSIADES. 'Tis true, by Posidon! but what names do you want me to give them?

SOCRATES. Term the female pigeonnette and the male pigeon.

STREPSIADES. Pigeonnette! hah! by the Air! That's splendid! for that lesson bring out your kneading-trough and I will fill him with flour to the brim.

SOCRATES. There you are wrong again; you make *trough* masculine and it should be feminine.

STREPSIADES. What? if I say *him*, do I make the *trough* masculine?

SOCRATES. Assuredly! would you not say him for Cleonymus?

STREPSIADES. Well?

SOCRATES. Then trough is of the same gender as Cleonymus?

STREPSIADES. Oh! good sir! Cleonymus never had a kneading-trough; he used a round mortar for the purpose. But come, tell me what I *should* say?

SOCRATES. For trough you should say *her* as you would for Sostraté.

STREPSIADES. *Her*?

SOCRATES. In this manner you make it truly female.

STREPSIADES. That's it! *Her* for trough and *her* for Cleonymus.

SOCRATES. Now I must teach you to distinguish the masculine proper names from those that are feminine.

STREPSIADES. Ah! I know the female names well.

SOCRATES. Name some then.

STREPSIADES. Lysilla, Philinna, Clitagora, Demetria.

SOCRATES. And what are masculine names?

STREPSIADES. They are countless—Philoxenus, Melesias, Amynias.

SOCRATES. But, wretched man, the last two are not masculine.

STREPSIADES. You do not reckon them masculine?

SOCRATES. Not at all. If you met Amynias, how would you hail him?

STREPSIADES. How? Why, I should shout, "Hi! hither, Amynia!"

SOCRATES. Do you see? 'tis a female name that you give him.

STREPSIADES. And is it not rightly done, since he refuses military service? But what use is there in learning what we all know?

SOCRATES. You know nothing about it. Come, lie down there.

STREPSIADES. What for?

SOCRATES. Ponder awhile over matters that interest you.

STREPSIADES. Oh! I pray you, not there! but, if I must lie down and ponder, let me lie on the ground.

SOCRATES. 'Tis out of the question. Come! on to the couch!

STREPSIADES. What cruel fate! What a torture the bugs will this day put me to!

SOCRATES. Ponder and examine closely, gather your thoughts together, let your mind turn to every side of things; if you meet with a difficulty, spring quickly to some other idea; above all, keep your eyes away from all gentle sleep.

STREPSIADES. Oh, woe, woe! oh, woe, woe!

SOCRATES. What ails you? why do you cry so?

STREPSIADES. Oh! I am a dead man! Here are these cursed Corinthians advancing upon me from all corners of the couch; they are biting me, they are gnawing at my sides, they are drinking all my blood, they are twitching off my testicles, they are exploring all up my back, they are killing me!

SOCRATES. Not so much wailing and clamour, if you please.

STREPSIADES. How can I obey? I have lost my money and my complexion, my blood and my slippers, and to cap my misery, I must keep awake on this couch, when scarce a breath of life is left in me.

SOCRATES. Well now! what are you doing? are you reflecting?

STREPSIADES. Yes, by Posidon!

SOCRATES. What about?

STREPSIADES. Whether the bugs will not entirely devour me.

SOCRATES. May death seize you, accursed man!

STREPSIADES. Ah! it has already.

SOCRATES. Come, no giving way! Cover up your head; the thing to do is to find an ingenious alternative.

STREPSIADES. An alternative! ah! I only wish one would come to me from within these coverlets!

SOCRATES. Hold! let us see what our fellow is doing. Ho! you! are you asleep?

STREPSIADES. No, by Apollo!

SOCRATES. Have you got hold of anything?

STREPSIADES. No, nothing whatever.

SOCRATES. Nothing at all!

STREPSIADES. No, nothing but my tool, which I've got in my hand.

SOCRATES. Are you not going to cover your head immediately and ponder?

STREPSIADES. Over what? Come, Socrates, tell me.

SOCRATES. Think first what you want, and then tell me.

STREPSIADES. But I have told you a thousand times what I want. 'Tis not to pay any of my creditors.

SOCRATES. Come, wrap yourself up; concentrate your mind, which wanders too lightly, study every detail, scheme and examine thoroughly.

STREPSIADES. Oh, woe! woe! oh dear! oh dear!

SOCRATES. Keep yourself quiet, and if any notion troubles you, put it quickly aside, then resume it and think over it again.

STREPSIADES. My dear little Socrates!

SOCRATES. What is it, old greybeard?

STREPSIADES. I have a scheme for not paying my debts.

SOCRATES. Let us hear it.

STREPSIADES. Tell me, if I purchased a Thessalian witch, I could make the moon descend during the night and shut it, like a mirror, into a round box and there keep it carefully....

SOCRATES. How would you gain by that?

STREPSIADES. How? Why, if the moon did not rise, I would have no interest to pay.

SOCRATES. Why so?

STREPSIADES. Because money is lent by the month.

SOCRATES. Good! but I am going to propose another trick to you. If you were condemned to pay five talents, how would you manage to quash that verdict? Tell me.

STREPSIADES. How? how? I don't know, I must think.

SOCRATES. Do you always shut your thoughts within yourself. Let your ideas fly in the air, like a may-bug, tied by the foot with a thread.

STREPSIADES. I have found a very clever way to annul that conviction; you will admit that much yourself.

SOCRATES. What is it?

STREPSIADES. Have you ever seen a beautiful, transparent stone at the druggists, with which you may kindle fire?

SOCRATES. You mean a crystal lens.

STREPSIADES. Yes.

SOCRATES. Well, what then?

STREPSIADES. If I placed myself with this stone in the sun and a long way off from the clerk, while he was writing out the conviction, I could make all the wax, upon which the words were written, melt.

SOCRATES. Well thought out, by the Graces!

STREPSIADES. Ah! I am delighted to have annulled the decree that was to cost me five talents.

SOCRATES. Come, take up this next question quickly.

STREPSIADES. Which?

SOCRATES. If, when summoned to court, you were in danger of losing your case for want of witnesses, how would you make the conviction fall upon your opponent?

STREPSIADES. 'Tis very simple and most easy.

SOCRATES. Let me hear.

STREPSIADES. This way. If another case had to be pleaded before mine was called, I should run and hang myself.

SOCRATES. You talk rubbish!

STREPSIADES. Not so, by the gods! if I was dead, no action could lie against me.

SOCRATES. You are merely beating the air. Begone! I will give you no more lessons.

STREPSIADES. Why not? Oh! Socrates! in the name of the gods!

SOCRATES. But you forget as fast as you learn. Come, what was the thing I taught you first? Tell me.

STREPSIADES. Ah! let me see. What was the first thing? What was it then? Ah! that thing in which we knead the bread, oh! my god! what do you call it?

SOCRATES. Plague take the most forgetful and silliest of old addlepates!

STREPSIADES. Alas! what a calamity! what will become of me? I am undone if I do not learn how to ply my tongue. Oh! Clouds! give me good advice.

CHORUS. Old man, we counsel you, if you have brought up a son, to send him to learn in your stead.

STREPSIADES. Undoubtedly I have a son, as well endowed as the best, but he is unwilling to learn. What will become of me?

CHORUS. And you don't make him obey you?

STREPSIADES. You see, he is big and strong; moreover, through his mother he is a descendant of those fine birds, the race of Coesyra. Nevertheless, I will go and find him, and if he refuses, I will turn him out of the house. Go in, Socrates, and wait for me awhile.

CHORUS (to Socrates). Do you understand, that, thanks to us, you will be loaded with benefits? Here is a man, ready to obey you in all things. You see how he is carried away with admiration and enthusiasm. Profit by it to clip him as short as possible; fine chances are all too quickly gone.

STREPSIADES. No, by the Clouds! you stay no longer here; go and devour the ruins of your uncle Megacles' fortune.

PHIDIPPIDES. Oh! my poor father! what has happened to you? By the Olympian Zeus! you are no longer in your senses!

STREPSIADES. See! see! "the Olympian Zeus." Oh! the fool! to believe in Zeus at your age!

PHIDIPPIDES. What is there in that to make you laugh?

STREPSIADES. You are then a tiny little child, if you credit such antiquated rubbish! But come here, that I may teach you; I will tell you something very necessary to know to be a man; but you will not repeat it to anybody.

PHIDIPPIDES. Come, what is it?

STREPSIADES. Just now you swore by Zeus.

PHIDIPPIDES. Aye, that I did.

STREPSIADES. Do you see how good it is to learn? Phidippides, there is no Zeus.

PHIDIPPIDES. What is there then?

STREPSIADES. 'Tis the Whirlwind, that has driven out Jupiter and is King now.

PHIDIPPIDES. Go to! what drivel!

STREPSIADES. Know it to be the truth.

PHIDIPPIDES. And who says so?

STREPSIADES. 'Tis Socrates, the Melian, and Chaerephon, who knows how to measure the jump of a flea.

PHIDIPPIDES. Have you reached such a pitch of madness that you believe those bilious fellows?

STREPSIADES. Use better language, and do not insult men who are clever and full of wisdom, who, to economize, are never shaved, shun the gymnasia and never go to the baths, while you, you only await my death to eat up my wealth. But come, come as quickly as you can to learn in my stead.

PHIDIPPIDES. And what good can be learnt of them?

STREPSIADES. What good indeed? Why, all human knowledge. Firstly, you will know yourself grossly ignorant. But await me here awhile.

PHIDIPPIDES. Alas! what is to be done? My father has lost his wits. Must I have him certificated for lunacy, or must I order his coffin?

STREPSIADES. Come! what kind of bird is this? tell me.

PHIDIPPIDES. A pigeon.

STREPSIADES. Good! And this female?

PHIDIPPIDES. A pigeon.

STREPSIADES. The same for both? You make me laugh! For the future you will call this one a pigeonnette and the other a pigeon.

PHIDIPPIDES. A pigeonnette! These then are the fine things you have just learnt at the school of these sons of the Earth!

STREPSIADES. And many others; but what I learnt I forgot at once, because I am too old.

PHIDIPPIDES. So this is why you have lost your cloak?

STREPSIADES. I have not lost it, I have consecrated it to Philosophy.

PHIDIPPIDES. And what have you done with your sandals, you poor fool?

STREPSIADES. If I have lost them, it is for what was necessary, just as Pericles did. But come, move yourself, let us go in; if necessary, do wrong to obey your father. When you were six years old and still lisped, 'twas I who obeyed you. I remember at the feasts of Zeus you had a consuming wish for a little chariot and I bought it for you with the first obolus which I received as a juryman in the Courts.

PHIDIPPIDES. You will soon repent of what you ask me to do.

STREPSIADES. Oh! now I am happy! He obeys. Here, Socrates, here! Come out quick! Here I am bringing you my son; he refused, but I have persuaded him.

SOCRATES. Why, he is but a child yet. He is not used to these baskets, in which we suspend our minds.

PHIDIPPIDES. To make you better used to them, I would you were hung.

STREPSIADES. A curse upon you! you insult your master!

SOCRATES. "I would you were hung!" What a stupid speech! and so emphatically spoken! How can one ever get out of an accusation with such a tone, summon witnesses or touch or convince? And yet when we think, Hyperbolus learnt all this for one talent!

STREPSIADES. Rest undisturbed and teach him. 'Tis a most intelligent nature. Even when quite little he amused himself at home with making houses, carving boats, constructing little chariots of leather, and understood wonderfully how to make frogs out of pomegranate rinds. Teach him both methods of reasoning, the strong and also the weak, which by false arguments triumphs over the strong; if not the two, at least the false, and that in every possible way.

SOCRATES. 'Tis Just and Unjust Discourse themselves that shall instruct him.

STREPSIADES. I go, but forget it not, he must always, always be able to confound the true.

JUST DISCOURSE. Come here! Shameless as you may be, will you dare to show your face to the spectators?

UNJUST DISCOURSE. Take me where you list. I seek a throng, so that I may the better annihilate you.

JUST DISCOURSE. Annihilate me! Do you forget who you are?

UNJUST DISCOURSE. I am Reasoning.

JUST DISCOURSE. Yes, the weaker Reasoning.

UNJUST DISCOURSE. But I triumph over you, who claim to be the stronger.

JUST DISCOURSE. By what cunning shifts, pray?

UNJUST DISCOURSE. By the invention of new maxims.

JUST DISCOURSE. ... which are received with favour by these fools.

UNJUST DISCOURSE. Say rather, by these wiseacres.

JUST DISCOURSE. I am going to destroy you mercilessly.

UNJUST DISCOURSE. How pray? Let us see you do it.

JUST DISCOURSE. By saying what is true.

UNJUST DISCOURSE. I shall retort and shall very soon have the better of you. First, I maintain that justice has no existence.

JUST DISCOURSE. Has no existence?

UNJUST DISCOURSE. No existence! Why, where are they?

JUST DISCOURSE. With the gods.

UNJUST DISCOURSE. How then, if justice exists, was Zeus not put to death for having put his father in chains?

JUST DISCOURSE. Bah! this is enough to turn my stomach! A basin, quick!

UNJUST DISCOURSE. You are an old driveller and stupid withal.

JUST DISCOURSE. And you a debauchee and a shameless fellow.

UNJUST DISCOURSE. Hah! What sweet expressions!

JUST DISCOURSE. An impious buffoon!

UNJUST DISCOURSE. You crown me with roses and with lilies.

JUST DISCOURSE. A parricide.

UNJUST DISCOURSE. Why, you shower gold upon me.

JUST DISCOURSE. Formerly, 'twas a hailstorm of blows.

UNJUST DISCOURSE. I deck myself with your abuse.

JUST DISCOURSE. What impudence!

UNJUST DISCOURSE. What tomfoolery!

JUST DISCOURSE. 'Tis because of you that the youth no longer attends the schools. The Athenians will soon recognize what lessons you teach those who are fools enough to believe you.

UNJUST DISCOURSE. You are overwhelmed with wretchedness.

JUST DISCOURSE. And you, you prosper. Yet you were poor when you said, "I am the Mysian Telephus," and used to stuff your wallet with maxims of Pandeletus to nibble at.

UNJUST DISCOURSE. Oh! the beautiful wisdom, of which you are now boasting!

JUST DISCOURSE. Madman! But yet madder the city that keeps you, you, the corrupter of its youth!

UNJUST DISCOURSE. 'Tis not you who will teach this young man; you are as old and out of date as Saturn.

JUST DISCOURSE. Nay, it will certainly be I, if he does not wish to be lost and to practise verbosity only.

UNJUST DISCOURSE (to Phidippides). Come hither and leave him to beat the air.

JUST DISCOURSE (to Unjust Discourse). Evil be unto you, if you touch him.

CHORUS. A truce to your quarrellings and abuse! But expound, you, what you taught us formerly, and you, your new doctrine. Thus, after hearing each of you argue, he will be able to choose betwixt the two schools.

JUST DISCOURSE. I am quite agreeable.

UNJUST DISCOURSE. And I too.

CHORUS. Who is to speak first?

UNJUST DISCOURSE. Let it be my opponent, he has my full consent; then I will follow upon the very ground he shall have chosen and shall shatter him with a hail of new ideas and subtle fancies; if after that he dares to breathe another word, I shall sting him in the face and in the eyes with our maxims, which are as keen as the sting of a wasp, and he will die.

CHORUS. Here are two rivals confident in their powers of oratory and in the thoughts over which they have pondered so long. Let us see which will come triumphant out of the contest. This wisdom, for which my friends maintain such a persistent fight, is in great danger. Come then, you, who crowned men of other days with so many virtues, plead the cause dear to you, make yourself known to us.

JUST DISCOURSE. Very well, I will tell you what was the old education, when I used to teach justice with so much success and when modesty was held in veneration. Firstly, it was required of a child, that it should not utter a word. In the street, when they went to the music-school, all the youths of the same district marched lightly clad and ranged in good order, even when the snow was falling in great flakes. At the master's house they had to stand, their legs apart, and they were taught to sing either, "Pallas, the Terrible, who overturneth cities," or "A noise resounded from afar" in the solemn tones of the ancient harmony. If anyone indulged in buffoonery or lent his voice any of the soft inflexions, like those which to-day the disciples of Phrynis take so much pains to form, he was treated as an enemy of the Muses and belaboured with blows. In the wrestling school they would sit with outstretched legs and without display of any indecency to the curious. When they rose, they would smooth over the sand, so as to leave no trace to excite obscene thoughts. Never was a child rubbed with oil below the belt; the rest of their bodies thus retained its fresh bloom and down, like a velvety peach. They were not to be seen approaching a lover and themselves rousing his passion by soft modulation of the voice and lustful gaze. At table, they would not have dared, before those older than themselves, to have taken a radish, an aniseed or a leaf of parsley, and much less eat fish or thrushes or cross their legs.

UNJUST DISCOURSE. What antiquated rubbish! Have we got back to the days of the festivals of Zeus Polieus, to the Buphonia, to the time of the poet Cecydes and the golden cicadas?

JUST DISCOURSE. 'Tis nevertheless by suchlike teaching I built up the men of Marathon. But you, you teach the children of to-day to bundle themselves quickly into their clothes, and I am enraged when I see them at the Panathenaea forgetting Athené while they dance, and covering themselves with their bucklers. Hence, young man, dare to range yourself beside me, who follow justice and truth; you will then be able to shun the public place, to refrain from the baths, to blush at all that is shameful, to fire up if your virtue is mocked at, to give place to your elders, to honour your parents, in short, to avoid all that is evil. Be modesty itself, and do not run to applaud the dancing girls; if you delight in such scenes, some courtesan will cast you her apple and your reputation will be done for. Do not bandy words with your father, nor treat him as a dotard, nor reproach the old man, who has cherished you, with his age.

UNJUST DISCOURSE. If you listen to him, by Bacchus! you will be the image of the sons of Hippocrates and will be called *mother's great ninny.*

JUST DISCOURSE. No, but you will pass your days at the gymnasia, glowing with strength and health; you will not go to the public place to cackle and wrangle as is done nowadays; you will not live in fear that you may be dragged before the courts for some trifle exaggerated by quibbling. But you will go down to the Academy to run beneath the sacred olives with some virtuous friend of your own age, your head encircled with the white reed, enjoying your ease and breathing the perfume of the yew and of the fresh sprouts of the poplar, rejoicing in the return of springtide and gladly listening to the gentle rustle of the plane-tree and the elm. If you devote yourself to practising my precepts, your chest will be stout, your colour glowing, your shoulders broad, your tongue short, your hips muscular, but your penis small.

But if you follow the fashions of the day, you will be pallid in hue, have narrow shoulders, a narrow chest, a long tongue, small hips and a big tool; you will know how to spin forth long-winded arguments on law. You will be persuaded also to regard as splendid everything that is shameful and as shameful everything that is honourable; in a word, you will wallow in debauchery like Antimachus.

CHORUS. How beautiful, high-souled, brilliant is this wisdom that you practise! What a sweet odour of honesty is emitted by your discourse! Happy were those men of other days who lived when you were honoured! And you, seductive talker, come, find some fresh arguments, for your rival has done wonders. Bring out against him all the battery of your wit, if you desire to beat him and not to be laughed out of court.

UNJUST DISCOURSE. At last! I was choking with impatience, I was burning to upset all his arguments! If I am called the Weaker Reasoning in the schools, 'tis precisely because I was the first before all others to discover the means to confute the laws and the decrees of justice. To invoke solely the weaker arguments and yet triumph is a talent worth more than a hundred thousand drachmae. But see how I shall batter down the sort of education of which he is so proud. Firstly, he forbids you to bathe in hot water. What grounds have you for condemning hot baths?

JUST DISCOURSE. Because they are baneful and enervate men.

UNJUST DISCOURSE. Enough said! Oh! you poor wrestler! From the very outset I have seized you and hold you round the middle; you cannot escape me. Tell me, of all the sons of Zeus, who had the stoutest heart, who performed the most doughty deeds?

JUST DISCOURSE. None, in my opinion, surpassed Heracles.

UNJUST DISCOURSE. Where have you ever seen cold baths called 'Baths of Heracles'? And yet who was braver than he?

JUST DISCOURSE. 'Tis because of such quibbles, that the baths are seen crowded with young folk, who chatter there the livelong day while the gymnasia remain empty.

UNJUST DISCOURSE. Next you condemn the habit of frequenting the market-place, while I approve this. If it were wrong Homer would never have made Nestor speak in public as well as all his wise heroes. As for the art of speaking, he tells you, young men should not practise it; I hold the contrary. Furthermore he preaches chastity to them. Both precepts are equally harmful. Have you ever seen chastity of any use to anyone? Answer and try to confute me.

JUST DISCOURSE. To many; for instance, Peleus won a sword thereby.

UNJUST DISCOURSE. A sword! Ah! what a fine present to make him! Poor wretch! Hyperbolus, the lamp-seller, thanks to his villainy, has gained more than ... I do not know how many talents, but certainly no sword.

JUST DISCOURSE. Peleus owed it to his chastity that he became the husband of Thetis.

UNJUST DISCOURSE. ... who left him in the lurch, for he was not the most ardent; in those nocturnal sports between two sheets, which so please women, he possessed but little merit. Get you gone, you are but an old fool. But you, young man, just consider a little what this temperance means and the delights of which it deprives you—young fellows, women, play, dainty dishes, wine, boisterous laughter. And what is life worth without these? Then, if you happen to commit one of these faults inherent in human weakness, some seduction or adultery, and you are caught in the act, you are lost, if you cannot speak. But follow my teaching and you will be able to satisfy your passions, to dance, to laugh, to blush at nothing. Are you surprised in adultery? Then up and tell the husband you are not guilty, and recall to him the example of Zeus, who allowed himself to be conquered by love and by women. Being but a mortal, can you be stronger than a god?

JUST DISCOURSE. And if your pupil gets impaled, his hairs plucked out, and he is seared with a hot ember, how are you going to prove to him that he is not a filthy debauchee?

UNJUST DISCOURSE. And wherein lies the harm of being so?

JUST DISCOURSE. Is there anything worse than to have such a character?

UNJUST DISCOURSE. Now what will you say, if I beat you even on this point?

JUST DISCOURSE. I should certainly have to be silent then.

UNJUST DISCOURSE. Well then, reply! Our advocates, what are they?

JUST DISCOURSE. Low scum.

UNJUST DISCOURSE. Nothing is more true. And our tragic poets?

JUST DISCOURSE. Low scum.

UNJUST DISCOURSE. Well said again. And our demagogues?

JUST DISCOURSE. Low scum.

UNJUST DISCOURSE. You admit that you have spoken nonsense. And the spectators, what are they for the most part? Look at them.

JUST DISCOURSE. I am looking at them.

UNJUST DISCOURSE. Well! What do you see?

JUST DISCOURSE. By the gods, they are nearly all low scum. See, this one I know to be such and that one and that other with the long hair.

UNJUST DISCOURSE. What have you to say, then?

JUST DISCOURSE. I am beaten. Debauchees! in the name of the gods, receive my cloak; I pass over to your ranks.

SOCRATES. Well then! do you take away your son or do you wish me to teach him how to speak?

STREPSIADES. Teach him, chastise him and do not fail to sharpen his tongue well, on one side for petty law-suits and on the other for important cases.

SOCRATES. Make yourself easy, I shall return to you an accomplished sophist.

PHIDIPPIDES. Very pale then and thoroughly hang-dog-looking.

STREPSIADES. Take him with you.

PHIDIPPIDES. I do assure you, you will repent it.

CHORUS. Judges, we are all about to tell you what you will gain by awarding us the crown as equity requires of you. In spring, when you wish to give your fields the first dressing, we will rain upon you first; the others shall wait. Then we will watch over your corn and over your vine-stocks; they will have no excess to fear, neither of heat nor of wet. But if a mortal dares to insult the goddesses of the Clouds, let him think of the ills we shall pour upon him. For him neither wine nor any harvest at all! Our terrible slings will mow down his young olive plants and his vines. If he is making bricks, it will rain, and our round hailstones will break the tiles of his roof. If he himself marries or any of his relations or friends, we shall cause rain to fall the whole night long. Verily, he would prefer to live in Egypt than to have given this iniquitous verdict.

STREPSIADES. Another four, three, two days, then the eve, then the day, the fatal day of payment! I tremble, I quake, I shudder, for 'tis the day of the old moon and the new. Then all my creditors take the oath, pay their deposits, swear my downfall and my ruin. As for me, I beseech them to be reasonable, to be just, "My friend, do not demand this sum, wait a little for this other and give me time for this third one." Then they will pretend that at this rate they will never be repaid, will accuse me of bad faith and will threaten me with the law. Well then, let them sue me! I care nothing for that, if only Phidippides has learnt to speak fluently. I go to find out, let me knock at the door of the school.... Ho! slave, slave!

SOCRATES. Welcome! Strepsiades!

STREPSIADES. Welcome! Socrates! But first take this sack (offers him a sack of flour); it is right to reward the master with some present. And my son, whom you took off lately, has he learnt this famous reasoning, tell me.

SOCRATES. He has learnt it.

STREPSIADES. What a good thing! Oh! thou divine Knavery!

SOCRATES. You will win just as many causes as you choose.

STREPSIADES. Even if I have borrowed before witnesses?

SOCRATES. So much the better, even if there are a thousand of 'em!

STREPSIADES. Then I am going to shout with all my might. "Woe to the usurers, woe to their capital and their interest and their compound interest! You shall play me no more bad turns. My son is being taught there, his tongue is being sharpened into a double-edged weapon; he is my defender, the saviour of my house, the ruin of my foes! His poor father was crushed down with misfortune and he delivers him." Go and call him to me quickly. Oh! my child! my dear little one! run forward to your father's voice!

SOCRATES. Here he is.

STREPSIADES. Oh, my friend, my dearest friend!

SOCRATES. Take your son, and get you gone.

STREPSIADES. Oh, my son! oh! oh! what a pleasure to see your pallor! You are ready first to deny and then to contradict; 'tis as clear as noon. What a child of your country you are! How your lips quiver with the famous, "What have you to say now?" How well you know, I am certain, to put on the look of a victim, when it is you who are making both victims and dupes! and what a truly Attic glance! Come, 'tis for you to save me, seeing it is you who have ruined me.

PHIDIPPIDES. What is it you fear then?

STREPSIADES. The day of the old and the new.

PHIDIPPIDES. Is there then a day of the old and the new?

STREPSIADES. The day on which they threaten to pay deposit against me.

PHIDIPPIDES. Then so much the worse for those who have deposited! for 'tis not possible for one day to be two.

STREPSIADES. What?

PHIDIPPIDES. Why, undoubtedly, unless a woman can be both old and young at the same time.

STREPSIADES. But so runs the law.

PHIDIPPIDES. I think the meaning of the law is quite misunderstood.

STREPSIADES. What does it mean?

PHIDIPPIDES. Old Solon loved the people.

STREPSIADES. What has that to do with the old day and the new?

PHIDIPPIDES. He has fixed two days for the summons, the last day of the old moon and the first day of the new; but the deposits must only be paid on the first day of the new moon.

STREPSIADES. And why did he also name the last day of the old?

PHIDIPPIDES. So, my dear sir, that the debtors, being there the day before, might free themselves by mutual agreement, or that else, if not, the creditor might begin his action on the morning of the new moon.

STREPSIADES. Why then do the magistrates have the deposits paid on the last of the month and not the next day?

PHIDIPPIDES. I think they do as the gluttons do, who are the first to pounce upon the dishes. Being eager to carry off these deposits, they have them paid in a day too soon.

STREPSIADES. Splendid! Ah! poor brutes, who serve for food to us clever folk! You are only down here to swell the number, true blockheads, sheep for shearing, heap of empty pots! Hence I will sound the note of victory for my son and myself. "Oh! happy, Strepsiades! what cleverness is thine! and what a son thou hast here!" Thus my friends and my neighbours will say, jealous at seeing me gain all my suits. But come in, I wish to regale you first.

PASIAS (to his witness). A man should never lend a single obolus. 'Twould be better to put on a brazen face at the outset than to get entangled in such matters. I want to see my money again and I bring you here to-day to attest the loan. I am going to make a foe of a neighbour; but, as long as I live, I do not wish my country to have to blush for me. Come, I am going to summon Strepsiades.

STREPSIADES. Who is this?

PASIAS. ... for the old day and the new.

STREPSIADES. I call you to witness, that he has named two days. What do you want of me?

PASIAS. I claim of you the twelve minae, which you borrowed from me to buy the dapple-grey horse.

STREPSIADES. A horse! do you hear him? I, who detest horses, as is well known.

PASIAS. I call Zeus to witness, that you swore by the gods to return them to me.

STREPSIADES. Because at that time, by Zeus! Phidippides did not yet know the irrefutable argument.

PASIAS. Would you deny the debt on that account?

STREPSIADES. If not, what use is his science to me?

PASIAS. Will you dare to swear by the gods that you owe me nothing?

STREPSIADES. By which gods?

PASIAS. By Zeus, Hermes and Posidon!

STREPSIADES. Why, I would give three obols for the pleasure of swearing by them.

PASIAS. Woe upon you, impudent knave!

STREPSIADES. Oh! what a fine wine-skin you would make if flayed!

PASIAS. Heaven! he jeers at me!

STREPSIADES. It would hold six gallons easily.

PASIAS. By great Zeus! by all the gods! you shall not scoff at me with impunity.

STREPSIADES. Ah! how you amuse me with your gods! how ridiculous it seems to a sage to hear Zeus invoked.

PASIAS. Your blasphemies will one day meet their reward. But, come, will you repay me my money, yes or no? Answer me, that I may go.

STREPSIADES. Wait a moment, I am going to give you a distinct answer. (*Goes indoors and returns immediately with a kneading-trough.*)

PASIAS. What do you think he will do?

WITNESS. He will pay the debt.

STREPSIADES. Where is the man who demands money? Tell me, what is this?

PASIAS. Him? Why he is your kneading-trough.

STREPSIADES. And you dare to demand money of me, when you are so ignorant? I will not return an obolus to anyone who says *him* instead of *her* for a kneading-trough.

PASIAS. You will not repay?

STREPSIADES. Not if I know it. Come, an end to this, pack off as quick as you can.

PASIAS. I go, but, may I die, if it be not to pay my deposit for a summons.

STREPSIADES. Very well! 'Twill be so much more to the bad to add to the twelve minae. But truly it makes me sad, for I do pity a poor simpleton who says *him* for a kneading-trough.

AMYNIAS. Woe! ah woe is me!

STREPSIADES. Hold! who is this whining fellow? Can it be one of the gods of Carcinus?

AMYNIAS. Do you want to know who I am? I am a man of misfortune!

STREPSIADES. Get on your way then.

AMYNIAS. Oh! cruel god! Oh Fate, who hath broken the wheels of my chariot! Oh, Pallas, thou hast undone me!

STREPSIADES. What ill has Tlepolemus done you?

AMYNIAS. Instead of jeering me, friend, make your son return me the money he has had of me; I am already unfortunate enough.

STREPSIADES. What money?

AMYNIAS. The money he borrowed of me.

STREPSIADES. You have indeed had misfortune, it seems to me.

AMYNIAS. Yes, by the gods! I have been thrown from a chariot.

STREPSIADES. Why then drivel as if you had fallen from an ass?

AMYNIAS. Am I drivelling because I demand my money?

STREPSIADES. No, no, you cannot be in your right senses.

AMYNIAS. Why?

STREPSIADES. No doubt your poor wits have had a shake.

AMYNIAS. But by Hermes! I will sue you at law, if you do not pay me.

STREPSIADES. Just tell me; do you think it is always fresh water that Zeus lets fall every time it rains, or is it always the same water that the sun pumps over the earth?

AMYNIAS. I neither know, nor care.

STREPSIADES. And actually you would claim the right to demand your money, when you know not a syllable of these celestial phenomena?

AMYNIAS. If you are short, pay me the interest, at any rate.

STREPSIADES. What kind of animal is interest?

AMYNIAS. What? Does not the sum borrowed go on growing, growing every month, each day as the time slips by?

STREPSIADES. Well put. But do you believe there is more water in the sea now than there was formerly?

AMYNIAS. No, 'tis just the same quantity. It cannot increase.

STREPSIADES. Thus, poor fool, the sea, that receives the rivers, never grows, and yet you would have your money grow? Get you gone, away with you, quick! Ho! bring me the ox-goad!

AMYNIAS. Hither! you witnesses there!

STREPSIADES. Come, what are you waiting for? Will you not budge, old nag!

AMYNIAS. What an insult!

STREPSIADES. Unless you get a-trotting, I shall catch you and prick up your behind, you sorry packhorse! Ah! you start, do you? I was about to drive you pretty fast, I tell you—you and your wheels and your chariot!

CHORUS. Whither does the passion of evil lead! here is a perverse old man, who wants to cheat his creditors; but some mishap, which will speedily punish this rogue for his shameful schemings, cannot fail to overtake him from to-day. For a long time he has been burning to have his son know how to fight against all justice and right and to gain even the most iniquitous causes against his adversaries every one. I think this wish is going to be fulfilled. But mayhap, mayhap, he will soon wish his son were dumb rather!

STREPSIADES. Oh! oh! neighbours, kinsmen, fellow-citizens, help! help! to the rescue, I am being beaten! Oh! my head! oh! my jaw! Scoundrel! do you beat your own father!

PHIDIPPIDES. Yes, father, I do.

STREPSIADES. See! he admits he is beating me.

PHIDIPPIDES. Undoubtedly I do.

STREPSIADES. You villain, you parricide, you gallows-bird!

PHIDIPPIDES. Go on, repeat your epithets, call me a thousand other names, an it please you. The more you curse, the greater my amusement!

STREPSIADES. Oh! you infamous cynic!

PHIDIPPIDES. How fragrant the perfume breathed forth in your words.

STREPSIADES. Do you beat your own father?

PHIDIPPIDES. Aye, by Zeus! and I am going to show you that I do right in beating you.

STREPSIADES. Oh, wretch! can it be right to beat a father?

PHIDIPPIDES. I will prove it to you, and you shall own yourself vanquished.

STREPSIADES. Own myself vanquished on a point like this?

PHIDIPPIDES. 'Tis the easiest thing in the world. Choose whichever of the two reasonings you like.

STREPSIADES. Of which reasonings?

PHIDIPPIDES. The Stronger and the Weaker.

STREPSIADES. Miserable fellow! Why, 'tis I who had you taught how to refute what is right, and now you would persuade me it is right a son should beat his father.

PHIDIPPIDES. I think I shall convince you so thoroughly that, when you have heard me, you will not have a word to say.

STREPSIADES. Well, I am curious to hear what you have to say.

CHORUS. Consider well, old man, how you can best triumph over him. His brazenness shows me that he thinks himself sure of his case; he has some argument which gives him nerve. Note the confidence in his look! But how did the fight begin? tell the Chorus; you cannot help doing that much.

STREPSIADES. I will tell you what was the start of the quarrel. At the end of the meal you wot of, I bade him take his lyre and sing me the air of Simonides, which tells of the fleece of the ram. He replied bluntly, that it was stupid, while drinking, to play the lyre and sing, like a woman when she is grinding barley.

PHIDIPPIDES. Why, by rights I ought to have beaten and kicked you the very moment you told me to sing!

STREPSIADES. That is just how he spoke to me in the house, furthermore he added, that Simonides was a detestable poet. However, I mastered myself and for a while said nothing. Then I said to him, 'At least, take a myrtle branch and recite a passage from Aeschylus to me.'—'For my own part,' he at once replied, 'I look upon Aeschylus as the first of poets, for his verses roll superbly; 'tis nothing but incoherence, bombast and turgidness.' Yet still I smothered my wrath and said, 'Then recite one of the famous pieces from the modern poets.' Then he commenced a piece in which Euripides shows, oh! horror! a brother, who violates his own uterine sister. Then I could no longer restrain myself, and attacked him with the most injurious abuse; naturally he retorted; hard words were hurled on both sides, and finally he sprang at me, broke my bones, bore me to earth, strangled and started killing me!

PHIDIPPIDES. I was right. What! not praise Euripides, the greatest of our poets!

STREPSIADES. He the greatest of our poets! Ah! if I but dared to speak! but the blows would rain upon me harder than ever.

PHIDIPPIDES. Undoubtedly, and rightly too.

STREPSIADES. Rightly! oh! what impudence! to me, who brought you up! when you could hardly lisp, I guessed what you wanted. If you said *broo, broo*, well, I brought you your milk; if you asked for *mam mam*, I gave you bread; and you had no sooner said, *caca*, than I took you outside and held you out. And just now, when you were strangling me, I shouted, I bellowed that I would let all go; and you, you scoundrel, had not the heart to take me outside, so that here, though almost choking, I was compelled to ease myself.

CHORUS. Young men, your hearts must be panting with impatience. What is Phidippides going to say? If, after such conduct, he proves he has done well, I would not give an obolus for the hide of old men. Come, you, who know how to brandish and hurl the keen shafts of the new science, find a way to convince us, give your language an appearance of truth.

PHIDIPPIDES. How pleasant it is to know these clever new inventions and to be able to defy the established laws! When I thought only about horses, I was not able to string three words together without a mistake, but now that the master has altered and improved me and that I live in this world of subtle thought, of reasoning and of meditation, I count on being able to prove satisfactorily that I have done well to thrash my father.

STREPSIADES. Mount your horse! By Zeus! I would rather defray the keep of a four-in-hand team than be battered with blows.

PHIDIPPIDES. I revert to what I was saying when you interrupted me. And first, answer me, did you beat me in my childhood?

STREPSIADES. Why, assuredly, for your good and in your own best interest.

PHIDIPPIDES. Tell me, is it not right, that in turn I should beat you for your good? since it is for a man's own best interest to be beaten. What! must your body be free of blows, and not mine? am I not free-born too? the children are to weep and the fathers go free?

STREPSIADES. But...

PHIDIPPIDES. You will tell me, that according to the law, 'tis the lot of children to be beaten. But I reply that the old men are children twice over and that it is far more fitting to chastise them than the young, for there is less excuse for their faults.

STREPSIADES. But the law nowhere admits that fathers should be treated thus.

PHIDIPPIDES. Was not the legislator who carried this law a man like you and me? In those days he got men to believe him; then why should not I too have the right to establish for the future a new law, allowing children to beat their fathers in turn? We make you a present of all the blows which were received before this law, and admit that you thrashed us with impunity. But look how the cocks and other animals fight with their fathers; and yet what difference is there betwixt them and ourselves, unless it be that they do not propose decrees?

STREPSIADES. But if you imitate the cocks in all things, why don't you scratch up the dunghill, why don't you sleep on a perch?

PHIDIPPIDES. That has no bearing on the case, good sir; Socrates would find no connection, I assure you.

STREPSIADES. Then do not beat at all, for otherwise you have only yourself to blame afterwards.

PHIDIPPIDES. What for?

STREPSIADES. I have the right to chastise you, and you to chastise your son, if you have one.

PHIDIPPIDES. And if I have not, I shall have cried in vain, and you will die laughing in my face.

STREPSIADES. What say you, all here present? It seems to me that he is right, and I am of opinion that they should be accorded their right. If we think wrongly, 'tis but just we should be beaten.

PHIDIPPIDES. Again, consider this other point.

STREPSIADES. 'Twill be the death of me.

PHIDIPPIDES. But you will certainly feel no more anger because of the blows I have given you.

STREPSIADES. Come, show me what profit I shall gain from it.

PHIDIPPIDES. I shall beat my mother just as I have you.

STREPSIADES. What do you say? what's that you say? Hah! this is far worse still.

PHIDIPPIDES. And what if I prove to you by our school reasoning, that one ought to beat one's mother?

STREPSIADES. Ah! if you do that, then you will only have to throw yourself along with Socrates and his reasoning, into the Barathrum. Oh! Clouds! all our troubles emanate from you, from you, to whom I entrusted myself, body and soul.

CHORUS. No, you alone are the cause, because you have pursued the path of evil.

STREPSIADES. Why did you not say so then, instead of egging on a poor ignorant old man?

CHORUS. We always act thus, when we see a man conceive a passion for what is evil; we strike him with some terrible disgrace, so that he may learn to fear the gods.

STREPSIADES. Alas! oh Clouds! 'tis hard indeed, but 'tis just! I ought not to have cheated my creditors.... But come, my dear son, come with me to take vengeance on this wretched Chaerephon and on Socrates, who have deceived us both.

PHIDIPPIDES. I shall do nothing against our masters.

STREPSIADES. Oh! show some reverence for ancestral Zeus!

PHIDIPPIDES. Mark him and his ancestral Zeus! What a fool you are! Does any such being as Zeus exist?

STREPSIADES. Why, assuredly.

PHIDIPPIDES. No, a thousand times no! The ruler of the world is the Whirlwind, that has unseated Zeus.

STREPSIADES. He has not dethroned him. I believed it, because of this whirligig here. Unhappy wretch that I am! I have taken a piece of clay to be a god.

PHIDIPPIDES. Very well! Keep your stupid nonsense for your own consumption. (*Exit.*)

STREPSIADES. Oh! what madness! I had lost my reason when I threw over the gods through Socrates' seductive phrases. Oh! good Hermes, do not destroy me in your wrath. Forgive me; their babbling had driven me crazy. Be my councillor. Shall I pursue them at law or shall I...? Order and I obey.—You are right, no law-suit; but up! let us burn down the home of those praters. Here, Xanthias, here! take a ladder, come forth and arm yourself with an axe; now mount upon the school, demolish the roof, if you love your master, and may the house fall in upon them, Ho! bring me a blazing torch! There is more than one of them, arch-impostors as they are, on whom I am determined to have vengeance.

A DISCIPLE. Oh! oh!

STREPSIADES. Come, torch, do your duty! Burst into full flame!

DISCIPLE. What are you up to?

STREPSIADES. What am I up to? Why, I am entering upon a subtle argument with the beams of the house.

SECOND DISCIPLE. Hullo! hullo! who is burning down our house?

STREPSIADES. The man whose cloak you have appropriated.

SECOND DISCIPLE. But we are dead men, dead men!

STREPSIADES. That is just exactly what I hope, unless my axe plays me false, or I fall and break my neck.

SOCRATES. Hi! you fellow on the roof, what are you doing up there?

STREPSIADES. I traverse the air and contemplate the sun.

SOCRATES. Ah! ah! woe is upon me! I am suffocating!

CHAEREPHON. Ah! you insulted the gods! Ah! you studied the face of the moon! Chase them, strike and beat them down! Forward! they have richly deserved their fate—above all, by reason of their blasphemies.

CHORUS. So let the Chorus file off the stage. Its part is played.

FINIS OF "THE CLOUDS"

Printed in Great Britain
by Amazon